Studies in International Performance

Published in association with the International Federation of Theatre Research

General Editors: **Janelle Reinelt** and **Brian Singleton**

Culture and performance cross borders constantly, and not just the borders that define nations. In this new series, scholars of performance produce interactions between and among nations and cultures as well as genres, identities and imaginations.

Inter-national in the largest sense, the books collected in the *Studies in International Performance* series display a range of historical, theoretical and critical approaches to the panoply of performances that make up the global surround. The series embraces 'Culture' which is institutional as well as improvised, underground or alternate, and treats 'Performance' as either intercultural or transnational as well as intracultural within nations.

Titles include:

Patrick Anderson and Jisha Menon (*editors*)
VIOLENCE PERFORMED
Local Roots and Global Routes of Conflict

Elaine Aston and Sue-Ellen Case
STAGING INTERNATIONAL FEMINISMS

Christopher Balme
PACIFIC PERFORMANCES
Theatricality and Cross-Cultural Encounter in the South Seas

Helen Gilbert and Jacqueline Lo
PERFORMANCE AND COSMOPOLITICS
Cross-Cultural Transactions in Australasia

Helena Grehan
PERFORMANCE, ETHICS AND SPECTATORSHIP IN A GLOBAL AGE

Judith Hamera
DANCING COMMUNITIES
Performance, Difference, and Connection in the Global City

Alan Read
THEATRE, INTIMACY & ENGAGEMENT
The Last Human-Venue

Joanne Tompkins
UNSETTLING SPACE
Contestations in Contemporary Australian Theatre

S. E. Wilmer
NATIONAL THEATRES IN A CHANGING EUROPE

Forthcoming title:

Adrian Kear
THEATRE AND EVENT

Studies in International Performance
Series Standing Order ISBN 978–1–4039–4456–6 (hardback)
978–1–4039–4457–3 (paperback)
(*outside North America only*)

You can receive future titles in this series as they are published by placing a standing order. Please contact your bookseller or, in case of difficulty, write to us at the address below with your name and address, the title of the series and the ISBN quoted above.

Customer Services Department, Macmillan Distribution Ltd, Houndmills, Basingstoke, Hampshire RG21 6XS, England

Performance, Ethics and Spectatorship in a Global Age

Helena Grehan

palgrave
macmillan

First published 2009 by
PALGRAVE MACMILLAN

Palgrave Macmillan in the UK is an imprint of Macmillan Publishers Limited,
registered in England, company number 785998, of Houndmills, Basingstoke,
Hampshire RG21 6XS.

Palgrave Macmillan in the US is a division of St Martin's Press LLC,
175 Fifth Avenue, New York, NY 10010.

Palgrave Macmillan is the global academic imprint of the above companies
and has companies and representatives throughout the world.

Palgrave® and Macmillan® are registered trademarks in the United States,
the United Kingdom, Europe and other countries.

ISBN-13: 978–0–230–51801–8 hardback
ISBN-10: 0–230–51801–X hardback

This book is printed on paper suitable for recycling and made from fully
managed and sustained forest sources. Logging, pulping and manufacturing
processes are expected to conform to the environmental regulations of the
country of origin.

A catalogue record for this book is available from the British Library.

Library of Congress Cataloging-in-Publication Data

Grehan, Helena.
    Performance, ethics and spectatorship in a global age /
Helena Grehan.
        p. cm.—(Studies in international performance)
    Includes bibliographical references and index.
    ISBN 978–0–230–51801–8
    1. Theater and society. 2. Theater – Philosophy. 3. Theater
audiences. I. Title.

PN2049.G74 2009
792.01'3—dc22   2008050869

Printed and bound in Great Britain by
CPI Antony Rowe, Chippenham and Eastbourne

Contents

List of Illustrations

Series Editors' Preface

In 2003, the current International Federation for Theatre Research President, Janelle Reinelt, pledged the organization to expand the outlets for scholarly publication available to the membership, and to make scholarly achievement one of the main goals and activities of the Federation under her leadership. In 2004, joined by Vice-President for Research and Publications Brian Singleton, they signed a contract with Palgrave Macmillan for a new book series, 'Studies in International Performance.'

Since the inauguration of the series, it has become increasingly urgent for performance scholars to expand their disciplinary horizons to include the comparative study of performances across national, cultural, social and political borders. This is necessary not only in order to avoid the homogenizing tendency to limit performance paradigms to those familiar in our home countries, but also in order to be engaged in creating new performance scholarship that takes account of and embraces the complexities of transnational cultural production, the new media, and the economic and social consequences of increasingly international forms of artistic expression. Comparative studies can value both the specifically local and the broadly conceived global forms of performance practices, histories and social formations. Comparative aesthetics can challenge the limitations of perception and current artistic knowledges. In formalizing the work of the Federation's members through rigorous and innovative scholarship, we hope to contribute to an ever-changing project of knowledge creation.

International Federation for Theatre Research
Fédération International pour la
Recherche Théâtrale

Acknowledgements

I have been thinking about this book for a long time and my thinking has developed and improved significantly as a result of conversations, responses and debates with many people over the last three years. I would particularly like to thank Anne Surma whose patience, insight and support has made it possible for me to survive and to write a much clearer book that I might otherwise have. Anne has lived through this book and has been there to provide guidance, friendship and advice on all aspects of the manuscript (and on living with it). I am deeply, deeply grateful. Peta Bowden and Patricia Harris have also read and re-read drafts and have spent hours talking to me about the performances, about Levinas and about questions of responsibility and ethics. Their responses were always wise and inspiring and at times wonderfully provocative. Jane Goodall, has read draft after draft and listened to me in times of crisis. She has advised me not only on the nuances of good argument but also on survival techniques that have allowed much needed laughter to re-enter the frame. Joanne Tompkins and Peter Eckersall have also read copious drafts and their feedback has been detailed, thoughtful, reassuring and invaluable. Yvonne Haigh has helped me come to a much clearer understanding of Levinas's work and she has done so in a way that did not discourage me, even when I was overwhelmed. I feel privileged to have such a community of scholars and friends around me and I thank them most sincerely.

There have also been many friends, colleagues and students who have helped source documents, discussed the material with me and been willing to engage in often heated debates about issues surrounding performance, ethics and responsibility. I would particularly like to thank Helen Gibson, Alex Kelly, Angela Campbell, Renee Newman-Storen, Lorraine Shea, Josephine Wilson, Bill Dunstone, Ed Scheer, Paul Rae, Margaret Hamilton, Jemma Hefter, Kirk Brandenburg, Andy McNeill, Lauren Grocott, Paula Calleja, Tony Mobily, Alexa Taylor, Pip Rundell, Nina Siew and the students in 'Literature in an Age of Terror'.

And of course this book would not have been at all possible without the help of Jim, Jenny Marie-France, Maurits and friends and family who provided childcare, food, wine and support of all kinds.

Most of all, I want to thank Hans-willem and Saoirse, who have lived with this project every day and have cajoled me and worked hard to dampen my uncertainties, as well as loving and caring for me through thick and thin. I promise I won't do this again for a while.

I would also like to thank Andrew Ross, Matt Marshall and Susan Moxham for agreeing to talk with me; your thoughtful responses to my questions have really enriched my understanding of the works. Sincere thanks to Patricia Piccinini, Beryl Korot, Jon Green and Socìetas Raffaello Sanzio for generously providing me with such wonderful images and Maryanne Nairn, Gilda Biasini, Finn Pedersen and Tom Gutteridge for assisting with this process. I'd also like to thank Marie-France van Hall, Gaston Avrillon and Françoise Avrillon for helping me get in contact with Michele Laurent.

Thanks to Brian Singleton and Janelle Reinelt for pushing me further with ethics and for your helpful advice and enthusiasm, and to Christabel Scaife, Steven Hall and all the staff at Palgrave Macmillan for your dedication and attention to detail.

An earlier version of parts of Chapter 4, '*Sandakan Threnody:* testimony and the dangers of polyphony', appeared as 'Testimony and Ambivalence in *Sandakan Threnody*' (2006), *Australasian Drama Studies*, 49, pp. 89–100.

Introduction

> Art expands the sympathetic imagination while teaching us about the limits of sympathy. Such teaching hopes to bring the cognitive and the emotional into alignment. There is no formula, however, for aesthetic education of this kind... It is rarely prescriptive, and, although it may schematize itself as a set of rules (as a poetics or a hermeneutics), the type of thinking involved seems to import a structural moment of indeterminacy that escapes the brain's binary wiring. (Hartman, 2001: 122–123)

> I go to theatre and performance to hear stories that order, for a moment, my incoherent longings, that engage the complexity of personal and cultural relationships and that critique the assumptions of a social system I find sorely lacking. (Dolan, 2001: 456)[1]

Jill Dolan points out that she wants 'a lot from theatre' (2001: 456); she is not alone. In a world of increasing individualism, where speed trumps time, it is essential to eke out a space in which spectators can experience the often confounding issues of our time, in a way that affords both the issues, and the spectators, the complexity they require or, in some circumstances, demand. It is at the theatre that we can find this space and that we can, in response to the ideas generated, consider how it is that aesthetic, ethical and political issues resonate with and affect us.

As Hans-Thies Lehmann, following Guy Debord, explains, we are living in a 'society of the spectacle', a society in which the media

1

(particularly news media) dominates and, as a consequence,

> the separation of the event from the perception of the event, precisely through the mediation of the news about it, leads to an erosion of the act of communication. The consciousness of being connected to others and thus being answerable and bound to them 'in the language', in the medium of communication itself recedes in favour of communication as (an exchange of) information. (Lehmann, 2006: 184)

Performance engages its spectators emotionally, viscerally and intellectually. It has the potential to generate a set of conditions within which linguistic or representational surfaces can be disturbed or interrupted in ways that allow spectators to reflect on and ask questions about the nature of any response to a work. In this regard, then, it provides an alternative space away from the mainstream, where the answerability that Lehmann thinks is being eroded can be reinvigorated. Performance opens up multiple, nuanced and often contradictory spaces for consideration and reflection. Within such spaces both the spectators and the performers can fight fatigue and continue to ask important questions.

The unsettled spectator

This book emerged from a desire to work-through a set of ambivalent – contradictory, thrilling and unsettling – responses to the Italian director Romeo Castellucci and Socìetas Raffaello Sanzio's production *Genesi: from the museum of sleep* (1999).[2] The performance had as its subject relationships between technology and humanity and a consideration of the extent to which humans will go in their experimentation with creation and destruction. It is a work about risk, about endurance and about suffering. In terms of its form the performance comprised three Acts. The first took place in the chamber of Marie Curie, the second at Auschwitz and the third in the presence of Abel and Cain. The performers included children, an older woman with a mastectomy scar, a disabled Cain, and a contortionist. There were barely any words spoken: the work was imagistic, shocking and sonically challenging. It affected spectators profoundly because it engendered an experience of shock, awe and confusion, as well as moments of beauty and profound disturbance.

Rachel Halliburton explains that Castellucci 'does not allow his audiences initially to react with their minds, but forces them into purely emotional territory' (Halliburton, 2001). She also points out that 'no moderate reaction is possible' in response to the work of Socìetas Raffaello Sanzio. As an individual spectator the perform- ance unsettled me by making me feel physically uncomfortable in my skin and urging me, as a consequence, to think through and feel through what might, and perhaps, what should not be represented within the context of performance. More specifically it made me question the function of representing the Holocaust at the end of the twentieth century and to wonder about how a company might invest or reinvest such a significant and traumatic event with meaning, for spectators. As Castellucci points out, the decision to use the Holocaust was a difficult one. He says, 'I wonder whether it is immoral. I won- der which degree of purity I might reach to get close to this horror, so difficult to be included among events, which are thoroughly human' (Castellucci, 1999).

I was not quite sure what it was about *Genesi: from the museum of sleep* that intrigued and irritated me so much, but I knew that it had something to do with the ways in which the work engaged spectators both cognitively and emotionally. Although I am not certain that I personally achieved an 'alignment' as Hartman sug- gests in the epigraph above, I do know that I got to a point of feel- ing radically unsettled, a point at which I was driven to reassess my understandings of both the power of theatre and the function of spectatorship in the context of a fraught, media-saturated world.

While many theorists and critics talk about performance and ana- lyse what happens, or provide ways of reading a work, not many feel comfortable with attempting to talk about or theorise the thing that makes us return to the theatre – the sense of an experience, of excite- ment, of identification or disruption – that thing that the live event offers, as it opens new ways of thinking and feeling, and as a result, bringing us back again and again and again. As Dolan astutely points out, 'how do we write about our own spectatorship in nuanced ways that capture the complicated emotions that the best theater experi- ences solicit?' (Dolan, 2005: 8).

Dolan's question is an important one and obviously one that a book such as this, on ethics and spectatorship, must address. As she explains, spectatorship, by its very nature is complicated. It involves visceral, emotional and intellectual reactions to images, ideas, symbols and lines spoken. These reactions are often impossible to describe, decipher or to explain. For this reason discussions about spectatorship continue to be a difficult (if not fraught) area for theatre and performance studies and one that is often avoided by theorists who prefer to focus on an engagement with a particular work without a substantial consideration on how the work impacted either on individual spectators or on audiences more broadly. This decision is understandable as there are risks involved in talking about spectatorship. These include the possibility of becoming too personal, of interpreting responses from the position of an 'ideal' spectator, or of making generalisations or assumptions that cannot be supported or proved.

In the context of this book, then, spectatorship must be understood as including the responses of individual citizens or subjects who go to the theatre to be challenged and who keep going back because of theatre's capacity to awaken and stimulate reflection on important topics and themes. Theatre has the potential to provide subjects with a space in which to engage in complex and often contradictory ways with key issues of our times. The impacts of this experience of being challenged are described beautifully by Claudia Castellucci when she says, 'the actor who looks at the spectator reveals to the spectator his own gesture, a form of mirroring that also creates a profound equivocation and puts in doubt the spectator's proper role' (Castellucci, 2007: 210–211).

What is distinctive about theatre, however, is that once a subject enters the performance space s/he becomes both an individual spectator and part of a collective. In this context each spectator negotiates between his or her own individual responses to a work and the responses, when discernible, of those others who are also in attendance. It is interesting to speculate or reflect on how the experience of spectatorship might affect the responses of an individual subject. For Nicholas Ridout, for example, it is a difficult process: 'When the promise of a direct face-to-face encounter between two human beings is made within the theatrical set-up, either the act of delivery or the act of collection is always compromised' (Ridout, 2006a: 32).

But there is another element of spectatorship that needs to be considered here and that is the idea of the audience as a collective. The audience is always a collective and while considering the relationship between the responses of an individual spectator and a group is not an easy task, it is even more complicated to ascribe reactions or responses to a group. Gleaning a collective response to a work is almost impossible. Observations can be made about applause, silence or awe (for example), but it is very difficult to judge what these actually mean in any objective sense. While surveys can be undertaken as an audience leaves the theatre, the act of selecting appropriate questions and then gauging whether or not or to what extent any responses assist in analysis is an almost impossible one. Textured responses cannot be evaluated in a scientific way because they are not reducible to empirical findings.

To overcome these difficulties it is important that I address a range of responses to the performances discussed in this book to tease out the diverse ethical questions these works raise and to avoid the risk of the book being read as positing an ideal spectator, an ideal form of spectatorship. In order to do this I will draw on the work of performance theorists, critics, reviewers, bloggers and the views of directors, performers and those associated with the productions, as well as my own responses as a spectator at these events. By engaging with the writings and reflections of these participants, I hope to provide the reader with an understanding of the ways in which a process of ethical reflection can liberate a range of nuanced, often contradictory and powerful readings of contemporary performance work for spectators.

Responsibility and ethics

The performance works I am interested in involve spectators in a play of seduction and estrangement where they must engage deeply in order to unravel the questions, ideas and feelings the works stimulate. They ask for active spectatorship, not in the sense that spectators might leap out of their seats and become politically active, but in the sense that they can become intrigued, engaged and involved in a process of consideration about the important issues of response and responsibility and what these might mean both within and beyond the performance space.

I am not only interested in describing the complexity of emotional and intellectual responses a performance might engender, I also want to understand how these responses, during and after the performance, liberate (or have the potential to liberate) certain kinds of ethical challenges for spectators as citizens in the wider world. In this regard I was drawn to the work of Emmanuel Levinas and Zygmunt Bauman. Bauman's work in *Postmodern Ethics*, in which he draws on Levinasian ethics, is particularly relevant to my understandings of both Levinas's ideas and the ways in which response and responsibility might work in the postmodern moment. I engage with Bauman's writings about ambivalence and extend these to talk about the difficulties of understanding the responses that can be engendered by complex and often oblique or quixotic political performances. Both Levinas and Bauman (to a lesser extent) guide my journey through the works addressed in this book. Whilst, as I will explain, there are problems with discussing Levinasian philosophy in the context of performance, his key philosophical insights are invaluable.

Levinas's philosophy is centrally concerned with the other and with the subject's responsibility for the other. This is, for him, the meaning of ethics. I draw primarily on his book *Otherwise than Being: Or Beyond Essence* as well his *Collected Philosophical Papers* to inform my discussions. He claims that when the other calls us we have no option but to respond. By engaging with his ideas I wanted to try to understand and describe the responses of theatre spectators and also to think about what spectators might do with their responses once they leave the theatre. This links to the concern I expressed earlier with understanding what it is that the theatre does to, or for, spectators. It also raises questions about the burden a work places on them.

I am not talking about didactic or overtly political work per se, but about work that is invested in exploring important social, political or cultural issues. This kind of work does not – if it works well – allow spectators to leave the space and enjoy a Chardonnay, feeling as if they have actually done something by attending. It does not, necessarily even provide them with the 'hope' that is central to Dolan's project (2005). Rather, it follows them, nags and irritates them, and although they might attempt either to suppress these responses or to establish ways of being in the world with them, the nagging remains and demands consideration. Eventually, if it cannot be soothed, the

irritation drives spectators to find ways of changing things personally or politically so that it is soothed. This is not, however, about
being charged with a political function and being ordered to change
the world. Instead it is about spectators working out how to respond
and ultimately what responsibility might mean for those who engage
with politically inflected work.

I draw on Levinas and Bauman in this book because I want to
apply ethics to performance, not in terms of a methodology but
rather as a departure point that helps tease out the complicated and
thrilling responses and ideas some works unleash, and to help me
talk about these in ways that might have meaning for others.

The works in question

For the purposes of this book I have selected five performances and an
installation that each causes an irritation. They are quite different in
terms of form and content (although of course there are some similarities of theme and method), and they are all concerned with different
issues. The first work is *Genesi: from the museum of sleep,* as outlined
above. The second, by Black Swan Theatre, is *The Career Highlights of
the MAMU* (2002). This production, directed by Andrew Ross, focuses
on the impacts of nuclear testing and various regressive governmental
policies imposed on a group of Indigenous Australians, the Spinifex
People. It uses testimony, documentary footage and a range of performance modes to enthrall and unsettle its spectators. The third, by
Ong Keng Sen and TheatreWorks, *Sandakan Threnody* (2004), deals
with Australian and British prisoners of war in Borneo at the end of
World War II. It is centrally concerned with questions of pain, memory, memorialisation and trauma. The fourth, *Le Dernier Caravansérail*
(2003), by Ariane Mnouchkine and Théâtre du Soleil, draws on painstaking research to tell (in spectacular fashion) harrowing stories about
the plight of refugees and asylum seekers as they flee regimes of terror
and despair. The fifth, *Three Tales* (2002), is a digital opera, by Steve
Reich and Beryl Korot, that returns to the themes of humanity and
technology but does so in a dramatically different fashion than *Genesi:
from the museum of sleep. Three Tales* explores the Hindenburg disaster,
the nuclear tests at Bikini Atoll in the Pacific in 1946 and, using Dolly
the sheep as a central icon, interrogates complex moral, scientific and
social issues surrounding genetic modification and cloning. The final

work addressed in this book is an installation entitled 'Undivided' in the (2004) exhibition *Nature's Little Helpers* by Patricia Piccinini. This considers the tangible (lived) effects of responsibility on human subjects as new, post-human lifeforms begin to emerge.

Ultimately, my desire is that readers gain some knowledge of, or insight into, works they may not have experienced 'live'. Or, if they did experience these works, that the ideas presented in this book combine with their own reactions to enrich or further complicate the range of responses possible. But there is another desire lurking here and it is that I hope this book opens up a dialogue between ethics and performance, particularly in terms of spectatorship. I would like this work to be seen as a starting point for scholars and practitioners who want to explore and push the limits of an exchange between performance, spectatorship and ethics.

While I have drawn on Levinasian philosophy there are, of course, many other philosophers whose ideas could have been used to liberate detailed and thought-provoking readings of the works addressed here. The point is that ethics offers an important language (or set of languages) for considering the deep, fraught and often unspoken responses contemporary politically inflected performance can generate. If we want to talk about what spectators do, and I think we should, then considering this 'doing' in terms of ethics specifically, or philosophy more generally, can open up a range of ways of reading our responses to significant performance works as well as to the often deeply troubling world around us.

1
Situating the Spectator

> It is a fundamental fact of today's Western societies that all
> human experiences (life, eroticism, happiness, recognition)
> are tied to *commodities* or more precisely their consumption
> and possession (and not to a discourse). This corresponds
> exactly to the civilization of images that can only ever refer
> to the next image and call up other images. The totality of
> the spectacle is the 'theatricalization' of all areas of social
> life. (Lehmann, 2006: 183; original emphasis)

Living in the affluent West I am constantly reminded of the ways in
which 'human experiences', as Lehmann so astutely argues, revolve
around the 'consumption and possession' of 'commodities'. For the
privileged there is the possibility of instant gratification at every
turn. This gratification, however exciting, is always briefly felt as the
next potential possession or moment of consumption rolls into view.
Fighting the desire (which I could argue is imposed, but perhaps this
suggests a lack of agency and an inability to resist) to possess and
consume seems almost impossible. Minor moments of guilt, shame
and embarrassment strike from time to time, but the process of
amassing (objects, information, ideas, etc.) seems to continue unre-
lentingly. It is from within this society that individual subjects often
clamour for meaning, for something less instant, more complex and
more sustaining.

Lehmann talks about postdramatic theatre and its role in proffer-
ing an alternative space, a space of presence rather than representation, a space in which theatre draws on different (technologised or

perhaps non-narrative) forms to forge a connection (albeit tentative) with its audiences; and his ideas are significant. My focus here is not on the 'postdramatic' per se, and although several of the works addressed in this book could be considered under that rubric, I explore the ways in which performance, particularly politically-inflected works, have the potential to generate a space in which more profound considerations of ethics and responsibility might be liberated. I want to consider what performance might offer for alternative ways both of being in the world and relating to others, as it seems that in the drive for consumption and possession actual relations with and responses to other people have the potential to become marginalised.

Globalisation and the postmodern subject

In his provocative essay 'The World Inhospitable to Lévinas', Bauman explores issues such as global freedom, mobility, poverty, justice and the separation of economic and political powers within states. He considers how these issues, as they currently exist, generate an environment in which 'collective action' becomes almost impossible and freedom from responsibility valorised. 'Shedding responsibility for consequences is the most coveted and cherished gain that the new mobility brings to free-floating, locally-unbound capital' (Bauman, 1999: 159).

Echoing Lehmann, Bauman argues that this is a world in which subjects are engaged 'primarily as consumers', and where 'to meet the norm, to be a fully-fledged member of society, one needs to respond promptly and efficiently to the temptations of the consumer market' (Bauman, 1999: 164).[1] It is a society in which 'the poor are unequivocally a liability, and by no stretch of the imagination can they be recorded on the side of present or future assets' (Bauman, 1999: 164). While Bauman paints a bleak picture of contemporary (Western) society, it is one that I believe reflects the experiences of many subjects. So what kind of society is this? If there is a 'shedding' of 'responsibility' and a focus on consumption, from where do subjects draw meaning? How might they respond to the dislocation, fracturing and uncertainty that surround them? And how, if at all, might they negotiate a sense of self-worth (beyond objects and symbols) or an understanding of the worth of others?

It seems, according to Bauman, that instead of taking action, sub-jects in affluent Western societies continue (for the most part) to 'close our eyes' to poverty and the plight of the other. Bauman draws on Ryszard Kapuscinski's work to explain this phenomenon. Kapuscinski identifies 'three interconnected expedients consistently applied by the media' (in Bauman, 1999: 165). It is important to briefly outline these here as they help to shape my understanding of contemporary subjects and to explain why it is that I find Levinas's work so compelling.

The first is the idea that the 'poor themselves bear responsibility for their fate. They could... choose a life of work and thrift instead – but apparently decided not to, due to inferior intelligence' (in Bauman, 1999: 165). The second concerns the simplification of news about the poor to the issue of hunger, thus denying the myriad other issues associated with poverty. Bauman cites Kapuscinski's story about 'wandering through African townships and villages and meet-ing children ' "who begged me not of bread, water... but a ballpoint pen" ' (Kapuscinski in Bauman, 1999: 166). Thirdly the 'spectacles of disasters, as presented by the media' present an image of the poor as existing in a 'subhuman world beyond ethics and beyond salvation.' In doing so it generates a frame in which their suffering, as por-trayed, suggests that 'attempts to save that world from the worst con-sequences of its own brutality may bring only momentary effects which in the long run are bound to fail; all the lifelines thrown even-tually become nooses for the poor to hang themselves' (Bauman, 1999: 166).

This third expedient is the most complex and disturbing, as it reflects a process of rationalisation or justification (aided or guided by the media) that is very unsettling. Bauman continues: 'the vic-tims of famine are not ethical subjects. Our own stance toward them is not a moral issue. Morality is for carnivals only, the spectacular, instantaneous, short-lived, explosive condensation of pity and com-passion' (Bauman, 1999: 166).[2] In writing this down I recognise myself in this assessment. I see how easily I am manipulated by images, by framing and repetition. I think back to times I have justi-fied action or inaction, and that I have contemplated giving up my comfortable life to work for or with the poor, only to sit back down and blush at the condescending (or potentially patronising) nature of this desire.

Kapuscinski's expedients thus reflect the complexities of the globalised landscape, in which those who are privileged by birth or circumstances can avail themselves of so many things and those who are not often experience an entirely different fate. The performances addressed in this book work to unsettle spectators in such a way that they have the potential to reflect in complex, contradictory and hence productive ways on the function of both response and responsibility in the context of this fraught environment.

Anxiety and Levinasian responsibility

For an ethical subject, subjectivity (following Levinas) emerges from responsibility. But responsibility, in Levinasian terms, is complex and not something that an individual subject has a choice about:

> Responsibility for the other, going against intentionality and the will, which intentionality does not succeed in dissimulating, signifies not the disclosure of a given and its reception, but the exposure of me to the other, prior to every decision. (Levinas, 1998: 141)

Responsibility comes before any conscious process of decision making; it is something that occurs for the subject in the pre-ontological realm, the realm of the sensible. As Leslie A. Wade points out: 'For Levinas, the Other is anterior to the self, prior to discourse (and knowledge), and the self comes into being only in relation to the Other' (Wade, 2008: 8). The ethical subject is not someone bound by universal truths or ideals. A Levinasian model of ethics reworks Enlightenment notions of self-sustaining ego, law, knowledge, and justice by arguing for an understanding of the individual subject as s/he exists within a 'face-to-face' relationship with the other.[3] As Levinas maintains:

> Communication would be impossible if it should have to begin in the ego, a free subject, to whom every other would be only a limitation that invites war, domination, precaution and information. To communicate is indeed to open oneself, but the openness is not complete if it is on the watch for recognition. It is complete not in opening to the spectacle of or the recognition of the other, but in becoming a responsibility for him. (Levinas, 1981: 119)

In responding to the other, a subject is caught in a process of ethical questioning that results from the interruption to his or her ongoing subjectivity, caused by the call of the other.[4] The subject is compelled to respond and perhaps even to move beyond the position of 'the tourist or the vagabond', described by Bauman as representing the people – circulating within the postmodern world – who 'are sensation-seekers and collectors of experiences; their relationship to the world is primarily *aesthetic*: they perceive the world as a food for sensibility' (Bauman, 1998: 94; original emphasis). In fact, Levinas goes so far as to say that 'the response is put forth for the other, without any "taking up of attitudes." This responsibility is like a cellular irritability; it is the impossibility of being silent, the scandal of sincerity' (Levinas, 1981: 143). He explains that the call of the other, the interruption, is something that is constantly occurring and that it is something that the subject has no option but to respond to.

If the call of the other, in Levinasian terms, is continuous and inevitable, and if the subject has no option but to respond, then it is necessary to consider how this call works and what role, if any, performance and theatre might play in this process? How might theatre, and the transition that occurs as an individual subject enters the space and becomes a spectator, impact on, or contribute to the relationship between the self and the other?

For Levinas the ethical relationship is understood as 'Saying *(le dire)*' and the 'Said *(le dit)*'. As he explains 'Saying is not a game. Antecedent to the verbal signs it conjugates, to the linguistic systems and the semantic glimmerings, a foreword preceding languages, it is the proximity of one to the other' (Levinas, 1988: 5).[5] In other words, the realm of the saying is the space in which the subject is confronted by the call of the other. It is in this space that my subjectivity is interrupted in a way that requires me to *listen* to and *hear* the other. As a subject I am not required to understand or decode what is said, and thus to engage in a process that denies alterity by attempting to reduce the other to the same.

The 'Saying' is the space in which each individual subject faces the other and engages in an exchange that occurs in the pre-ontological realm. In this realm the focus is on the tactile, the proximate. It is the realm of openness where the other calls the subject in a way that is not necessarily predetermined by the confines of language or of rules. It is a realm before the closure of the 'Said', which is the movement into ontology, narrative and ultimately fixity of meaning. This focus on the 'saying' as it occurs in the realm of the sensible is one of the elements of Levinas's ethics that makes it so important for this project, because performance also occurs in or activates this realm. There are myriad opportunities for the 'saying' to rupture the 'said', to refuse closure, to contradict and to mobilise the realm of the senses in the works addressed here, and in theatre more generally. As Peggy Phelan explains:

> If Levinas is right, and the face-to-face encounter is the most crucial arena in which the ethical bond we share becomes manifest, then live theatre and performance might speak to philosophy with renewed vigor. (Phelan, 2004: 577)

Phelan points out that theatre can facilitate a 'face-to-face' engagement; it is, however, important to note that this is not a literal movement of Levinas's philosophical discussions of the 'face-to-face' encounter into the theatre and onto the face of the performer. Alan Read, for example, in his book *Theatre, Intimacy & Engagement*, reconsiders his earlier work on Levinas and theatre and cautions against any 'rash theorizing of theatre as a "face-to-face" encounter' (Read, 2007: 227). Rather, this relationship is understood here as a way of thinking about the interruptions generated for spectators (interruptions that are felt bodily as we experience fear, close our eyes, feel a chill or perhaps a surge of emotion in response to images or scenes), through the complex processes of representation employed in contemporary performance. Spectators engage with a work on a number of levels and these levels effectively confuse any distinctions between thinking and feeling.[6]

The experience of seduction and estrangement (for example) results from the complex bodily responses elicited by a work for spectators. It is an experience that is not finite, is often difficult to describe in language, and is about the ways in which each individual spectator negotiates his or her vulnerability, exposure, sadness, trauma, despair as well as joy, warmth, exhilaration and hope in response to the work and the artists within it, as well as to the responses (where discernible) of other spectators. The 'saying' operates in performance alongside (or underneath) the said, and together, they generate an environment where the spectators and the performance or the performers are bound together in a process of exchange. Although the individual spectator's vulnerability is exposed by 'the saying' it is important to understand that each spectator exists in a constant state of trauma as s/he covers over 'the saying', or the call of the other, in the realm of the said in order to keep his/her sanity. The saying cannot exist without the said and this is what makes the relationship useful for theatre. The trauma, for an individual spectator, occurs in the constant movement between the self and the other, between responsibility and reluctance.

Despite the covering over of the saying by the said, performance, with its use of fragmentation, physicality, presence, shock, heightened emotional states and spectacle, offers myriad moments in which the saying can interrupt or pierce each spectator's sense of self so that a process of ethical questioning about response and responsibility can emerge powerfully. As Wade explains, 'what intrigues me is the possibility of performing the Saying, the address to the Other that invites, that demands no closure or thematizing, that serves less to interpret than to interrupt' (Wade, 2008: 18).

Politics and responsibility

This experience of responsibility is further complicated by the fact that each subject's relationship to the other must also be considered within a political context. In this regard, I again turn to Levinas, and his use of the idea of 'le tiers/the third party' (by which he refers to society, law, government and politics) to explain that the ethical relationship with the other is not a singular or isolated relationship; it is one between the other and other others, in the social domain.[7] The tension that exists between the other and 'le tiers', is interesting as it describes the difficulties of responding to the other in an environment where other forces or institutions constantly call for our participation or attention. As Levinas explains 'the third party looks at me in the eyes of the Other – language is justice' (Levinas, 1969: 213). This also raises the coincident requirement that we make judgments about the order of our responses. He points out:

> I don't live in a world in which there is but one single 'first comer'; there is always a third party in the world: he or she is also my

other, my neighbor. Hence, it is important to me to know which of the two takes precedence. (Levinas, 2001: 166)

This is an environment in which there are multiple levels of difference operating at once, and where these levels of difference cannot be reduced to a singular concept. For Levinas, politics must be conceived of not as a totalising structure but as something obliged to acknowledge (and extending out from or existing in a dynamic association with) the face-to-face relationship with the other.[8]

This interplay of ethics and politics informs the ways in which subjects read events as they unfold in the world around them, as well as ways in which they might respond to or engage with political performance as spectators.

This book is concerned with subjects as citizens and as spectators who are interested in negotiating pathways through the contemporary media-saturated globalised landscape. These subjects, look to the theatre to provide a space in which there is a rejection of totalisation in favour of a pluralism of views or responses, and they are informed by and motivated in response to this to find new ways of thinking about or responding to, important political, historical and social questions. That is not to say that the subjects in question necessarily come to the theatre with predetermined ethical positions. They tend to want more than a recognition of the other's difference or otherness; they want a reconsideration of the ideas of justice, law and power beyond 'abstract systems of obligation' (Nealon, 1998: 34), and they seek out political theatre as space that has the potential to provide this reconsideration.[9]

As a spectator at the performance, *Le Dernier Caravansérail*, Alison Croggon experienced numerous moments in which the political realm was profoundly rendered via the performance. This rendering allowed or perhaps provoked Croggon to probe the complexities and personal costs of oppression in new ways. As she explains:

[The play's] politics exist outside gross generalizations of power as understood, for example, in the public world of mass media, reaching instead into the intimate and complex space of our own lives. It is here that we can understand longing and desire, love and hatred, hope and betrayal and despair. (Croggon, 2005)

I also attended this performance and I experienced a moment in which the significance of the political realm came literally crashing into the performance in a way that released a sense of deep shame for me as an Australian citizen. It was also a moment where Levinas's understandings of the relationships between ethics and politics, and in this case my own relationships to the other as represented on stage, and to other others within the political domain, became abundantly clear.

Part II of the spectacular six-hour epic, *Le Dernier Caravansérail*, 'Origines et destins' (Origins and Destinies) opens with a small raft attempting to stay afloat on an angry sea. It is crammed with refugees and asylum seekers and it catches fire. A helicopter is heard overhead and Australian Special Air Services (SAS) personnel begin to descend on ropes. It seems as if help is at hand. Instead of helping, however, the SAS announce on a megaphone that the refugees should go home. They repeat loudly through the megaphone: 'Australia does not accept you'. This devastating statement reverberates around the performance space. I am not sure if there is such a thing as acute shame but I certainly felt it as I watched this scene. The shame was acute because this was not mere fiction; this scene echoed the real political actions of the Australian Government in response to refugees stranded in distress in international waters close to Christmas Island (Australian territory) in 2001. The Government steadfastly refused entry of the damaged vessel into Australian waters. The Norwegian ship, The MV Tampa, eventually rescued the refugees and asylum seekers on board.

The act of witnessing this in performance, and the cruelty inherent in the rejection and the loss of life that resulted, generated a feeling of shame so profound that I wanted to flee the performance space and indeed the nation. Similar reactions are discussed by other respondents to the performance, Philippa Wehle, for example states that:

> After five hours of intense encounters with lives lived and lost in countless odysseys, one is left inevitably with a deep sense of indignation and sorrow coupled with the determination to try to find some answers to the complex refugee situation. (2005: 85)

These complicated responses, of shame, of indignation and of understanding reflect the intricate weave of this production and allow a consideration of the kinds of ethical questions the performance raises. As Wehle points out, we leave the performance space with a 'determination'. The combination of responses – the emotional and personal as well as the more politically driven – indicate the ways in which this performance works to engender responsibility both in the Levinasian sense, where we feel it in and on our bodies: shame, indignation, understanding; and in the practical realm, where we leave with a desire for change.

Anxiety and practical responsibility

Levinas is primarily concerned with the face of the human other, but he does not prescribe a particular type of response as *the* ethical one. In fact the only thing that is certain is that the subject will respond. However, a response may be to ignore the call of the other or to acknowledge it and decide not to act in response to it in practical terms. As Rosalyn Diprose states: 'while the other's alterity transports me beyond myself, this does not imply that I accept the other's ideas, the content of what is said. It implies only that I think again' (Diprose, 2002: 141).

This lack of direction or detail on what an ethically productive response should entail, or indeed how to make it applicable within the ontological realm, is troubling. It highlights the fact that while Levinas's understanding of ethics based on responsibility is essential to my own ideas about ethics and my understanding of responsibility, it just will not work on its own. It does not reveal or uncover what responsibility should feel like, or how it might be activated for spectators in the current globalised environment (either within or beyond the performance space). As Nicholas Ridout in his eloquent discussion of Levinasian philosophy argues, 'for Levinas, it seems, the face is not actually any face in particular, but rather the figure of the pre-ontological possibility of an encounter between subjects' (Ridout, 2006: 30) and for Ridout this is unhelpful. He goes on to explain that

> an ethics that does not permit the theatre-maker or spectator to make meaningful distinctions between, say, a performance by Guillermo Gómez-Peña and a piece of racist propaganda would seem not to be an ethics at all. (Ridout, 2006: 30–31)[10]

Ridout is right to suggest that the lack of direction causes difficulty and has the potential to render Levinasian ethics useless within the context of theatrical production and analysis (or indeed in any concrete situation), and therefore, for him at least, it is necessary to jettison this approach. Levinas did not, however, write a philosophy for theatre; he described an ethics that is situated in terms of the relationship between the self and the other. I believe that given the significance of Levinas's work in rethinking ethical relations and positioning them firmly within the subject-other relationship, it is more useful to extend this ethics so that it can have relevance for subjects and for spectators in the contemporary context, than it is to abandon it.

I propose an extension of Levinasian ethics so that it can make the distinctions that Ridout feels it is currently incapable of. Levinasian ethics moves the focus from the subject to the other and demands that the subject respond to the other. I would like to extend this response (this moment of rupture where the saying interrupts the said) by situating it firmly in the context of the contemporary moment. While Levinas does not guide the subject in terms of how the response might operate, subjects, who function in the ontological realm, who have specific cultural, racial, social and other affiliations, draw meaning from the world, and are shaped by it.

They may be disturbed by injustice, poverty and war (for example), but they may also experience a sense of impotence or insignificance in the face of such an overwhelming array of pressing global problems. These subjects embody a combination of responses (or desire for response) from inaction to outrage, from immersion to alienation. Considering this, then, there is more than one sense in which responsibility operates for them. They may be moved by a desire to do something in response to the world around them, and consequently to activate their responsibility in some way. It may be this desire that inspires them to go to the theatre or performance space (in the first place) and to engage with a work.

This kind of responsibility involves choice, and the decision to take action. It sits, therefore, outside of a Levinasian notion of responsibility, which operates at a pre-ontological or even existential level. Practical responsibility, as I explained in response to *Le Dernier Caravansérail* above, allows spectators (or, in some instances, compels them) to take action, to respond (in a physical or active sense) to

responsibility, to the call of the other. The action that these spectators might take can vary from engaging in discussions with people to
generate awareness of issues, to participating in direct political action
to alter a situation, to changing the ways in which they relate to various others as they encounter them. Or even to thinking differently
about events, situations or ideas.

These practical actions are mobilised, I believe, by contemporary
politically inflected performances and any understanding of responsibility must acknowledge that there is always the potential for the
pre-ontological disturbance to emerge into the ontological realm,
even if this emergence only manifests itself as a moment of reflection or reconsideration.

This idea of practical responsibility is not, however, always achieved
in the contemporary moment, where (as Bauman pointed out)
responsibilities are being shed. Nor is it always achieved within the
performance-spectator relationship. Despite this, the crucial issue is
that practical responsibility has the *potential* to work for subjects who
seek a way beyond the status quo. Interested subjects have the capacity to use the performance space as a space in which to build relationships and engage with the other in all of his/her complexity and
also to think about what the implications of this engagement might
be for the individual spectator's own relationship to, and place
within, the world.

I am not trying to develop a formula that claims that political
performance *necessarily* generates the face of the other and that, in
response, every spectator hears the call and leaps into action, either
on a physical or reflective level. However, I am attempting to understand and perhaps reveal or uncover the ways in which performance (particularly politically inflected performance) provides an
alternative space of resistance, of calm, or even of radical unsettlement within which spectators may hear the call of the other (in a
different way).

Because this is not a formula, it is difficult to describe what this
call might look or sound like in any singular sense; it simply doesn't
occur in this way. Each of the performances considered in the following chapters activates the senses and generates myriad spaces
for ethical reflection. Each uses different techniques, both in terms
of form and content, to generate this experience. Each work draws
on historical or political themes to grapple with significant social

and/or cultural questions. They do not present singular answers or tell unified stories; instead, they destabilise or interrupt dominant ideologies and challenge spectators in ways that encourage them to probe difficult concepts surrounding their positions in the world and their relationship to others.

The focus of this process of interruption is not to uncover finite or 'correct' answers that might help an individual spectator understand or decode the other, but to use performance to unsettle assumptions and to strive for a 'plurality' of views about and responses to the challenging questions of our time. The works in question deal variously with the refugee crisis (*Le Dernier Caravansérail*), the oppression (and triumph) of Indigenous Australians (*The Career Highlights of the MAMU*), the impacts of war (*Sandakan Threnody*), and the limits of technology, science and experimentation (*Three Tales, Genesi: from the museum of sleep* and *Nature's Little Helpers*).

The spectator and ambivalence

Levinas is a profoundly important and a profoundly difficult philosopher, and, as I have highlighted, there are many problems with the use of his philosophical insights within my project. Nonetheless, the fundamental focus of his ethics is responsibility and therefore it is central to this book, which aims to understand the fragile position of contemporary subjects as both citizens and spectators.

Despite the dangers of using Levinasian philosophy, I continue with his philosophy because I explore the ways in which performance can stimulate active engagement, reflection, action, response and responsibility for spectators. For Levinas this activity is the opposite of 'participation', for me, however, it is *participation* (I will discuss this in detail below). I also persist with his philosophy because of its fundamental focus on ethics as it exists in, and in response to, the other. I want to extend this focus here by considering how responsibility can or might be engendered through performance. This issue is of crucial importance in the current environment with its increasing media saturation, and 'war on terror', and the attendant claims these events make on our emotional energies.

Political performance (or any art that is engaged politically and seeks to pierce the cult of individualism by rupturing complacency and provoking spectators or viewers) is all very well, but my focus is to consider *how* it is that spectators become involved in, and respond to, this kind of work. The spectators in question are also subjects who exist in the globalised world, for whom performance offers an alternative space in which to act, to confront ethical questions and to get beyond the potential paralysis of the contemporary moment. But what kind of action am I proposing, and what shape might this or any action take? The performances addressed in this book engage spectators in a range of response processes. They may, for example, move between experiences of complete corporeal and intellectual immersion in a work, through the ideas it is grappling with or through the proximity to the performer or performers, to moments of dislocation when the ideas, images or bodily presence of the performer or performers are experienced as repulsive, traumatic, disturbing or perhaps alienating. These processes occur (to varying degrees and in different ways for individual spectators) throughout the performances discussed here. It is the ability of these works to generate these dynamic (if at times uncomfortable) sets of responses that make performance such a useful and productive space within which spectators can become imaginatively involved with the works and the ethical questions they provoke.

What is not clear is what happens once the spectators leave the performance space. I am not suggesting that they will take up arms against a cause or that there will be a frenzied or group response to any performance, I am suggesting, rather, that responsibility can lead to (or, in the best performances, will lead to) ambivalence. This is an ambivalence about what to do with the responsibility produced by and in response to the work. If a performance is successful in terms of its ability to engage spectators in a process of ethical reflection, it will leave them feeling ambivalent. This is not an ambivalence that means they will necessarily flounder or that they occupy a position of inertia, but instead it is understood as a productive space that allows for the ideas, traces, concepts and concerns in the performance to percolate.

Ambivalence, as I understand it, then, is a form of radical unsettlement, an experience of disruption and interruption in which the anodyne is challenged. Ambivalence keeps spectators engaged with the other, with the work, and with responsibility and therefore in an ethical process, long after they have left the performance space. Nicholas Ridout speaks of another similar engagement with and in the theatre and he describes this as 'embarrassment'. He talks in some detail about the relationships between this and shame, and while Ridout's embarrassment is slightly different in focus from my notion (following Bauman) of ambivalence, his description of its effects can be usefully applied to the experience of ambivalence, Ridout says

> there is something in the appearing that takes place in the theatre that seems capable of activating in an audience a feeling of our compromised, alienated participation in the political and economic relations that make us appear to be who we are. (Ridout, 2006a: 94)

Ridout also quotes Helene Keyssar who talks about the experience of being 'wholly befuddled' in response to a performance (2006a: 78). He goes on to explain that 'It seems that it is when we find ourselves in a grey area, where the lights could, as it were, be either on or off, or both, that embarrassment... is most likely to arise out of face-to-face encounters of this kind' (Ridout, 2006a: 79). This point is important as it signals that while ambivalence or befuddlement or embarrassment can be temporarily confusing (and can result in an experience of floundering), this is, mostly, a momentary experience. As Ridout continues 'the moment, or even, in fact, the possibility of the moment of embarrassing self-disclosure in the event of the theatrical face to face, is essential to the self-recognition that we enjoy' (Ridout, 2006a: 79). Ambivalence is about these moments of self-recognition but also about the internal processes of doubt, anxiety, reflection and consideration individual spectators go through in their attempts to make sense of, or to respond to a work.

Because performance engages its spectators on multiple levels, it has the potential to open up a space in which an echo or reverberation of the other's call might penetrate in ways that it may not in the media-saturated realm outside the performance space. Performances that generate ambivalence open up the 'Saying' (le dire) so that it can interrupt spectators, fracture any finite responses, expose their vulnerabilities, and create an experience of seduction and estrangement.

This experience of seduction and estrangement can take many forms. Carol Middleton, for example, describes the audiences' responses to Socìetas Raffaello Sanzio's production *Genesi: from the museum of sleep* as follows:

> Bewildered, overwhelmed, shocked and awed, the audience
> drifted from the State Theatre... We had been visually and orally
> confronted by imagery and sound that peeled away the layers
> that normally act as filters to our senses, and been exposed to the
> cacophony of chaos, the rawness of creation and the pain of
> human existence. (Middleton, 2002)

This work elicited a range of complex emotions for me also. In Act II
'Auschwitz' I was confronted with child performers who were, apparently, waiting to be exterminated. Nothing was said (in either sense):
there were images of listless children, eerie sounds of gaiety and
music off stage, a star, a toy train and a scream. This Act was left
open; it jolted me out of any sense of recognition, yet at the same
time it was familiar, and it punctured me. I was vulnerable, wounded
and lost. Nonetheless, I did not flounder in this state because once
the shock of the wound eased, I became incensed and wanted to do
something practical in response. This was a moment in which
response and responsibility collided and ambivalence was unleashed.
It was a moment in which I wanted to escape from the theatre but
did not know in what direction to run, think or feel. It was a moment
of profound and disturbing ambivalence that continues to resonate.
For Alan Read, in his discussion of this performance, and particularly of Act II, something slightly different, yet no less profound,
occurred,

> the theatre machine in the hands of Romeo and Claudia
> Castellucci, Chiara Guidi, and their children, insists on the theat-
> ricality of the unthinkable. By refusing to offer any explanation
> in language, but an enthusiasm of effects, sound, light, gesture
> the inexplicable becomes palpable. (Read, 2007: 163)

For Read the 'inexplicable becomes palpable' and he goes on to say
that 'there is no secure outside within which the audience sit safely
removed from the implications here of what they see' (Read, 2007:
163). It is precisely this lack of safety that engages spectators in a process of continued reflection and response, a process of productive
ambivalence. I am not suggesting, however, that ambivalence results

in a set of responses that are the same for every spectator. Instead, ambivalence is about acknowledging the complex, often contradictory and multilayered questions and responses political performances can trigger for spectators.

It is important to acknowledge that Levinas sees his philosophy as a philosophy of ambivalence. His emphasis is slightly different from my own use of the term but it is worth considering his use of ambivalence as it helps to explain some of the complexities of his philosophy. He writes that:

> Philosophy is called upon to conceive ambivalence ... Even if it is called to thought by justice, it still synchronizes in the said the diachrony of the difference between the one and the other, and remains the servant of the saying that signifies the difference between the one and the other as the one for the other, as non-indifference to the other. (Levinas, 1998: 162)

Robert Eaglestone draws attention to this affirmation of ambivalence when he talks about the fact that Levinas's work is full of 'double-nesses'. He provides a number of examples, the most relevant of which is his reference to Robert Bernasconi's argument that 'Levinas has an understanding of the face which is both "empirical" and "transcendental"' (Eaglestone, 2004: 269). While there is nothing ambivalent for Levinas about the call of the other (the act of calling or of being called) what that call implies is potentially ambivalent. This is significant as I agree that while the call is not ambivalent, how spectators respond, or have the potential to respond, is with ambivalence. And this is why it is necessary to extend Levinasian ethics into the ontological realm and the domain of practical responsibility.

The limits of Levinas

Although I have been primarily concerned here with spectatorship and the ways in which spectators can be engaged ethically in order that they might find a space for response, stimulation and responsibility in performance, away from the stasis and saturation of the 'outside' world, the dangers (already alluded to) of utilising Levinas's philosophy within this project cannot be overlooked. There are three areas that are of specific concern. Firstly there is a risk in the concentration on the other that the subject (the active spectators imagined here) might be silenced in the process. Secondly, Levinas is suspicious of art (and representation more generally) as he sees it as obfuscating the face of the other and this is obviously something that I must respond to. Thirdly, one of the most perplexing problems with art, for Levinas, is its ability to elicit 'participation' and while, as I have stated, we have different (oppositional) understandings of participation, it is necessary to interrogate the concept 'participation' before proceeding to the analytical chapters of this book.

In exploring these problems I have the opportunity to acknowledge the limitations of his ideas when they are used in the context of discussions about performance (and of course to consider the possibility that the limitations are, in the use of his philosophy within this context, not necessarily in the philosophy itself).

The 'scandal of sincerity' and the dangers of silencing the subject

Levinas's focus on the other has been criticised as leading to a negation of the self and therefore to an inhibiting of the possibility of an ethical exchange. It is important to interrogate this position as it has implications for an understanding of the notions of response and responsibility for spectators, both within and beyond the performance space. Paul Ricoeur, for example, argues that Levinas's philosophy places too much emphasis on the other at the expense of the subject and the possibility of reciprocity. Ricoeur is concerned with the potential for extreme individualism involved in ultimate alterity. He states 'in reality this initiative establishes no relation at all, to the extent that the other represents absolute exteriority with respect to an ego defined in the condition of separation' (Ricoeur, 1992: 188–189). It would also seem that without reciprocity the act of spectatorship becomes redundant. Surely that is what the spectator does – give back, responds, and participates in an exchange? I think that while Levinas is adamant that the focus needs to move from an exchange between the self and the other, where the self is prioritised, he is not arguing that the self be negated. Instead, I read his philosophy as one that positions the relationship as one of susceptibility, where the self is motivated by the necessity of responding to the other, instead of by a desire for reciprocity. As Levinas explains:

> Responsibility for the other, in its antecedence to my freedom, its antecedence to the present and to representation, is a passivity more passive than all passivity, an exposure to the other without this exposure being assumed, an exposure without holding back, exposure of exposedness, expression, saying. This exposure is the frankness, sincerity, veracity of saying. (1998: 15)[11]

Levinas is proposing a shift that demands the positioning of the other at the centre of any exchange process rather than a necessary negation of the self. This shift from an absorbing focus on the self to the other is urgently needed in a Western culture preoccupied with 'possession and consumption.'

How this reorientation takes place and what it implies for contemporary (secular) subjects needs further explanation, since the idea of the subjugation of the self (or the potential for this through ethical action) generates a sense of unease and results in detailed criticism of Levinas's work. What Levinas proposes is a complicated and powerful philosophy that demands great commitment from subjects. It is not an ethics that admits a symmetrical or reciprocal relation to the other; in fact Levinas cautions against Martin Buber's reciprocal ethics 'because the moment one is generous in hopes of reciprocity, that relation no longer involves generosity but the commercial relation, the exchange of good behavior' (Levinas, 1999: 101). The other, for Levinas, cannot be reduced to the same. On this matter, Jeffrey Nealon makes the point that the process of 'subjection' that occurs for the subject in the face of the other is not one of 'ham-fisted determinism, where subjection merely creates slaves or automatons.' It is, instead, a process whereby 'subjection necessarily happens in response itself, in responding to the other by saying I: performative responsibility is subjectivity itself' (Nealon, 1998: 50). This is an aspect of Levinas's work that can be difficult to decipher.

Notwithstanding this concern, it is central to an understanding of the relationship between the self and the other and to a Levinasian notion of ethics as responsibility, as well as to understanding why his approach (despite its complexity in the context of performance) is so useful for this project. If this repositioning of the self-other relationship is considered within a performance context it would mean that spectators do not participate in a desire for acknowledgement, or indeed in order to decode the other and reduce him/her to the same. Instead, they engage in a process of giving, in which the complexity and alterity of the other is responded to without the desire to decode, contain or categorise. In the scheme of Levinasian ethics the subject does not attempt to contain the other, but gives him/herself to the other in an act of 'radical generosity' (Levinas, 1987a: 92).[12]

This sense of generosity was created for Tony Hughes-d'Aeth in response to the alterity of the Indigenous elders who told their stories via documentary footage in the midst of a multi-modal energetic performance of Scott Rankin and Trevor Jamieson's *The Career Highlights of the MAMU*. Hughes-d'Aeth explains that the work allowed him to experience 'the vectors of separate histories' (Hughes-d'Aeth, 2002) and 'the *punctum*' occurred for him when Trevor Jamieson

> disguised in black Kendo robes danced around a distraught Japanese woman who was declaiming a poem about Hiroshima ... at this moment I comprehended that the Spinifex people and the residents of Hiroshima were bonded – as few other people in the world could be – in their first-hand experience of nuclear assault. (Hughes-d'Aeth, 2002)

This understanding allowed Hughes-d'Aeth to gain insight into, but not necessarily an ability to contain or own, the experiences being negotiated or represented in the performance space. Thus, if the relationship between the self and the other is understood not as one in which the subject is negated or sidelined in response to the call of the other, but as one in which the focus shifts from the subject to the other – to hearing, connecting and being open to (or touched by) the other – then this is precisely the kind of relationship that I see as operating productively for spectators (such as Hughes-d'Aeth above) in response to the performances discussed in this book. It is a relationship that allows for multiple and often contradictory responses. It is one that occurs in the realm of the sensible where the performance (and or performers) can reach out to spectators and engage them bodily through touch and the generation of an intimate space: it is a relationship of proximity.

As Bauman points out, for Levinas

> 'proximity' stands for the unique quality of the ethical situation –
> which 'forgets reciprocity, as in love that does not expect to be
> shared'. Proximity is not a very short distance, it is not even the
> overcoming or neglecting or denying distance – it is, purely (though
> not at all simply), 'a suppression of distance'. (Bauman, 1993: 87)

In this regard, Levinasian ethics, with its focus on the other and the
subject's responsibility for the other, provides a framework for subjects
who feel compelled to respond but who also understand that any action
or response is contingent. It is a framework in which both responsibility
and ambivalence are generated. Levinas's philosophy is one that resists
the desire to understand (in a singular or definitive sense by reducing
the saying to the said), or to decode the other, or to simplify his/her suffering, experience or identity to something containable.

The limits of art

The question or idea of art (in the broadest sense) is a complex one for
Levinas and one that elicits a range of (at times contradictory)
responses throughout his writings. The majority of his responses to
art describe his mistrust or outright condemnation of it. For example,
in his *Collected Philosophical Papers*, he says: 'there is something wicked
and egoist and cowardly in artistic *enjoyment*. There are times when
one can be ashamed of it, as of feasting during a plague' (Levinas,
1987: 12; my emphasis). Despite this misgiving, he draws on a range
of artists throughout his work, including Paul Celan, Fyodor
Dostoyevsky, S.Y. Agnon and Sasha Sosno.[13] Art and representation in
general trouble Levinas, and in 'Reality and its Shadow' he outlines a
number of reasons for his mistrust. Firstly he fears the ways in which
art has the ability to interfere with the face of the other. As Robbins
points out:

> Art consists in substituting for the object its image... it is an
> obscuring or a shadow of reality. Whereas 'a concept is the object
> grasped, the intelligible object,' and thus a 'living' relationship
> with that object, 'the image *neutralizes* this real relationship'.
> (Robbins, 1999: 51–52)

This may be interpreted as assigning literalness to the face, that it is, when presented to the subject, outside of representation. While I have signalled the dangers of a literal approach earlier it is also worth questioning what this then means for an understanding of the face. Surely the face in itself (its rawness or flesh) cannot exist beyond representation? Doesn't the face represent the person, the body? Levinas addresses this concern:

> The epiphany of the face is alive. Its life consists in undoing the form in which every entity, when it enters into immanence, that is, when it exposes itself as a theme, is already dissimulated. The other who manifests himself in the face as it were breaks through his own plastic essence. ... His presence consists in *divesting* himself of the form which, however, manifests him. His manifestation is a surplus over the inevitable paralysis of manifestation. (Levinas, 1986: 351–352; original emphasis)

For Levinas, representation gets in the way of the subject's ability to respond to this manifestation. The face cannot be held 'captive', and the danger of art is that it attempts to do this and therefore denies the possibility of responsibility.

Because Levinas's specific references to theatre concentrate on work that is mimetic, they are therefore quite different in focus from the performances addressed here, although his concerns cannot be dismissed. In many of his references to both theatre and poetry, for example, he highlights a larger concern, and that is his relationship to the aesthetic in general. He is concerned that aesthetic practices act in such a way that 'the numinous or the sacred envelops and transports man beyond his powers and wishes' (Levinas, 1969: 14). While this is possibly true, and may indeed have been the case for much of the art (broadly understood) Levinas was exposed to, in the current environment and with the proliferation of sophisticated media technologies art does not have the central position of influence or indeed of potential for distraction that it once had. The function of art (particularly political art) is rather different in the contemporary sphere.[14]

I experience some anxiety about Levinas's critique of art on the grounds that this critique suggests that art gets in the way of a 'true' (prior or real) ethical relationship with the other. For him there is a space or moment (the pre-ontological realm) in which an unmediated relationship between the self and the other will or can occur. Although this belief is admirable, it can only work on a theoretical level as relationships are always mediated. Levinas's position in this regard does not fully acknowledge the 'real' or lived contexts within which human relationships and exchanges operate and it is for this reason that his philosophy needs to be extended if it is to be considered in terms of actual relationships between the subject and the other, whether these occur within or beyond the theatre.

The question of participation

Another aspect of art that Levinas fears is its ability to move the subject away from a focus on responsibility by both obscuring the face, and by generating an environment in which the individual spectator or the audience as a whole *participates* in the work.[15] Participation, for Levinas, signals a submission, loss or paralysis that exists in opposition to ethics.[16] He states: 'The relaxation in intoxication is a semblance of distance and irresponsibility. It is a suppression of fraternity, or a murder of the brother' (Levinas, 1998: 192). This fear of participation is explained by Robert Eaglestone as a fear of both 'individual drunken, stoned, poetic delirium', and of the 'same blinding, mass-or-mob-intoxicating effect of, for example, marching or chanting rhythmically in a carefully designed rally' (Eaglestone, 2004: 262).[17] This is a crucial clarification. It is Levinas's fear, that through 'participation' the subject will somehow become deaf to the need for responsibility, and, as a consequence, will not be able to hear the call of the other, that most powerfully informs his mistrust of art. It is as if the fact of participating in a collective (for example as an audience member) negates any possible individual responses.[18]

I counter these concerns with the argument that each of the works discussed in this book performs the function of disrupting any desire for participation in the Levinasian sense. While there are, of course, moments of collective response, which can be discerned by audible gasps, increased tension, or laughter, these do not occlude the possibility of alternative individual responses. In fact, these works generate rupture upon rupture, the kind of 'rupture' Levinas assigns to language when he says 'language is "rupture and commencement, breaking of rhythm which enraptures and transports the interlocutors–prose" ' (in Eaglestone, 2004: 262). These ruptures of the performances take many different forms and include the 'irruption of the real', as discussed by Lehmann:

> The irruption of the real becomes an object not just of reflection (as in Romanticism) but of the theatrical design itself. This operates on a number of levels, but in an especially revealing way through a strategy and an *aesthetics of undecidability* concerning the basic means of theatre. (Lehmann, 2006: 100; original emphasis)

This 'irruption of the real' is something that emerges to varying degrees in each of the works addressed here. In *Genesi: from the museum of sleep* and *Tragedia Endogonidia Br.#4* (2003) for example, director Romeo Castellucci and Socìetas Raffaello Sanzio use spectacular devices and techniques to challenge spectators viscerally. The productions convey with vivid imagery scenes of horror, shock and bewilderment that continually push the boundaries of theatre and performance as well as the emotional tolerance of spectators.

As Ridout suggests 'the work becomes an investigation of the conditions under which something might be possible: in this case, how it might be possible to make theatre' (Ridout, 2006: 178). In *Le Dernier Caravansérail* tragic, heart-wrenching testimony, collected via interviews with refugees over a two-year period, is used as the basis of a performance that highlights the plight of refugees and displaced people as they cross the globe. In this production, Ariane Mnouchkine and Théâtre du Soleil use repetition and spectacle to attempt to puncture participation in the Levinasian sense. Testimony is also used in *The Career Highlights of the MAMU, Sandakan Threnody*, and in *Three Tales* to present and complicate the process of representation and the ways in which spectators might engage with, respond to, or recognise the 'face of the other'. Giorgio Agamben's work on testimony and bearing witness is also invaluable in these three chapters as his ideas complicate and extend Levinasian ethics by asking questions about the ways in which testimony and witnessing function to hide, reveal, challenge and add depth to processes of representation.

Each of these works activates 'an *aesthetics of undecidability*' that results in the kind of participation I propose as a counter to the Levinasian understanding of the term. These performances realise

'the *mutual implication of actors and spectators in the theatrical production of images*', an activity Lehmann sees as both 'aesthetic' and
'ethico-political', and an activity that makes 'visible the broken
thread between personal experience and perception' (Lehmann,
2006: 186; original emphasis). They also operate in the pre-ontological
realm, the realm of the sensible (as discussed earlier), where spectators
are engaged in an exposure to the other that occurs, as Levinas
explains, 'on the surface of the skin' (1998: 15).

I do not want to imply that each performance seamlessly fractures
the idea of participation by successfully engaging every spectator
continuously and/or by unveiling an essentialist or singular exposure to the face of the other. Although all of the works manage to
engender responsibility and have the capacity to engage spectators
in a process of ethical reflection, they do not all do this with ease
and they are experienced in a range of ways by different spectators.

Responding to Levinas's claim that art gets in the way of the relationship with the 'face of the other' both causes me considerable
anxiety and provides added complexity to this project. It is also one
of the areas in which I depart from or seriously question Levinas's
philosophy. This occurs for a number of reasons. Firstly, I could argue
that in at least three of the works addressed here (*Sandakan Threnody,
The Career Highlights of the MAMU* and *Three Tales*) spectators confront the (literal) face of the other via documentary footage, as each
of these works uses documentary to fracture the performance and to
allow for the story or 'testimony' of the other to be heard within the
performance. The use of this footage interrupts the representational
process, and I could read this approach as allowing the 'face of the
other' to be seen, although not captured. This strategy is used in
Sandakan Threnody when, in the middle of the performance, documentary footage of Susan Moxham is projected into the complete
darkness of the performance space. Moxham talks about loss and
about despair. She explains what it was like to be the child of a prisoner of war and about post-traumatic stress and its impact. She speaks
calmly and without much affect. There is no artifice here, and amidst
the unfolding spectacle of the performance this moment is haunt-
ingly evocative and disturbing.

While the documentary footage, particularly in *The Career
Highlights of the MAMU* (Chapter 3) and *Sandakan Threnody* (Chapter 4),
works to pierce the performance by introducing a radically different

element (both in terms of form and content), it is not offering spectators literal access to the truth of the other's experience in any singular sense. It is worth considering Michael André Bernstein's concerns
with the limits of this form in his discussion of Holocaust testimony.
He cautions that 'one of the most pervasive myths of our era, a myth
perhaps even partially arising out of our collective response to the
horrors of the concentration camps, is the absolute authority given
to first-person testimony' (Bernstein, 1994: 47). While it is important
to consider this caution, the use of footage in these performances
provides an alternative version or way of seeing (via 'evidence') of
the other's experiences of loss and horror associated with war and
oppression. This serves to complicate the relationship between
representation and the other. The others who speak in the documentaries (despite their mediation by the filmic form) call spectators in
particular, specific and personal ways, to hear their stories and to
take responsibility. The documentary sequences work in play with
the other elements of the performance to complicate the parameters
within which the 'face of the other' is understood.

The issue of the face of the other becomes even more complicated
in *Three Tales* (Chapter 6), as it both obscures and then moves beyond
any current conceptualisations of who the other might be. Through
the introduction of cyborgs, robots and machines the possibility of
defining or even identifying the face becomes even more difficult in
this performance. As well, the limitations of Levinas's assumption
that only humans can have a face become apparent in the twenty-
first century context, with its considerations of the post-human, the
prosthetic and the machine. As the final chapter of the book, the discussion unveils important questions about ethics, responsibility and
the other as s/he or it might be made manifest in a current or future
environment. It also provides a space in which to think about the
limits and potentiality of ethics and responsibility in a landscape in
which the 'human' as an identifiable figure may become obsolete.

Unsettled spectators

Ambivalence is a key aspect of contemporary life. Instead of seeing
ambivalence as something that leads to stasis or inertia, it should be
reimagined as an unsettling and productive space. Neither ambivalence nor undecidability necessarily imply that the subject will

flounder or experience paralysis in terms of decision making (or if they do this is likely to be a temporary condition); rather, it may generate an environment in which subjects become aware of their obligation to respond, as well as of the unstable or contingent nature of any response they might make. Ambivalence is understood here as a radical unsettling.

Not all of the works discussed in this book manage to create this feeling in a singular or sustained way. Each does, at least in places, generate various experiences of ambivalence for a range of spectators about the ethical decisions, or the potential for ethical action they might experience or undertake. Ambivalence involves negotiating between the real bodily feelings unleashed by a work (for example, goosebumps, the retreat behind clasped hands, the feeling of nausea, the audible gasp, etc.), and the intellectual responses to what those reactions might mean both in terms of the performance and its ramifications outside the space and into the 'real' world.

Ultimately an individual subject's responses, while contingent, fragile and potentially unstable, are always politicised, as s/he delves deeply into a work and uses the ideas and experiences it generates to shape moments of resistance to the fatigue and fear that dominate feelings about the contemporary global order.

Spectators who leave the performance space feeling some degree of ambivalence are likely to continue to reflect on and consider the work for some time. Through these responses they remain open to the call of the other outside the theatre. So, far from being 'sensation seeker[s]' or 'collector[s] of experiences' (as Bauman points out), they becomes people who are interested in and open to the other; they consider the ramifications of these responses beyond their own self-reflexive engagement and out into the community.

2
Genesi: The Spectator and 'Useless Suffering'?

> The suffering for the useless suffering of the other person, the just suffering in me for the unjustifiable suffering of the Other, opens upon suffering the ethical perspective of the inter-human. ... It is this attention to the Other which, across the cruelties of our century – despite these cruelties, because of these cruelties – can be affirmed as the very bond of human subjectivity, even to the point of being raised to a supreme ethical principle – the only one which it is not possible to contest – a principle which can go so far as to command the hopes and practical discipline of vast human groups. (Levinas, 1988: 159)

Since its inception Socìetas Raffaello Sanzio 'has explored the creation of artificial and non-verbal languages, the possibilities of an "iconoclastic" theatre, the boundaries and excesses of the use of the body in performance, as well as aspects of ritual and myth' (Giannachi and Kaye, 2002: 137).[1] It produces work that is both difficult to describe and at times difficult to endure. It is work that takes spectators on myriad journeys and that, in the process, stretches established or preconceived notions of what theatre can or might do.

Although each performance is different, each shares similarities with the others in terms of its aesthetic and focus. There is a concentration on generating a sense of presence, toying with representation, creating imagistic 'scenes', using spectacular devices, playing with artifice and at the same time paring it back to reveal hidden symbols or ideas. The desire is not to uncover 'truth' or meaning in any singular sense.

'Scenes' can be read on multiple levels; they often slowly emerge and unravel before perplexed or perhaps bewildered spectators. They appear as beautiful and disturbing installations, images, or montages. There is very little or no dialogue; words mostly seem unnecessary.

The aesthetic is the core, and the work functions to stimulate spectators viscerally. Socìetas Raffaello Sanzio makes spectators vulnerable. They often feel engaged, inspired, but at the same time out of their depth in any attempt at interpreting the work. Once (or if) they realise that any unified 'decoding' of meaning is both impossible and unnecessary then the performance takes on another dimension and it can be experienced as a journey into an unknown landscape of harrowing and exquisite images, of pain, trauma, silence and sonic ferocity, of strange bodies and strange encounters between bodies, of endurance (for both performers and spectators) and, ultimately, of profound and radical unsettlement. As Castellucci makes clear:

> Theatre is not something that must be 'recognised': 'I-go-to-the-theatre-to-recognise-the-Shakespeare-studies-that-I-have-completed'. It is not [or should not] be like that. Theatre is rather a journey **through** the unknown, **towards** the unknown. What myself and those of a similar mind have tried to do over the years has been to hold high the scandal of the stage and to keep it constantly vibrating. (Marshall, 2003: 7; original emphasis)

I explore a range of at times contradictory and emotional (as in bodily) reactions to the company's production, *Genesi: from the museum of sleep,* in this chapter to tease out how it is that a performance which affects spectators so profoundly at a sensory level can be responded to. In the process the relationships or similarities between what Castellucci calls his 'pre-tragic' theatre and Levinas's pre-ontological realm are considered. There is no attempt to fit one idea into the other, or to 'apply' Levinas, as this is something that is impossible. Neither is there an attempt to come up with solutions or answers to what Socìetas Raffaello Sanzio might be doing. Instead I am interested in trying to describe, analyse and understand (or make an incursion into) what happens or might happen for spectators while they 'watch' a work like *Genesi: from the museum of sleep.*

Genesi is a performance in three acts. It deals with and reinterprets the idea of Genesis. Castellucci, who directed the work, points out: 'this

Genesi is not only the biblical one, but is also one which gives birth (on stage) to my own rhetorical presumption to remake the world' (Castellucci, 1999). The first Act, 'At The Beginning', is concerned with a 'reality **outside of time**. The Creation occurs **before the invention of time'** (Castellucci in Marshall, 2003: 11; original emphasis). It concentrates on the chamber of Marie Curie and the invention of radium and it introduces *the museum of sleep*. The second Act, 'Auschwitz', which is considered the 'fulcrum' of the piece, takes place in Auschwitz and is performed by children. 'Auschwitz, precipitates the action into a **historical** time' (Castellucci in Marshall, 2003: 11; original emphasis); it reflects a time that 'seems suspended, swathed in the wadding of a nursery and the unctuous melodies of Luis Mariano' (Castellucci in Marshall, 2003: 12). The third Act, 'Abel and Cain', 'evokes a **mythical** time' (Castellucci in Marshall, 2003: 11; original emphasis). It deals with the story of Abel and Cain and 'the original homicide', where Cain faces the 'dramatic duel between the 2 fundamental polarities of human action: the Beginning and the End' (Castellucci in Marshall, 2003: 12–13).

Presence versus representation: disturbing 'representational schemes'[2]

There is a detailed focus in the work produced by Socìetas Raffaello Sanzio on the ways in which the language of the theatre can interrogate its very operations as well as the ways in which it can play with or mine representation. In fact, much of the scholarly material written about the company attempts to understand, analyse, challenge or explain its use of representation. Gabriella Giannachi and Nick Kaye, for example, talk about the 'rhetorical aspects of performance' (Giannachi and Kaye, 2002: 139) and the ways in which it is informed by Greek theatre, particularly tragedy, as well as contemporary movements such as *'arte provera'* (Giannachi and Kaye, 2002: 138; original emphasis). They go on to say that 'Raffaello Sanzio's performances work to challenge the *representational order* of the theatre's various rhetorical strategies through the "material reality" of the performed act' (Giannachi and Kaye, 2002: 141). Alan Read explains that he is drawn to the work because it

> resists representation…and things that have deliberately been kept from representation. This work suggests to me that, contrary

to academic emphases of the last decade, performance might be reasserting the possibilities of the intensely visual, yet unaddressed. (Read, 2007: 105)

Joe Kelleher in an essay on *Tragedia Endogonidia C.#01* (2002) suggests that 'this is not theatre as mirror to the world, but theatre as oven, where scraps and traces of human imagining (call these language, or legend, or idea) are cooked up until they discover themselves altered' (Kelleher, 2002: 11). And Nicholas Ridout argues that it is the company's skill with representation that leads scholars and critics to make the claim that they are dealing with the 'real' rather than the representational. For Ridout this 'tendency in critical responses to the work to emphasise "the real" as opposed to "the pretend" is testimony to the success of the pretending' (Ridout, 2006: 177). These points reveal that it is the play with representation – the tension between the 'real' and the 'pretend', the cooking of 'scraps of human imagining' – that involves spectators in a process of reflection about the emotional, visceral and intellectual implications of the images, stories and ideas contained (or secreted) in the performance. But what do spectators do with these ideas, images and stories? How do they negotiate these complicated, contradictory and often upsetting images as they leave the theatre with them? How do they avoid floundering in response to the work? My desire is to probe some of these questions or to encourage other spectators or theorists to deal with them, and this desire shapes my focus in this chapter.

I interrogate the ways in which work that toys with, explores or exceeds representation through its use of 'pre-tragic' theatre and its play with both form and content, as Ridout, Kelleher, Read and others describe it, has the potential not only to stimulate a process of reflection (or generate a bodily sense of unease) but to raise ethical questions and to provoke responsibility and a productive ambivalence for or within spectators.

Pre-tragic theatre and the realm of the sensible

For Castellucci 'pre-tragic theatre signifies, *a priori,* an infantility, an infantile theatre, in which "infantility" refers to a condition beyond language' (in Giannachi and Kaye, 2002: 164; original emphasis).

He laments the fact that tragedy is no longer part of contemporary life and says, 'redemption, pathos and ethos are words that cannot be reached, having fallen into the coldest of abstractions. The theatre [I] respect, now, is a theatre that makes you cry' (Castellucci, 2002). Socìetas Raffaello Sanzio is deeply concerned with creating work that has the power to reach spectators emotionally.[3] There is a desire in the company's work to reclaim tragedy as something that has *affect*, rather than as a concept that has lost its meaning. In order to generate theatre that has this power, Castellucci turns to 'pre-tragic' theatre. This is demonstrated in the company's decision to create works that include animals, children and the 'dis-human' performer. Live animals are used to show 'the ontological inadequacy' in the 'actor's occupation of the stage', and children are included because they can occupy a 'pre-linguistic' state (Giannachi and Kaye, 2002: 151–152). This state (of infantility) 'beyond language' is, or can also be a state of innocence, where children and animals play or frolic. Yet it is a fragile innocence, at times ruptured and at other times smoothed over by both the bodies and actions of the performers.

Castellucci argues that his work 'relies on the body of the actor' (Valentini and Marranca, 2004: 20). He sees the actor's body as having the potential to radically affect spectators, as a force more powerful than an adherence to narrative structure or written text or an allegiance to an idea of 'tradition'. There is a concern with keeping the performance open, therefore avoiding a re-presentation of a text/ script. It would seem that through the actor 'the truth of the body becomes inscribed quite precisely in the fiction of the spectacle' (in Valentini and Marranca, 2004: 20).

In each of its productions Socìetas Raffaello Sanzio casts a range of performers who sit outside traditional ideas of the 'actor', thus *exposing* spectators to a range of bodily forms that are themselves at times exposed, vulnerable, innocent and provocative. In *Giulio Cesare* (1997), for example, the focus is not on power but on rhetoric and, as with *Genesi*, on 'concepts of the "pre-tragic"' (Giannachi and Kaye, 2002: 156). Many of the performers were chosen because of their bodily characteristics, for the ways in which their bodies and their presence could enact the 'pre-tragic'. For Castellucci, 'what makes an actor important in this experience is the soul, the face, and the body' (in Valentini and Marranca, 2002: 20). In *Giulio Cesare*, a man who has a laryngotomy performs Mark Anthony. Castellucci believes that an actor who has undergone a laryngotomy can perform with a 'new voice...from the viscera, from deep inside' (in Valentini and Marranca, 2002: 21) and this allows him to recall Caesar's wounds, from his own 'wound' and to stimulate emotion 'by a consciously rhetorical use of the body and voice.' There is a sense here that the technology and the wound combine, as Castellucci explains, 'to make the speech truthful, outrageous, and moving' (in Valentini and Marranca, 2002: 21) and to unsettle expectations surrounding bodily and representational forms and limits. Two anorexic performers play Brutus and Cassius while Cicero who 'drives forward Shakespeare's text the most, who has the most weight because he inspired the conspiracy' (in Valentini and Marranca, 2002: 21) is performed by a man weighing 240 kilograms. Matthew Causey explains this interest in exploring the limits of the human form as follows:

> The **Dis-Human** and the **Dis-real**, [is] a performative strategy employed, and a theory espoused by Castellucci, which acts as an erasure of traditional constructions of human-ness and identification on stage. The supplements of the performing machine, animal, child and the 'disabled/perfect' actor, establish an aesthetic that resists acting, metaphor, and narrative, in favour of performance/enactment, metonymy, and image. (Causey, 2001: 202; original emphasis)

Castellucci thinks that these performers can, because they 'retain a capacity of surprise' achieve 'an amazing "truth" in their acting' (in Marshall, 2003: 3). The bodily presence of the 'dis-human' performer who, for the most part exists in silence on the stage, circumvents the potential of verbal language to seduce or persuade, and as a consequence, it engages spectators in a different realm, outside of or beyond language.

I read this desire of Castellucci to resurrect the pre-tragic as commensurate with Levinas's insistence that the call of the other occurs within the pre-ontological realm, the realm of the sensible. It seems that both Castellucci and Levinas want to acknowledge (or, in Castellucci's case, recreate) a realm that is not overpowered by discourse, where communication can occur through proximity and where spectators (in this case) can be 'exposed to the other as a skin is exposed to what wounds it, as a cheek is offered to the smiter' (Levinas, 1998: 49). By disturbing representational frames through the inclusion of non-actors, animals, children and the dis-human, Socìetas Raffaello Sanzio generate conditions within which spectators are involved intimately, bodily and through the senses.

There is, for Castellucci, a focus on and interest in 'finitude: not "speech before words", but the "silence" that precedes it; not "transcendence", but the mortality implied within our linguistic condition' (Giannachi and Kaye, 2002: 144). This interest in 'finitude' and 'mortality' can be linked directly to Levinas's notions of the saying and the said. 'Pre-tragic' theatre with its focus on the materiality of bodies and the pre-linguistic occupation of spaces functions to interrupt (or to constantly disrupt) the 'said' in a way that allows individual spectators to respond to the face of the other as it appears in the child, the dis-human performer and perhaps even the animal.[4]

The use of 'pre-tragic' theatre or theatrical devices complicates the work and perhaps begins to explain why it demands an abandonment of any preconceived ideas about spectatorship. It is also what makes the performance such an exhilarating experience. *Genesi: from the museum of sleep,* for example, challenges spectators on a number of levels and calls for a reconsideration of the very idea of theatre. For Alan Read, *Genesi*, and particularly Act 2 'Auschwitz', had a profound impact. He explains that in its insistence on the 'theatricality of the unthinkable' it is a theatre that 'refuses' to offer any 'explanation in language', instead presenting sound and lighting effects in which 'the inexplicable becomes palpable' (Read, 2007: 163).

My reactions to this performance echo Reads, as they were primarily visceral, emotional and sensory. They generated deep consideration about how I might respond, how I might unravel my responsibility for the various others I encountered in the work, and what I might do with the feeling of radical ambivalence that emerged as I attempted to negotiate these responses.

Genesi: from the museum of sleep: is response possible?

As I pointed out in the introduction to this book, my attendance at a performance of *Genesi* challenged (and expanded) my understanding of the parameters and potential power of theatre and performance as well as the ways in which theatre could work to stimulate a process of ethical reflection.[5] I contend that a work such as *Genesi: from the museum of sleep,* with its deeply embedded historical material, its political tone and its avant-garde style, creates a dance of intimacy and displacement in which spectators must continually negotiate and re-negotiate their responses and reactions to the performance in order to make provisional sense of the experience. In this regard it is interesting to think about Marshall's contention that:

> *Genesi* strives to be very nearly, if not actually impossible to consciously understand, a work which one must apprehend, experience or perhaps merely endure. It exists in a radical, Dionysian realm beyond tragedy, beyond description and possibly beyond language itself. It is a work as complex as it is compelling, as bizarre as it is raucous. ... It is a work as full of piety as it is full of sacrilege, as dense with allusive meanings as it is a deliberate staging of the absence or failure of meaning. (Marshall, 2003: 2)

The performance with its use of bodies, images, technical devices, sound and animals is spectacular and shocking. *Genesi* makes any consistent or unified response difficult, as Marshall's comments attest. However, rather than silencing its spectators, all of this begs or perhaps even compels them to respond. Castellucci states that he is centrally concerned with 'penetrat[ing] [the spectator's] shell' (Castellucci, 1999). *Genesi* jolts spectators out of any readily identifiable reaction to the work and engages them in a dangerous game of contradictory responses. It is the combination and play of elements – the probing of the limits of representation, the intertextual references and the ways in which the performance provokes a range of (often muddled) responses from devastation to adoration – that makes this work so intriguing and so difficult.

Genesi engages spectators in a process of seduction and estrangement where they find themselves at times enthralled, wounded and overwhelmed by the images and actions of the performers, and at other times repulsed and alienated by them. These are difficult responses that are sensed both bodily and cognitively as spectators experience the desire to embrace, protect or even 'save' performers (however problematic this response is) as well as a desire to hide, flee and erase aspects of the performance from my memory. Read writes that, in response to Act 2 'Auschwitz' there is no zone of safety outside the performance for the audience. They exist instead, 'in the same camp, we dwell in the same state of exception that allowed for those conditions, not being played out in front of us, to become the rule' (Read, 2007: 163–164).

This is a work of such complexity that it will reach spectators in different ways. It is likely that someone who is primarily interested in the aesthetic or spectacular quality of the work will read it differently than I, or Read, did; or, indeed, if a spectator is overtly sentimental or, conversely, uninterested or tired (for example) the performance will have different resonances for them. There is no core or definitive response to *Genesi*, but there is a desire to consider what the work does (or has the potential to do) in terms of generating both response and responsibility (in both the Levinasian and 'practical' senses of the term) in and for spectators.

How, for example, does *Genesi* manage to stimulate or liberate new ways of thinking about (or connecting emotionally with) the Holocaust? How does the use of the 'dis-human' performer challenge spectators to reflect on the idea of bodies and the politics of representing bodies? How might all of the complex, overwhelming images generated by this performance be responded to beyond silence or a suggestion that *Genesi* sits outside interpretation? The performance plays with the vulnerabilities of spectators and, through a process of concealing and revealing (bodies, ideas, emotions), it unsettles them.

There is no space for participation in the sense abhorred by Levinas; rather, *Genesi* works to reveal the face of the other and, in the process,

> it *calls* me – or interpellates me *[il m'interpelle]* – and signifies an order to me by its very nudity, its denuding [or destitution] *[dénûment]*. Its presence is a summation to respond. The I does not simply become conscious of this necessity to answer, as if it were a matter of an obligation or duty which it would have to decide of. (Levinas in Robbins, 1999: 9; original emphasis)

This interpellation occurs, for this spectator at least, through the ways in which this performance engages me bodily, in the realm of the senses, beyond the confines of language. This engagement occurs most profoundly via my connection with the performances by 'dis-human'

(Causey, 2001: 202) performers, the generation of the spectacular and dramatic images as well as a recuperation of Auschwitz as 'the nadir of human experience after which nothing exists' (Castellucci, 1999). Castellucci sees Auschwitz as 'the extreme and inconceivable consequence of Man's *Genesis*' (1999) and he positions it in the middle of this performance work as a comment on the dangers of 'man's' genesis. He points out that in *Genesi,* and particularly in 'Auschwitz', he wants to re-awaken the horror so that the audience can experience anew (and perhaps *directly,* in a homage to Artaud), the complexities and profound inhumanity of the concentration camp. For Castellucci, the idea of theatre is to 'comprehend the heights and the abysses of human experience – but not through illustration, nor by means of the production of information. The experience of abomination is too deep to be consumed on the surface' (in Marshall, 2003: 8).

As a director, he passionately asserts that his interest lies in creating a space for interpretation rather than presentation (in Marshall, 2003: 3). He believes in the power of terror when dealt with creatively, and rejects the literal presentation of information. This, for him, would imply a closing-off of ideas. Such an approach does not allow the event to generate emotional or imaginative responses for or from spectators, however complex and disturbing those responses might be.

'Beyond' artifice?

In the programme notes for *Genesi* Castellucci admits: 'I can't get my head around the concept of Genesis without thinking about creation as a crisis: it's the only way of fixing the kind of images that I always thought might interest someone like God' (1999). This aim to capture images that might be of interest to God is lofty indeed; however, it signals a tension within *Genesi* that permeates the entire production. Castellucci seems to want to move beyond artifice, to strip the theatrical experience bare and to expose its very workings so that the spectator can be penetrated. Yet the work is spectacular.[6] Some of the most arresting and disturbing elements of the performance emerge as the spectacular bleeds into the sparse, or when the work is visually spectacular and at the same time deeply traumatic. This is most evident in 'Auschwitz' and 'Cain and Abel' (and I will expand on these points as the chapter progresses).

Castellucci, according to Causey, sees three ways of approaching a text: 'burn it, evaporate it, or absorb it. The idea is not to perform the text but to use it as a channel for exploration' (Causey, 2001: 205). Castellucci also talks about the difficulties of viewing (as in actually seeing) theatre, and he regards viewing as 'an act of victory' (Eckersall, 2006).[7] Given the complexity of *Genesi*, he runs the risk of presenting something so densely layered with rich and complicated images that it becomes almost impossible to interpret and has the potential to lose the audience in the process. This is certainly a risk worth taking as it allows multiple, tragic, provocative and emotionally unsettling ideas to emerge. Perhaps *Genesi* could be read as a work in which Castellucci, uncovering the pre-tragic and/or operating in homage to Artaud, attempts to create a spectacle of avant-garde complexity in favour of a kind of transparency that might indicate failure as it might too easily engage audiences and lead to resolutions or simplistic responses. Alternatively, his choices might be read as a sign that this desire for opacity is in fact something more, a desire for a 'truly' Artaudian theatre that is felt, experienced and potentially impenetrable.

For Artaud, theatre will impact on the audience 'on condition it releases the magic freedom of daydreams, only recognisable when imprinted with terror and cruelty' (Artaud, 1993: 65).[8] This layering of presence, representation, body and image and the desire to achieve an Artaudian theatre that touches spectators directly/bodily, are the elements that work together in an attempt to move the 'dis-human' bodies beyond the idea of pure presence. On first encounter these bodies may appear to mobilise 'pure presence', but through the intricate layers of assemblage, machine and image it becomes apparent that they are in fact playing with presence via representation.

The museum of sleep

In Act One, which opens in the chamber of Madame Marie Curie in nineteenth century Paris, radium has just been discovered and the green iridescent light permeates the space. Lucifer steps forward and chants in Hebrew a prayer for the dead, from the Torah. He is anorexic, tall, gaunt and ghost-like. The performers stare at the discovery, unaware of the extent of its danger. Castellucci says 'radium is the only substance in the world that emits light. A light that gets into the bones. It's with radium ... that, little by little, you penetrate the nucleus of things until they break' (Castellucci, 1999). The potential horror of radium is unveiled to frame the performance.

This act introduces spectators to one of the results of 'man's *Genesis*', a substance that leads to the birth of 'modern physics' and that has the potential to end the human race. Lucifer strips naked and then forces his gaunt and angular body through two very narrow parallel bars. It is as if he is performing an act of birthing, an emergence though into what we are not sure. Perhaps he is trying to burst through into the twentieth century, to invade us (our space) in order that we might be alerted to the horror of the situation. Carol Middleton describes the scene as follows:

> Underscored by a soundscape that assaults the ears, Lucifer's pain is palpable as he squeezes through the narrow door from one abyss to another. The text has by now given way to sound and movement and we are swept into a vortex where words are superfluous. (Middleton, 2002)

The sight of this fragile giant whose almost translucent skin is taut on his bones generates a feeling of pity and dread as we watch him squeeze through the tiny gap in the bars (see Figure 2.1).

As Lucifer departs the stage he is replaced with dust, smoke, flashing images and machines and an excruciating soundtrack as the museum unfolds. Two mechanical sheep copulate in a glass case and a mechanical hand writes on the floor, marking the space, as a performer revolves on the top of a turntable. There is the skinned head of a cow positioned in a glass case, and 'Adam' (contortionist Franco Pistoni), in another case, performs a range of convoluted twists that appear as if he is sitting at times aside his own legs. As Adam performs, a vice crushes the cow's head in the adjacent box. For Matthew Causey:

> The grotesque stage-poetry of this moment brings a visceral corporeality to the stage. The body of the animal mutilated in the vice as the limbs of Adam are bent and distorted bring a 'cruel' presence that spirals the biblical notion of creation (Adam's rib) toward a violence that bleeds and exists within pain. (Causey, 2001: 205)

Eve appears, naked, middle-aged, and with one breast and a mastectomy scar. I am drawn to examine her body, specimen-like: we don't

Figure 2.1   Lucifer in the Chamber of Marie Curie, *Genesi: from the museum of sleep*, 1993. (Photograph: Luca del Pia; courtesy Socìetas Raffaello Sanzio)

often see naked post-mastectomy women 'in the flesh' and I chastise myself for wanting to absorb/consume/know this body. As I look, I confront again the narrowness of my own gaze and wonder: is Castellucci shattering the idea of a moral safe ground for looking through his use of the 'dis'-human performers? I play the game of looking/not-looking as I gaze at Eve with her long white hair. She is carrying white thread or wool that is connected to a labrynthine machine to which she also seems connected by her hair. Her performance is homage to Masaccio's frescoes in the Brancacci Chapel.[9] Castellucci says 'I chose Masaccio, for Eve. I love her as a unique being' (1999). He has also commented that the 'performers of Socìetas Raffaello Sanzio with special traits of anorexia, obesity, deformities and post-operative conditions, are 'perfect', and that these performers present 'a lost beauty of the body' (Castellucci in Causey, 2001: 208).

The museum and Eve's departure from the stage in tears generates a host of responses. The emotional connection facilitated in this scene is profound. The bodies 'on display' circumvent the idea of looking as consumption and challenge ideas about the museum and its function, about display and about artifice. For Causey 'the effect is captivating and disturbing...Meanings elide, evade, appear and merge in a labyrinth of images that are evocative and draw the spectator in' (Causey, 2006: 133). We become aware of the beauty of bodies, the intimacy their exposure might generate and the limited (or narrowly prescribed) parameters within which we conventionally ascribe notions of beauty and skill. This act reveals the face of the other, not in the form of a documentary or literal presentation of the 'face'. Rather, as Jill Robbins argues,

> because the face *is* a face, and not a mask, because it is without clothing or covering or attributes, because it divests itself of its form and signifies as expression, *kath 'auto,* as Levinas has said, having reference only to itself, it appears in the world as naked and destitute. In its extreme vulnerability, in the supplication of its gaze, it commands me. (Robbins, 1999: 9)

We are commanded by Eve to move beyond any consumption of this act (or indeed of her) and to reflect on our relationships with the other, in this case, the other as 'dis-human'. Responding to Eve is difficult. As with Causey I too am drawn in, I experience a sense of distress or unease and attempting to frame my responses, or to write them down (to capture them) within the confines of this book is also difficult. I think about the relationships between Eve's 'vulnerability' (if this is the case) and Levinas's ethics (in the form of sensibility) as it plays out for me in the context of this 'pre-tragic' scene. As I sit in the audience the movement between a feeling of awe and sadness or pity is compounded by a feeling of guilt that I let myself experience the performers in these conflicting ways. Rachel Halliburton's suggestion that 'Castellucci takes the audience to an area where only prolonged thought can deal with each individual's disorientation' (Halliburton, 2001) resonates as I wrangle with Eve.

Does language deaden our responses? In the transition from the saying to the said, the act of writing or stating rather than feeling, do we close off our responses to this other in a way that we yearn not to? In the act of translation or transcription, does the immediacy, shock and vulnerability we experience become something else? Managed, contained and closed.

As with most of the work the company produces Socìetas Raffaello Sanzio refuses to allow spectators an easy position where they can comment straightforwardly on the value of the use of the 'dis-human' body in performance. Although these bodies may appeal to a kind of truthfulness that Castellucci believes actors cannot access, they also challenge spectators in terms of the ways in which they are touched by, or look at and respond to 'the body'. A desire to stare, to see what is usually hidden, is initially rewarded by a visual feast of bodies. As spectators at this performance we may be torn between the wish to consume these figures and the shame of knowing that consumption of these others is deeply problematic. Yet nobody is censoring us and we find ourselves positioned in a play between the desire to look or absorb and the responsibility to see. It is this positioning that denies (or challenges) any simplistic reading or moralising of the dis-human body in the work.

Auschwitz: silent horror

> The theatre which tries to produce a resolution is unacceptable. It gives me the impression of being back at school. It's worse, actually, because this type of theatre would like us to believe it's telling us the truth. Even Brecht made the mistake of dogmatic pretension. It is much more accurate for the theatre to convey anxiety. It's preferable because then we ask the people who are watching to continue the story, to produce the missing part. (Castellucci in Tackels, 2001)

There is no attempt at resolution in Act 2 'Auschwitz'. In fact, this act is so intense that it is difficult to know how to respond at all, or indeed to put any response into words. It is in Act 2 that Levinas's ideas about suffering (quoted at the outset of this chapter) and the revelation of the suffering of the other can be most clearly grasped. In 'Auschwitz' there is a depiction (or more accurately, an excavation of loss, pain, trauma and memory) in which spectators come to understand (or at least approach an understanding of) the suffering of children during the Holocaust. This is revealed in a way that makes the pain palpable. There is no representation or 're-presentation'. There is, rather, an exquisite process of revelation that, in the tradition of Samuel Beckett and Franz Kafka (and following Theodor Adorno's dictum), imbricates us – through sparse images, silences and a piercing scream – in Auschwitz and in coming to terms with its implications in a way that is truly profound.

This is an act which creates dramatic shifts in emotional response and responsibility for spectators as they reflect on the act and on its positioning within the work. The decision to use Auschwitz must be read in the context of the intense discussion about the representability of the Holocaust. In addressing this debate it becomes possible to see function of *this* Auschwitz. Between Adorno's statement 'to write poetry after Auschwitz is barbaric' (Adorno, 1967: 34) and Paul Virilio's desire that we return to Auschwitz to remember the function of art (Virilio, 2003) there is a litany of material on the role of memory and documentation versus the importance (or the possibility) of interpreting the horror artistically.

There is anxiety about the ability of contemporary artists to understand and to respond to something they did not experience first-hand. There is a tension between the use of testimonial material and the act of artistic interpretation. There is also a fear that representation will result in the banalisation of the Holocaust or, alternatively, that it has the potential to 'create[ ] the possibility for sadistic identification in members of the audience because it contains a surplus of pleasure' (Rothberg, 2000: 41).[10] This idea is informed by Adorno who, in one of his later essays entitled 'Commitment', states: 'the so-called artistic rendering of the sheer physical pain of people beaten to the ground with rifle butts contains, however remotely, the power to elicit enjoyment out of it' (Adorno, 1978: 312). He goes on to talk about the relationship between art and sensation and, as Thomas Trezise writes,

what is most noteworthy here is the correlation between aesthetic success and ethical failure: the artistic mediation of experience, whether its purpose be pleasure, understanding, or both, is

considered tantamount to moral betrayal, to a renewed obliteration or silencing of victims. (Trezise, 2001: 44–45)

Theorists also caution against the dangers of silence.[11] If artists are to respond to the Holocaust, then it must be in an attempt to understand and make sense of it for our own lives rather than to recuperate something we cannot directly experience. As Andreas Huyssen points out 'remembrance shapes our links to the past, and the ways we remember define us in the present. As individuals and societies, we need the past to construct and anchor our identities and to nurture a vision of the future' (Huyssen, 1995: 249). This is an important point but also one that becomes both increasingly complicated and urgent as time passes and generations of people with no tangible link to the atrocities are born. Huyssen further develops his argument by stating that:

> The criteria for representing the Holocaust cannot be propriety or awe as would be appropriate in the face of a cult object. Awed and silent respect may be called for vis-à-vis the suffering of the individual survivor, but it is misplaced as a discursive strategy for the historical event, even if that event may harbour something unspeakable and unpresentable at its core. (Huyssen, 1995: 256)

The question of how to represent the Holocaust without falling into these traps and still managing to evoke a response without trivialising, generating pleasure or awe, or indeed a closing off of the potential for engagement and response, is a difficult one. In his important book *Staging the Holocaust*, Claude Schumacher provides what he considers the parameters for the production of 'Shoah drama':

> The successful Shoah drama or performance is one that disturbs, offers no comfort, advances no solution; it is a play that leaves the reader or spectator perplexed, wanting to know more although convinced that no knowledge can ever cure him of his perplexity. It must be a play that generates stunned silence. (Schumacher, 1998: 8)

And for Adorno it is only artists such as Beckett and Kafka who demonstrate a radicalism that has the power to approach the subject. Comparing the work of these artists with that of 'committed art',

Adorno proclaims that: 'by dismantling appearance, they explode from within the art' and 'the inescapability of their work compels the change of attitude which committed works merely demand' (Adorno, 1978: 314–315).

Castellucci, with his desire to 'penetrate your shell' carries on the tradition of work begun by Beckett and Kafka. He and Socìetas Raffaello Sanzio, with their manipulation of representation and presentation of iconoclastic performance pieces, 'explode from within the art' and 'compel' rather than 'demand' the kind of response Adorno suggests is appropriate. 'Auschwitz', by Castellucci, does much more than reproduce a familiar (yet horrific) tale; it 'dismantles illusion' and shows it to the audience with fresh eyes. The imaginative potential of the work moves beyond the event to stimulate reflection on the power of performance to create visceral responses that are politically, socially and culturally resonant.[12] As Schumacher states: 'theater which has true integrity and the highest artistic standards – does not try to create an illusion of reality... and it is precisely in the absence of mimetic *tromp-l'oeil* that the real strength of the theatrical performance lies' (Schumacher, 1998: 4; original emphasis).

As spectators we are variously inspired and shocked by 'Auschwitz.' We move between feeling that we are being visually and aurally assaulted, estranged, perturbed and seduced as the images progress and the act unfolds. 'Auschwitz' is literally shrouded in a white veil, so spectators view it through a curtain, never gaining complete clarity on the images as they appear and disappear. The sound of sentimental music wafts in from somewhere beyond the stage: it is reminiscent of the music of 1930s and 1940s and it is disconcerting. It is as if there is a party going on just outside the space. There is a sense of foreboding, of subterranean terror that might erupt at any moment. This act sits in a realm of ordinariness, a realm that seems unframed, 'honest', innocent or somehow outside of representation, and at the same time as highly constructed artifice. The representation of the Holocaust occurs here through absence, silence and play. As Castellucci explains: 'in the moment in which the characters and maybe even the spectators are at the highest level of emotional intensity, history decays, corrupts itself as reality and enters into representation' (in Giannachi and Kaye, 2002: 164). The performances by the children seem to attempt to puncture the constructed nature of the act, yet of course they cannot escape it entirely (see Figure 2.2). Read describes them as follows,

> the children in 'Auschwitz', the scene that is, are certainly not authorised to 'speak' of Auschwitz the historical event, and they resolutely do not. They are precisely enthusiastic in this scenario, literally irresponsible... While unable to quite identify themselves in speech these children would appear to be so many mediating agents between this stage, that historical reality, and the god or gods who let this happen. (Read, 2007: 163)

These 'literally irresponsible' children, dressed in white tunics, sit around the space and play games silently. There is something completely ordinary about their actions; they are innocents playing together, yet as we know this is Auschwitz, we dread what might be about to happen. Some of the children rock on a mechanical chair that emits a sound similar to that of a steam train as it rocks.

There is an eerie silence. A young boy arrives on the stage; he is riding a toy train. He is dressed in a white suit with a big yellow star on it; he reminds me of characters from *Alice in Wonderland*. But this is not funny; it is sinister and unsettling. He dismounts and begins to gather up rubber bodily organs that are hanging around the space. He carefully places these organs into compartments of his train before he leaves the stage. 'Sleep' is written in blood or faeces on the plastic scrim hanging at the back of the space. The mood changes from innocence to blame, revenge or cruelty. Three of the children gather together and kill one of the others: they slit his throat, in the process recalling Levi's 'gray zone'. Finally a group of children gather closely together under a shower and they gradually fall 'asleep' as they are covered in a white powder or fine mist. This is a moment in which I experience a sense of deep sadness. The significance of the children-as-performer-prisoners is stunningly evocative, and the horrors of Auschwitz are reinforced as we see innocence participating in a game of death. Artaud's 'body without organs' is realised in an avant-garde spectacle of horror.

The silences of the children and their dream-like presence bathed in white light reinforce for me the real bodily impacts of this act of genocide. As Read continues, 'the children swarm and mourn because they do not know they are mourners, while we know that

Figure 2.2 Children in Auschwitz, *Genesi: from the museum of sleep*, 1993. (Photograph: Luca del Pia; courtesy Socìetas Raffaello Sanzio)

they are' (Read, 2007: 163). The silence is punctured by a sudden, violent and shocking scream by Artaud (from beyond the grave). We hear 'je ne suis pas fou, je ne suis pas fou' (I am not mad, I am not mad). The children panic and scream. There is white light everywhere; it is devastating. The children's ghost-like presence in this act is profoundly disturbing. They are naïve and innocent, yet this is a qualified innocence. Their silenced bodies, crumpled under fine mist, speak to the spectators on a sensory level about Auschwitz, about the possibilities of its representation, about the relationship between horror and the ordinary, and about limits. This is profoundly disturbing theatre. Castellucci (echoing Adorno and Levi) points out in the programme notes that 'Auschwitz is the extreme and inconceivable consequence of Man's *Genesis*. We know that for the whole of human kind, a 'grey zone' now exists. ... It is the nadir of human experience after which nothing else exists.' He goes on to say 'I must disguise the horror with a lamb's skin. Only like this can it penetrate your shell' (Castellucci, 1999). In a work full of excesses and 'dis-human' performances, it is the moment where the all-too human-children arrive that pierces and wounds most profoundly.

This act stimulates the kind of participation that ruptures any simplistic or singular response to horror. It generates an instance in which 'the useless suffering' of the other is felt stingingly on the spectator's skin as s/he wonders how to react. It is the threatening absence of violence, and then the slitting of a child's throat that invades us as we watch it unfold. The play and movement between simplicity and complexity of the children and their games heightens innocence and reinforces the violence of the senseless murder of children in Auschwitz. As Carol Middleton explains, 'the musical score is unbearably sweet, as we await the inevitable – the turning on of the showers. The effect is chilling as the innocents play, unaware, in a senseless void where God is silent' (Middleton, 2002). We become both participants in and witnesses to this 'chilling' act.

Abel and Cain: violent artifice/artificial violence and the ordinary

> Our subjectivities and privileges can no longer be freed from the internalisation of implicit racism and suppressed violence. In this regard, the exposition of violence in the work of Sòcietas Raffaello Sanzio, it seems to me, is a shining beacon of the courage involved in subjecting the vision of theatre to the most rigorous test of *unsettling its assumed ethics*. In this unsettling, we are made to see the possibilities of envisioning ethics anew. (Bharucha in *Performance Paradigm*, 2007; my emphasis)

Act Three, 'Abel and Cain', is in some respects quite different from the previous two Acts. The stage is relatively sparse; it comprises the negotiations, struggles and despair of Abel and Cain as they move through a range of emotional responses to one another. In this Act it seems that the company's apparent desire to unfold the 'truth' of history results in a pathetic act of gratuitous play. Abel and Cain toy with one another as they writhe on the floor. When Cain kills Abel, it is for Castellucci, 'the saddest story in the world' (1999). Cain, a performer with an 'un-grown limb', strangles Abel with his un-grown arm, and once Abel has fallen to the floor Cain attempts to 'coax him' back to life before he 'lies on top of his brother' (Marshall, 2003: 4). As Cain and Abel struggle and Abel dies, two dogs run around the stage: they sniff, bark and shit as the non-speaking Cain and Abel writhe around (see Figure 2.3). The portrayal of Cain as 'innocent' is for Castellucci a way of demonstrating that

> the shorter arm bears witness to the fact that this is a game which, unlike all other games, cannot be started again, because its result has been fixed once and for all with the act that causes death, in the same way in which the arm has remained fixed in its childlike size. (Castellucci in Marshall, 2003: 4)

The performers silently toy with one another as the soundtrack and an oratorio by Henryk Górecki fill the space. They dance or wrestle quasi-erotically, and this engagement leads to the weaker 'innocent' killing his brother. Their actions are mundane and childlike but they are underscored by eerie and evocative music, and the way in which they struggle is both understated and overwhelmingly threatening.

There is a feeling of dread about what might or could happen, what might erupt from some underground layer, as the struggle unfolds. This feeling is reinforced by the silences, the pace, and timing of the act which are painfully slow. So slow in fact that each moment pierces and pushes the audience as they will it to be over. The symbolism is rich and the limits of the human relationships it reveals are unsettling. The dogs are repulsive and the act of Cain lying on Abel in griefstricken realisation is the ultimate tragedy when combined with the return of Eve to crown her triumphant son. Eve's return encourages us to question where the work was attempting to position us as we watch it unfold. As a spectator I wanted to rush to ethical judgement (in the conventional sense), to chastise Castellucci for playing with my emotions, to leave. For Middleton, however, the

Figure 2.3   Abel and Cain, *Genesi: from the museum of sleep*, 1993. (Photograph: Luca del Pia; courtesy Socìetas Raffaello Sanzio)

experience was a more optimistic one. She says 'there is some hope: in the third act death brings with it the promise of new life. In a brief moment of relief from the hellish realms, the stage is bathed in gold light and the music of Henry Gorecki soars joyously' (Middleton, 2002). There are echoes of this Act in the company's later work *Tragedia Endogonidia*, and particularly a scene in *Tragedia Endogonidia Br.#04*, where violence works to push spectators to the limit of their endurance.[13]

While the violence in *Tragedia Endogonidia Br.#04* is slightly different in that the artifice is heightened (in the extreme), it elicits a similar painful anxiety in spectators. The scene in question depicts three policemen who enter the stage which comprises a very large marble box lit with fluorescent lights. They position crime scene numbers around the space. One of the officers takes off his clothes and sits on the floor in his underwear. The other two proceed to pour a large bottle of fake blood all over him and to beat him with a length of rubber. The rubber is wired for sound so that every time he is struck the sound is much larger than the act and it echoes and reverberates throughout the space. This is obviously fake; it is artifice at its best. However, perhaps because of our knowledge of the 'unreal' nature of the act and the sight of the blood smeared all over the performer and on the white floor, as well as the intense and repeated sounds of the beating, this scene is almost intolerable. For Nicholas Ridout this is a 'simple scene of routine violence' but what makes this particular version unusual is its theatrical rendering. Ridout explains that 'the theatrical effect of the action's duration (it felt like fifteen minutes) makes it unusually intense and difficult to endure' (Ridout, 2003: 1). It is a scene of hyper violence, and each time the performer is struck the act of beating becomes more difficult to watch. I sat in silence squirming as the beatings continued, eventually resorting to hiding behind my hands, as I could no longer witness the scene.[14] Artistic Director of the Zürcher Theater Spektakel in Zurich, Maria Magdalena Schwaegermann describes her response as follows:

> The scene is in effect unbearably violent. For me as a spectator, the entire time it is clear that it's about the act. Perhaps that's why I tolerate the image to the bitter end. The timing of this brilliant performance group from Italy is grandiose. I am just about able to endure this scene, that is, just long enough so that the image is burnt into my brain. I cannot imagine that a single spectator that witnesses this scene would not react in the future, if they saw a violent scene like this one in reality. (Hamilton, 2007)

As with this scene in *Tragedia Endogonidia Br.#04* 'Abel and Cain' is difficult to endure. Not only because of the pathetic and painful nature of their struggle but also because it followed two Acts that were extremely powerful and emotionally challenging. It is not that

'Abel and Cain' goes on forever, but it is slow, and almost empty in comparison with 'Auschwitz.' It is hard to absorb, to engage with and respond to all of the stimulation experienced in the previous Acts, while also attempting to interrogate the function of this spectacle. In this final Act there is a stripping away, or a honing of spectacle – to Cain and Abel. Apart from the dogs, there are no hydraulic hands, skinned animal heads, or contortionists, to create a tension. We are suddenly left to our own devices. Cain and Abel are surrounded by an absence, a vast stage of emptiness.

This act jolts spectators out of the comfort of or reliance on the abundance of the spectacular or indeed a tension between the spectacular and the ordinary. Although there is a sense of anxiety about the possibility of some subterranean irruption at the outset of the act, this tension does not seem to build in the same way that it did in Act Two. Here we can see the starting point of the work: Castellucci's exploration of the devastating limits of humanity. Yet its position at the end of an extravagant journey as an act in which 'imitative illusion' is most definitely 'circumvented' makes it difficult. The power of the act relies on Abel and Cain, on the 'truth' of their story and the skill of their performance to engage. However, this stripping-back is risky. There is a sense that Castellucci is hoping for the clarity of this act to leave the spectator profoundly wounded, and also knowing, as Read makes clear, that there 'is no secure outside' (Read, 2007: 164). Indeed I leave the theatre feeling dis-abled or profoundly unsettled and totally insecure in response to these acts.

A fierce theatre, the spectator and ambivalence

My initial reaction to *Genesi* was one of confusion and dismay, as I felt pulled emotionally in myriad ways, and found my responses to be unclear and at times contradictory. This is not unusual, as Halliburton explains, 'perhaps it is precisely because of the confusion he arouses that he [Castellucci] represents an important force for maintaining the excitement in theatre today. The result is viscerally and turbulently unforgettable' (Halliburton, 2001). As an individual spectator *Genesi* positioned me (and it still does) in an ambivalent space, at once frustrated and at the same time pricked, wounded and inspired. This sense of confusion, and my subsequent more considered responses encouraged me to think about the ways in which we 'read', experience, interpret, or physically respond to performance.

While Castellucci is concerned with the 'the terror of sheer possibility' (1999) and wants to return to a fierce theatre, a pre-tragic or an almost Artaudian theatre that has the power to alienate, to challenge and provoke, it is the play of the spectacular elements (the form of the performance) against the content of the performance (and at times the ordinary) that makes the work so difficult. Although the apparent desire to truly provoke the audience might, at times, have collided with the machinic assemblages used, this collision had the potential to both alienate and challenge. The work stimulates nuanced and often contradictory responses as spectators negotiate between the spectacular and the provocative, between presence and representation and as they navigate the experience of seduction and estrangement it engenders. While this process is one of *Genesi's* strengths it is also one of the risks the production takes with its audiences.

The performance challenges each spectator to think through his/ her relationship with their own body, the ideas of beauty and, perfection and of course, with the other. As Castellucci points out, 'I believe that, in the end, what's very important is the idea. ... and the actual possibility of another parallel world, another language which, suddenly, as Alice knew, stops being "other"' (in Valentini and Marranca, 2004: 25). While *Genesi* may be difficult to read it disturbs on many levels and produces a range of responses – sensed or felt responses as well as emotional and intellectual ones – which keep spectators asking questions about life and art and the relevance of these at the beginning of a violent, globalised media-saturated century.

The dance of intimacy and distance it creates is a layered and complicated dance that has at least two interrelated movements. Firstly, it refers to the ways in which *Genesi* involves us in an interrogation of the kinds of bodily reactions a work might elicit. It engages spectators in Levinasian terms in the realm of the sensible. Through the use of a 'pre-tragic' theatre the work troubles representation and elicits feelings of vulnerability, tension, fear, desire and admiration.

For Levinas 'in language qua said everything is conveyed before us, be it at the price of betrayal' (1998: 6). In *Genesi* 'everything' and nothing is conveyed before us and the work mobilises, via the proximity it generates, a space in which we, the spectators, are confronted by the call of the other. This occurs, not in the sense that we must decode the call or understand it, and indeed, in response to *Genesi* understanding in a singular or unified way would be impossible, but instead that we respond. Thus the saying is 'antecedent to all thematization in the said, but it is not a babbling or still primitive or childish form of saying. This stripping beyond nudity, beyond forms, is not the work of negation' (Levinas, 1998: 15). It is instead 'vulnerability, exposure to outrage, to wounding' (Levinas, 1998: 15) that the work elicits, as described above. *Genesi* urges spectators to respond to the ideas and stories generated within the frame of the performance and it activates their responsibility for the others (particularly child, animal and dis-human) as the work unfolds. So while the dance is about the jolting between a sense of being seduced by and feeling deeply estranged from *Genesi*, it is also a seduction and estrangement that resonates both intellectually and emotionally in ways that are mutually and deeply imbricated.

Secondly, because of the tropes, symbols and aesthetic processes involved in the performance, there is a denial of any response that attempts to consume the other. The expedients outlined by Kapuscinski in Chapter 1 are subverted here, as are Lehmann's anxieties about contemporary society. This is a work that neither encourages nor condones voyeurism, instead it is, according to Mark Fisher, 'the closest a piece of theatre can come to a nightmare. Like a nightmare, any attempt to describe its impact crumbles into fragments of impotent language' (Fisher, 2003). There is none of the tourism, Bauman finds worrying at play here, instead, spectators are involved corporeally and intellectually in this 'nightmare', and detailed concentration is required in order that they might wake up and see how the work implicates them, beyond the moment of provocation, in a process that both unsettles the 'assumed ethics' of theatre (Bharucha, 2007) and challenges the stability of notions of representation, spectatorship and responsibility.

3
The Career Highlights of the MAMU: Alterity and Shame

> Our ontological relationship to land, the ways that country is constitutive of us, and therefore the inalienable nature of our relation to land, marks a radical, indeed incommensurable, difference between us and the non-Indigenous. This ontological relation to land constitutes a subject position that we do not share, and which cannot be shared, with the postcolonial subject whose sense of belonging in this place is tied to migrancy. (Moreton-Robinson, 2003: 31)

The Career Highlights of the MAMU[1] charts the story of the Spinifex people of the Great Victoria Desert in Western Australia. It is a multimodal performance that uses stand-up comedy, traditional Aboriginal dance and song, live rock and roll numbers, documentary footage of the Aboriginal elders speaking in Pitjantjatjara from their land, and autobiographical-style storytelling. It depicts the triumphs and tragedies of the Spinifex community recounting a range of stories, including those that detail the impacts of the British-led nuclear tests on the community and on the land in the 1950s and 1960s; the subsequent movement of the people to other communities; the battle to reclaim ownership of the land; the significance of sacred lands and traditions; and the impacts of Western culture on the Spinifex youth.

MAMU moves swiftly between modes of telling and it is anchored by the presence of Trevor Jamieson, who is the narrator of the piece. While the performance could be read as messy, or as critic Helen Thomson suggests 'untidy' (2002) the use of multiple modes adds to its power. As Hans-Thies Lehmann points out: 'it is not through the direct thematization of the political that theatre becomes political but through the implicit substance and critical value of its *mode of representation*' (Lehmann, 2006: 178; original emphasis).

This chapter considers how the modes of representation used in *MAMU* have the potential to encourage reflection on the experiences of the Spinifex people and the possibilities of both response to, and responsibility for those experiences. The performance's modes merge Western theatrical forms with Aboriginal performance techniques (which involve the use of traditional and sacred dance and song; different understandings of, and relationships with, time and space; and a less formal dramaturgy) with powerful content, to liberate a range of complex feelings and reactions in spectators.

In the title of this chapter I use two key terms: alterity and shame. My understanding of these terms is informed primarily by Levinas and my aim is to apply these to *MAMU* to allow me to read the work and the ethical questions it generates in particular ways. The work's ability to uncover the absolute alterity of the Indigenous elders is facilitated by the constant shifting of artistic modes. It is the juxtaposing of the documentary footage of these old people at their sacred sites, speaking calmly and poetically about their relationships with the land, with a hectic, humorous performance that allows this footage to puncture the performance. This approach also reinforces the significance of their stories and, as a consequence, the fact that their lives are governed by profoundly different cultural and spiritual concerns than those of the majority of spectators. As Levinas explains 'before any attribute, you are other than I, other otherwise, absolutely other! And it is this alterity…that is your alterity' (in Poirié, 2001: 49). James Meffan and Kim Worthington describe the implications of this experience of alterity for the subject when they state that, for Levinas, 'the demands made by alterity are self-applied and not directed to the Other except as that Other effects the process of self-critique' (2001: 135). The alterity of the Indigenous others in this production is complicated by the intimacy created in and in response to the performance.

There is no blame levelled at spectators despite the breadth of political material dealt with and the failure of successive Australian governments to respond to the plight of the Spinifex people. Instead there is a feeling of warmth in the performance space, and Trevor Jamieson uses his narration to create an experience of camaraderie and shared storytelling. This engages spectators in a set of difficult and at times contradictory emotional responses to the performance. These are responses that may include joy, shame, delight and despair.

The experience of shame is one that, for Levinas, is centrally concerned with the responses of the subject to the other. In this regard shame unleashes a deeply felt desire to escape blame, to come up with a rationale that might excuse inaction, or the refusal to hear or respond to the call of the other. Shame pierces excuses and attempts to cover over passivity, and it can reveal a lack of both response and responsibility that is painful. Levinas sees shame as something specific to the subject. He states 'if shame is present, it means that we cannot hide what we should like to hide. The necessity of fleeing, of hiding oneself, is put in check by the impossibility of fleeing *oneself*' (Levinas, 2003: 64). This indicates that the question of responsibility for the other is heightened as the subject reckons with him/herself.

While Levinas is concerned with the shame experienced by individual subjects it is also something that, within the parameters of a performance, has the potential to be experienced by the audience collectively. This is a difficult claim to make, because, as I discussed in the introduction to this book, assessing or determining collective responses to a performance can be a fraught process. However, in the context of a political performance that raises issues of national significance; and in this case issues that have resulted in a series of debates which are now termed the 'history wars' (I will elaborate on this period and its impact a little later in this chapter), the possibility of ascribing shame as a response to collective feelings (or the potential for collective feelings) engendered by *MAMU* is not too far fetched.

The most obvious danger in making any claims to collective shame is that they may imply an homogeneity of audience members and a singularity of response to a work. This is not what I am suggesting here, instead I want to explore how the sophisticated layering of emotional registers and political content in *MAMU* has the potential to create an intimacy in the space that, rather than directly shaming the audience, invites or seduces them into letting down their guard. Once this occurs and they are relaxed and engaged with the work the political impact of its stories (and a sense of shame they might elicit) can resonate on the body as Levinas suggests (1998: 15) in a way that can provide no escape from the difficulty of the situation.

Utilising the notion of shame to describe or account for responses to political performance is difficult because it necessitates a question about the function of shame. Raimond Gaita talks at length about shame as an appropriate response to the treatment of Australian Indigenous people; he carefully differentiates between guilt and shame and explains that 'pride and shame...are fundamental to the kind of fellowship that makes community possible' (1999: 99). He argues that shame on its own, as an emotional response or an expression of collective responsibility is not enough. Gaita asks

> would anyone seriously say that shame is of itself an adequate response to the terrible plight suffered by most Aborigines, or that shame amounts to anything when it is separated from a serious concern with reparation? Relief of the material and psychological misery of many of the Aborigines will not count as reparation, however, unless the spirit in which that relief is given is informed by a recognition of the wrongs they have suffered. (1999: 100–101)

While it is appropriate to suggest that there is the potential for collective shame (and therefore heightened responsibility) in response to political performance, the discussion of where this might lead must also be addressed. Because, in Levinasian terms, subjectivity always exists in relation to the other, shame can provide a means to open up this relationship. In this regard I argue following Gaita, that shame has the potential to lead to a deeper understanding of 'the wrongs they have suffered' and the responsibilities spectators have in responding to those wrongs.

It is important to acknowledge that in terms of a shame response to this production, and to the experience of Australian Indigenous people more generally, shame will only function for audiences or individual spectators who are invested in the issues addressed and the ways in which these issues shape the nation. As Gaita makes clear 'the attachment that makes shame appropriate and sometimes called for is inseparable from the desire to celebrate achievements which shape an historically deep sense of communal identity' (1999: 101). And as Freddie Rokem argues: 'The theatre "performing history" seeks to overcome both the separation and the exclusion from the past, striving to create a community where the events from this past will matter again' (Rokem, 2000: xii). Perhaps then the shame responses elicited, or potentially elicited, for spectators at *MAMU,* contribute in some way not only to making the treatment of Indigenous Australians matter 'again' but also in some cases making it matter at all. A reading of the reviews *MAMU* received when it toured Germany supports Gaita's point about the need for investment in the issues, as they suggest that while powerful, the performance was read primarily as a humorous 'honest' work about reconciliation.[2]

Cultural context: proximity and distance

In Chapter 1 I drew on Zygmunt Bauman's engagement with Ryszard Kapuscinski's three expedients to talk about the disjunction between media representations of poverty and the experience of the same. While Kapuscinski's focus was on 'Third World' countries, the conditions he witnessed and documented also operate within some 'first world' countries. In Australia, for example, the life expectancy of Indigenous people is 20 years less than non-Indigenous Australians. Infant mortality in Indigenous communities is three times higher than in non-Indigenous Australia and it is 'more than 50 percent higher than for Indigenous children in the USA and New Zealand'.[3] These statistics, along with high levels of unemployment, mental and physical illness, are unacceptable, yet they are tolerated (or glossed over) in this wealthy nation. Mainstream media representations of Indigenous Australians tend to focus primarily on behaviours that are illegal or damaging, or alternatively on sporting achievements or traditional painting (which often contributes to the museum-ification of Indigenous culture).

There is widespread ignorance about Indigenous culture (in both its traditional and contemporary contexts) and languages, and this does not generate an environment in which change, reconciliation or collaboration are easily achievable. In fact, there is a schism that seems to operate among the Australian public in the sense that most non-Indigenous Australians have little or no contact with Indigenous Australians, and both groups often feel that they do not have a framework or context within which to approach each other. There is, in effect, an experience of closeness in terms of a generalised sense of proximity with regard to the shared inhabitation of the land, but this is coupled with a mutual sense of remoteness or alienation at the same time.

This social reality is situated alongside a fierce debate amongst scholars about the numbers of Aboriginal people 'deliberately killed on our frontier and the subsequent genocidal practice of stealing Aboriginal children from their parents' (Thomson, 2004: 3). During the 1990s prominent right wing scholars, who were heavily supported by the then Prime Minister, John Howard, argued that responsibility for wrongs of the past was not the domain of contemporary Australians and therefore apologising to Aboriginal people was unnecessary.[4] The 'wars' raged for many years and resulted in numerous essays, newspaper articles and other documents debating the function of history, the significance and legitimacy of oral storytelling, and the need, or not, for a national apology to Indigenous Australians, and particularly to the Stolen generations.[5]

Understanding this context makes a performance such as *MAMU* both remarkable and unsettling. It also provides a challenge to directors and performers working with Indigenous stories because it means that creative works have to serve a number of functions. They are not 'free' to be (solely) works of art; instead, particularly when dealing with social or political themes, they carry the dual burden of engaging an audience and at the same time attempting to provide knowledge about the history and often about the social disadvantage experienced by many Indigenous Australians.

The desire to mobilise the performance space as a site for change and for drawing attention to political or social issues has to be balanced with a focus on craft and on generating work that is layered, sophisticated and has resonance for a range of audiences. This means that how a work is judged or responded to can be complex and can raise questions about the relationships between process and product, the value of judgement (on the part of spectators or theatre scholars), and the role and function of the creative work.

Helen Gilbert and Jacqueline Lo suggest that *MAMU* and other Australian Indigenous theatre at the Adelaide Festival, 'generally elicited positive reviews and were noted for their significance in raising the profile of Indigenous culture in general'. They say that the praise 'mostly focussed on the political and moral value of the stories/ themes dramatized while the criticisms were largely directed at production values' (Gilbert and Lo, 2007: 123). In this vein, critics, such as Murray Bramwell, point out that *MAMU* is not as tightly focussed as it needs to be, commenting that 'Jamieson has imagined a terrific project that is astutely anti-theatrical and a marvellous story. However, he needs to provide more narrative focus and fluency before this show is the breakthrough it promises to be' (2002). In brief, because it veers between melodrama, slapstick, comedy, documentary and realism, *MAMU* could be read as a work that runs the risk of trivialising the material. It could also be argued that it needs more dramaturgical intervention to smooth out the kinks and render the performance slick or polished. But this would fail to acknowledge the fact that the performance sits slightly outside mainstream (Western) notions of theatre and in doing so would miss the dual burden experienced by makers of theatre that deals with or responds to Indigenous issues. It also disallows the fact that it is precisely its messiness and its use of multiple modes that allows the performance to fracture any preconceived ideas about reception and to generate a powerful sense of intimacy and proximity within the space.

This leads into even muddier territory as such an attitude may imply that theatre and performance dealing with Indigenous stories needs special consideration or that it cannot be scrutinised or critically engaged with. This is an issue that causes much anxiety for those involved in both the production and reception of work that is concerned with these stories. It is not enough for a performance to generate intimacy, nor is it enough for it to allow spectators to emerge from the work feeling forgiven, or feeling that their presence at a performance is sufficient.

What is important, particularly in terms of any response to *MAMU,* is that readers, critics or spectators are aware of the complexity of forces informing the generation (and the reception) of work and that they remain open to the fact that performances such as *MAMU,* because they are attempting to do so many things, must be judged cautiously, and only after careful reflection.

How to respond?

The performance showcases the culture, language and traditions of the Spinifex people, while at the same time narrating their battles for land rights, freedom and compensation for the pain, suffering and death they experienced as a result of the nuclear tests. It is a work that is, as I have mentioned, difficult to define or respond to as it uses several devices to destabilise the 'usual' boundaries between spectators and performance. The combination of performance modes and cultural styles means that spectators are often unsure about how to read the work. They may also have difficulty reconciling the intimacy created by the performance, and particularly by Jamieson's narration, with the stories of hardship, oppression and exploitation experienced by the Spinifex people (see Figures 3.1 and 3.2).

MAMU commands a very different order of response to that of *Genesi: from the museum of sleep* (Chapter 2). It engages spectators overtly on specific political issues to do with race, culture, oppression and belonging. It also engages them emotionally through the connections they make with the Spinifex people as they tell their stories during the performance. These connections subvert any literal or one-dimensional response to the production. In fact, the impact of the performance as it engages spectators on both political and sensory levels means that it is almost impossible for spectators not to feel responsibility in the ontological *and* in the Levinasian pre-ontological realm in response.

As discussed in Chapter 1 Levinasian ethics is concerned with the call of the other and the ethical obligation of the subject to respond. Levinas does not prescribe what kind of response this might be, so it is fair to suggest that a subject may respond by hearing and then deciding to ignore the call of the other. Subjects may find refuge in a range of self-comforting ideas about their participation (understood in this context as the act of attending the performance). For example they might argue that their presence at the performance in itself is a political act and this means that any further action is unnecessary. While this may work for some spectators and would still mean that the response is ethical in Levinasian terms, I believe that in *MAMU* the intimacy generated by the performers and the significance of the documentary footage used in the work mean that an individual subject's sense of 'practical' responsibility is also mobilised. By this I mean that for many spectators who attend the performance the question of response becomes one that occurs in the ontological realm, where they feel the urge to actively think about the complex issues the work raises and to consider the relevance of these, in terms of how they respond to or take responsibility for the other. While responses vary, performances such as *MAMU* encourage spectators to talk about

Figure 3.1 Trevor Jamieson, narrator, *The Career Highlights of the MAMU,* 2002. (Photograph: Jon Green)

Figure 3.2 Trevor Jamieson and Milton Hansen perform a traditional dance, *The Career Highlights of the MAMU*, 2002. (Photograph: Jon Green)

the oppression of Indigenous Australians and to think about how ideas of proximity and distance operate in their own lives.

The production *Ngapartji Ngapartji* written by Scott Rankin in collaboration with Trevor Jamieson, which followed *MAMU* and extended its themes and ideas, is one example of a work that calls for concrete practical responsibility. Interested spectators can enrol in an online language course and can study the Pitjantjatjara language before attending a performance of *Ngapartji Ngapartji* so that they can participate in the parts of that work that are conducted in Pitjantjatjara. This provides a tangible forum for people, who may be interested in, yet disenfranchised from Indigenous culture, to feel as if they are doing something practical that is both socially and culturally useful.

Spinifex people/Spinifex country[6]

MAMU explores some of the complex historical and cultural experiences of the Spinifex people. Spinifex country spans 55,000 square kilometres covering the southern part of the Great Victoria Desert, it crosses the Western Australian/South Australian border.[7] The Spinifex people descended from the people of 'The Sun and The Shadow' and were

> an almost invisible people in modern Aboriginal Australia, known only by rumour to observers of Aboriginal culture and absent from virtually all Western Desert anthropological scholarship. Hidden from European eyes until the 1950s, the last of the Spinifex nomads remained uncontacted in their homelands until 1986, making them perhaps the last hunter-gatherers on earth. (Cane, 2002: 1)

The Spinifex people lived through colonisation, the British-led nuclear tests at Maralinga from 1956 to 1967 and the (government initiated) movement of families off the land to Cundeelee Mission in the 1960s and to the Coonana community in the 1980s. These sites were hundreds of kilometres away from their homeland, and community members experienced dispossession and fragmentation as a result of these moves. In the mid 1990s the Australian Government held a 'Royal Commission' to investigate the impact of the Maralinga atomic tests on the community.[8] The commission found that the Spinifex people were directly affected by the tests and they were afforded some monetary compensation. They used the compensation to (literally) build a road home. As the programme notes for the performance of *MAMU* at the Perth International Arts Festival explain:

> 22 bombs were tested in this forgotten land, far away from Western civilisation. We know now this place was not terra nullius but home to another civilisation, one who had lived in the desert for over 20,000 years.... Far removed from the board-rooms and conferences of powerful men, these people were left to feel the aftershocks of this explosion for many years to come. Displaced, sick and ignored, these people wandered through the physical and emotional fallout in search of their homeland. (Black Swan Theatre, 2002)

In the 1990s, after years of struggle, the Spinifex people achieved native title.[9] The Premier of Western Australia flew to Spinifex country and declared that the rights of the Spinifex people to the land had not been extinguished nor in any way impaired, and that they were the traditional owners of the reclaimed land.

MAMU – the performance

MAMU makes a crucial contribution to the re-writing and the re-presentation of Australian history. The performance recuperates (for a wide audience) the stories of hardship and survival experienced by the Spinifex people. As I outlined earlier, the juxtaposing of modes of telling reinforces the power of the documentary sequences. These sequences, filmed in Spinifex country, show the elders speaking about the significance of their land, traditions and culture in their language. Their narration is poetic, sparse and metaphoric. The documentary footage sits in stark contrast to (or interrupts) the live elements of the performance, as the sequences are calm, quiet and reflective and connections are made with the elders without overt theatrical devices or performance techniques. The images are projected onto a large screen at the back of the performance space, while many of the community members involved (ranging from small children to elders), who feature in the film sequences, sit at the front of the stage around a campfire.

The community members perform traditional songs to accompany the storytelling. Some of these performers live traditional lives in Spinifex country and visit the city rarely, if at all. Despite this they participate in all aspects of the performance and do not seem anxious about their roles as performers. In fact, the positioning of the community members at the front of the stage around the campfire is significant as they sing, chant and play instruments as well as interact with other performers. This interaction, which takes the form of laughing, adding words or responding to Trevor Jamieson's antics, adds to the intimacy in the space and fractures any expectations spectators might have about the form of the work. Children and adults participate in the traditional dances throughout the performance, and they act as extras in some of the stand-up sequences. As Samela Harris, who attended the Adelaide performance explains, 'Mamu is not strictly theatre. It is a sharing. The Spinifex people have come to us, a large extended family of them, and camped around a fire upon the stage' (Harris, 2002).

The performance is provocative on numerous levels; however, many of the most profound moments of provocation emerge in response to the political and personal implications of the stories performed and represented via the documentary sequences. The issue of both response and responsibility looms large as spectators wonder how governments could have allowed people to be left out in the desert and exposed to nuclear tests, and more importantly how they, the survivors, can share their stories with an audience without a tone of castigation or bitterness.

Joanne Tompkins's fine work on 'Contamination' in her book *Unsettling Space* helps to explain the motivation behind the tests; however, her explanation is also unsettling, as it seems that governments acted in the interest of governments rather than of people. Tompkins points out that

> the Australian government and scientific communities encouraged the explosion of nuclear bombs on Australian soil in the 1940s and 1950s to secure a greater role in international politics, as well as for protection from its neighbours during the Cold War. (Tompkins, 2006: 91)

Tompkins goes on to explain that the Australian government was later abandoned by both the British and the American military and left to deal with a site that would remain contaminated for the next 24,000 years.

The community was seriously affected by the testing, the subsequent movement of people from their traditional lands, and the impacts of contact with Western society on both adults and children. Yet they seem willing to perform, share and engage in a way that might suggest that the significance (or necessity) of telling the stories, of educating the public outweighs any bitterness. *MAMU* neither commodifies nor attempts to apportion blame for this situation; instead, it begins a process of engagement, and dialogue across boundaries (be they boundaries within the Spinifex community or between the community and the 'outside' world) so that (despite or perhaps because of the treatment of the community at the hands of various Australian governments and the lack of awareness among the general public) knowledges can be preserved and cultural understanding increased. This willingness to share, this generosity, heightens the potential for feelings of shame and responsibility in response to the stories of death, hardship and loss.

The significance of process: creating the archive

Through the recuperation and archiving of their stories the Spinifex elders hope to prevent the destruction of their cultural memory. For the elders it is crucial to create this repository so that the stories can be preserved. Stories are central to the maintenance of culture. As Laura Marks, in *The Skin of the Film*, eloquently explains:

> Storytelling crosses and recrosses between private life and politics, making the boundary between them impossible to locate. As Benjamin suggests, storytellers' knowledge is of a different order from that which passes as official information. As 'the communicability of experience decreases,' as official knowledge diverges from community experience (or vice versa), the storyteller's practical information becomes increasingly rare and precious (Benjamin, 1968: 84–87). Old people are thus repositories of virtual images; their death is like the loss of a past-that-is-preserved. Their stories, again, are like those 'radioactive fossils' that cannot be explained in terms of the geological layer on which they are found. (Marks, 2000: 70)

The act of creating this archive of the Spinifex people is one way of allowing their 'rare and precious' cultural stories and traditions to continue, at least as traces, long after the performance has finished and the elders have passed away. If the young people have the opportunity to return to the land and 'keep up the law' they will at least have this record to guide them. Positioning the archive as an extension of the performance signals the difference between this work and the kinds of art that Levinas feared would use representation to obscure the face of the other. *MAMU* and its associated documentation participates in a process of redressing the obscuring of the other (particularly the Indigenous other) in Australian culture and society. It uses the performance space as a site in which the call of the other can be not only heard but responded to by a 'live' audience, and also records, stores and protects the stories of the elders, the 'repositories of virtual images'. Thus, the complex cultural stories and the experiences of loss, survival, triumph and pain can be preserved and remembered.

According to Andrew Ross, the (then) director of Black Swan Theatre, film was initially chosen so that the elders could tell their stories from the places where they occurred. Ross states that 'the idea of the storytellers getting up on stage each night and repeating their stories in performance mode wasn't an appropriate approach' (Grehan, 2003). The documentary footage, when juxtaposed with the live performance, highlights the depth of Spinifex culture in a way the repeated telling of these stories within a performance context may not have. Indeed, part of the focus for the production was to assist in the creation of an archive documenting the stories and experiences of the Spinifex people. Black Swan Theatre wanted to work with the elders to establish this archive so they travelled out to Spinifex country and spent time with the elders, listening to their stories and creating documentary footage.

Hundreds of hours of footage was recorded with the aim of storing this footage at the proposed 'education centre' at Tjuntjuntjara so that it could be accessed by the community as well as interested scholars and students. The footage included interviews with elders, cultural stories, images of the landscape, as well as a record of the performance and rehearsals. A careful selection process took place so that the community elders were happy with the material chosen for *MAMU*. Ross told me that the aim was to 'create a situation whereby the community felt that they owned the work, that they were co-collaborators' (Grehan, 2003). When the production was finished much material remained and it was hoped that future projects would be developed to extend the work done in *MAMU*.[10]

Documentary as testimony

Through the play of elements *MAMU* becomes a performance where moments of dissonance and connectedness are created for spectators. In this regard, then, the performance moves away from the idea of participation that Levinas found so objectionable as it does not generate any kind of frenzied or group response or involve spectators in a process that might engender passivity. Feelings of responsibility, privilege, shame and despair are most apparent in response to the documentary footage as it emerges in the sequencing of images and in the storytelling process. This footage works in a similar way to some of the filmmaking practices discussed by Marks. She suggests that in certain intercultural filmmaking processes, techniques are utilised whereby the images and the narrative do not necessarily match. Through the disjuncture created, film can stimulate reflection and elicit an embodied response in spectators as they search for meaning within a piece. Such film can also provide a space for alternative voices that refuse to be absorbed into the mainstream. Marks's ideas about film and its potential for embodiment are interesting when the types of storytelling used through the documentary sequences in *MAMU* and the juxtaposition of these with the 'live' elements of the performance are considered.

In this performance the filmmakers and the filmic documents themselves 'trouble the relationship between vision and knowledge' (Marks, 2000: 133). This occurs both through the sharing of many previously untold Indigenous stories in often poetic and metaphorical language (in Pitjantjatjara and translated via subtitles without the inclusion of a voice-over to narrate or direct our understanding of the story). The documentaries refuse to provide information simply and didactically, preferring to use the material performatively in a manner that supports Marks's description of documentaries which 'frustrate the passive absorption of information, instead encouraging the viewer to engage more actively and self-critically with the image'

(Marks, 2000: 133). While Marks is specifically concerned with generating a critical (and particularly self-critical) engagement, there are also parallels to be drawn with Levinas's discussions of the relationship between the saying and the said.

What Marks sees as the ability of documentary to 'frustrate' 'passive absorption' by spectators, is what I read as performance's ability (through its mobilisation of the senses) to engage spectators viscerally and at a sensory level. In *MAMU* it is not just the documentary that does this but, as I pointed out at the outset, it is also its positioning in the midst of (or juxtaposing against) the live event.

Julie Salverson makes a similar point in an essay discussing the use of refugee testimony in her creative work. Drawing on Levinas she explores the use of testimony within the framework of a performance. She points out that 'the act of performance, then, would ask artist and listener to attend to the "said"...and the "saying"' (Salverson, 1999) and she goes on to explain, quoting Levinas that 'within these terms, artist and audience are asked to become a "here I am...a witness that does not thematize what it bears witness of, and whose truth is not the truth of representation, is not evidence"' (in Salverson, 1999).

Testimony emerges, in this chapter, as an important mode of telling because the documentary sequences serve as testimonies to the experiences of the Spinifex people. These testimonies have not been heard by the majority of the non-Indigenous population. They are poignant and poetic and provide a space in which the Spinifex elders talk in their own way about their relationships to land, country, tradition and culture, and the deeply held sense of loss that the destruction of this relationship has had on the people. There is no attempt to coerce, redress, challenge or confront; instead spectators are invited to share the poetic narration of the elders as they describe their stories in Pitjantjatjara. Shoshana Felman, in her exploration of Holocaust testimony, focuses on its impact; her account beautifully describes the ways in which the testimony in *MAMU* works. She writes that

> testimony is...a discursive *practice,* as opposed to a pure *theory.* To testify – to *vow to tell,* to *promise* and *produce* one's own speech as material evidence for truth – is to accomplish a *speech act,* rather than to simply formulate a statement. As a performative speech act, testimony in effect addresses what in history is *action* that exceeds any substantialized significance, and what in happenings is *impact*

that dynamically explodes any conceptual reifications and any constative delimitations. (Felman, 1992: 5; original emphasis)

The elders use metaphor and image to tell their stories, but these are not mere devices. Instead they reflect the ways in which the Spinifex elders see the world. The land and its spirits dominate, and as they share their experiences spectators begin to gain a sense of the profoundly different worlds inhabited by these people and the 'mainstream' population. The elders 'bear witness', in the manner outlined by Giorgio Agamben, when he states that

> to bear witness is to place oneself in one's own language in the position of those who have lost it, to establish oneself in a living language as if it were dead, or in a dead language as if it were living – in any case, outside both the archive and the *corpus* of what has already been said. (Agamben 1999: 161)

Although I argue here, following Levinas, Marks, Felman and Agamben that the testimony used in *MAMU* is not designed to produce singular answers, or to be 'thematized' (as Levinas explains), and that it 'explodes conceptual reifications' as Felman points out, it is also important to acknowledge that there can be problems with the use of documentary theatre. As Carol Martin makes clear, 'because so much documentary theatre has been made in order to "set the record straight" or to bring materials otherwise ignored to the public's attention, we ought not to ignore its moral and ethical claims to truth' (Martin, 2006: 14). While *MAMU* is not strictly documentary theatre, (it is described by Gilbert and Lo as a 'multimedia performance' (2007: 123)) it is essential to consider what this means or might mean for spectators responding to the filmic testimony in this performance.

The documentary sequences (particularly those that involve testimony) function to provide a sense of both the depth and alterity of Spinifex culture, and of the elders in particular. Because the elders speak in poetic terms, they do not attempt to deliberately make (obvious) truth-claims, or present counter arguments, or even demand that we read their stories in particular ways. Given this context we can understand that while there are undoubtedly emotional and moral investments made in determining what to show and how to position it within the performance, the testimony in this work reveals via the alterity of the elders the significance of their culture to Spinifex people. It does not urge a particular singular response on moral, ethical or political grounds. Instead what is urged is just that we respond, that the material and the lives associated with it are acknowledged and considered.

James Hatley, speaking of Levinas's interest in the poetic nature of the writing of Levi and Celan, states that: 'the poem, like philosophy, is called upon to reduce its thematization, to remain ambivalent in the saying of its said' (Hatley, 2000: 144). Agamben also draws on poetry in his discussion of testimony. He argues, quoting Hölderlin, that 'what remains is what the poets found' (in Agamben, 1999: 161), however he goes on to explain that this

> is not to be understood in the trivial sense that poets' works are things that last and remain throughout time. Rather, it means that the poetic word is the one that is always situated in the position of a remnant and that can, therefore, bear witness. (Agamben, 1999: 161)

This is akin to the ways in which the poetic testimony of the elders operates in *MAMU*. It disrupts any easy reading of the performance and more specifically of the deeply held spiritual and cultural experiences of the Spinifex people. The strength of the testimony is reinforced by its positioning in the midst of a work that moves dramatically and suddenly between artistic forms and emotional registers. These dramatic shifts and the intimacy created in the space by the performers reinforces the power of the testimony shared in the documentary sequences.[11]

As explained earlier the elders have a very different relationship to and understanding of the land than non-Indigenous people. It is not just that they are different in cultural terms, however; it is that seeing and hearing them speak generates (or has the potential to generate) an awareness of their absolute alterity in the sense that it stimulates 'a subjective acknowledgement of the limits of the percipient's knowing, of his or her inability to contain all that is perceivable within the ambit of understanding' (Meffan and Worthington, 2001: 135). Given the often-fraught relationships between Indigenous and non-Indigenous Australians explained at the outset of the chapter, the privilege of being addressed by the elders from their land is a significant and at times deeply disturbing experience.

I am not suggesting that the 'face' of the other, as it is made manifest in the documentary sequences is unmediated or troubled by framing in a way that fixes the 'problem' of representation and demands a singular reading. I am suggesting, however, that these sequences, because of their positioning and their use of poetic language and metaphor, rupture the representational order and allow spectators to come face to face with the other and to gain a much more profound sense of the significance of the land, culture and loss experienced by the Spinifex people.

Disarming the audience: humour and emotion

The performance is prefaced with the creation story of the Spinifex people. This story, as well as the traditional dance which follows and the first interview projected on the screen, establishes the breadth of tradition and ritual within the Spinifex community. This material frames entry into the performance in a way that does not explain or translate every aspect of Spinifex cultural life. Instead it provides spectators with a series of fragments and begins the process of underscoring for them the importance to the community of custom, ritual and traditional law.

Before the lights are dimmed the creation story is projected onto the video screens. This story documents the shaping of the land 7,000 years ago and the ways in which the spirits of the Sun and Shadow people saved the land from disappearance in the face of floods.

> The people of the Sun and Shadow are the Spinifex people today. The duality embodies their association with the land, defines their kinship and is the vertebrae of their religion. That association with land, law and people continued, cocooned within the spinifex plains of the Western Desert, for another 200 generations until the Spinifex people were shaken from their nomadic solitude by the atomic shock of Maralinga. It was in 1952 and the Spinifex people were about to meet white Australia. (Rankin and Jamieson, 2002)[12]

The performance commences with a traditional dance or 'Inma'. The entire cast gradually becomes visible, painted white and dancing. This is a poignant and beautiful sacred dance. As the dance unfolds the first interview is projected onto the screen. This interview is with Spinifex elder Roy Underwood, and whilst spoken in Pitjantjatjara it is translated into English via subtitles. The story, although translated, retains the mythical quality of the original and is about the spirits who shaped the Spinifex country. We see Underwood seated at a rockhole. He states:

> This is an old man. He is a devil spirit.
> He heard the old lady, Alukawati,
> She went across here shouting. They heard her
> They're all the same spirits … family …
> They heard some bad news, that old lady's grandson had killed the old man,
> So they exploded out from the earth.
> They knew they had lost a loved one.
>
> (Rankin and Jamieson, 2002)

The poetic language used by Underwood, as he talks about the spiritual formation of the land and his country, is evocative. The sounds of the language are unfamiliar, the stories (and the mode of telling) are different and new, and the sense of presence exuded by Underwood in his spiritual place is unsettling. This is such a 'foreign' experience that it disallows any potentially shallow ideas of cultural awareness or proximity. There is no corrective view of history here. Underwood's story, as he sits at the rockhole, fractures the representational space of the performance. As Rosalyn Diprose argues, following Levinas, 'the other's teaching of alterity solicits a response and is the basis of my ability to respond at all to anything' (Diprose, 2002: 137). Or as Levinas puts it: 'It is through the condition of being a hostage that there can be pity, compassion, pardon, and proximity in the world – even the little there is, even the simple "after you, sir" ' (Levinas, 1996: 91). This alterity is striking, as Underwood engages spectators through the simplicity of his words. There is no decoration here, no artifice. Any drama that may have been generated by the sacred dance that precedes this scene is abandoned.

There seems to be an invitation issued by or through the documentary to share the story but also a caution to be aware of its sacredness. This interview mobilises generosity, in the Levinasian sense, as 'a generosity born of an affective corporeal response to alterity, that generates rather than closes off cultural difference' (Diprose, 2002: 146). The fact that the stories are not altered in translation to make them more readily accessible to a non-Indigenous audience is a powerful aspect of the work.

Through the process of engagement with these dreaming or creation stories, as well as the stories from those who experienced (in a literal, embodied sense) the nuclear testing, spectators are encouraged to think critically about the stories being told and to begin to sense the depth of this resilient culture. The footage demonstrates that there are other ways of knowing and sharing history aside from the dominant Western official document. The multiple stories and voices in *MAMU* effect a challenge to any preconceived ideas about Aboriginal culture in general, and the Spinifex people in particular. They deny any simplistic understanding of Spinifex culture as an authentic (read singular) hermetically sealed community. Instead, the documents, both live and filmic, work together to create a layered portrait of a community in which traditional and contemporary knowledges and cultural practices exist in a dialogic relationship that is dynamic and continually evolving.

Jamieson's devilish charm

Jamieson's presence is crucial, as through his narration the multiple and diverse elements of the work are threaded together. He uses song and story to remind spectators of the key themes of *MAMU* and, despite the difficult nature of some of the material, his warmth and personality create the intimacy within the performance space that is maintained throughout the work. Jamieson explains his movements across Western and South Australia as he was growing up and shows these on a map projected onto the backdrop. He moves from here to introduce his family. This is a complicated process, as Aboriginal kinship systems differ markedly from non-Aboriginal systems. Each member of the family is introduced and their relationship to Jamieson explained.[13] While this is happening the projections depict Spinifex country and some of the community members who could not make it to the show. The mood shifts again, and the men and boys perform a traditional emu dance dressed in their tribal costumes. This is followed by an emu dance performed by the women. The elders accompany the dancing by clapping boomerangs and singing.

A traditional Spinifex painting is projected during the performance of the men's emu dance, and this is followed by an image of a sacred waterhole during the women's emu dance. Next documentary footage shows Roy Underwood discussing the significance of the waterhole and telling us that it is the emu place:

> I came back and found this place so we can keep it. The people had forgotten about it. I want to keep the men here but they still go off to Kalgoorlie. Our ancestors walked around here. They were not sick, no medicine. This is the emu place. (Rankin and Jamieson, 2002)

Once the documentary has finished, Jamieson explains to us that the dances we have just witnessed have not been performed for outsiders before. There is an interesting shift here between the way in which the documentary positions spectators with its depiction of the radical alterity of the Spinifex elders and Jamieson's more intimate and warm engagement. It is as if with Jamieson that spectators are being privileged, and with Underwood that they learn that, despite the privilege, they will never fully know the Spinifex people. Jamieson goes on to tell us that the dances are being 'looked after' by Djamu Roy and that they come from his mother's country. He then explains the responsibility that he and his brothers face when they become the keepers of their community's cultural knowledge as Djamu Roy passes it on to them. Here we gain a brief insight into the complexity of this task faced by Jamieson and his brothers. Retaining all the cultural knowledge and stories of the Spinifex people whilst also surviving in a contemporary world will be a challenge for these men but one that they seem to embrace. Jamieson explains what 'looking after country' means:

> Physical things like clearing out rockholes. Mental things like learning the Tjukurrpa, the stories and ceremonies And the spiritual things – the songs, dances, the public, the secret, the women's

the men's – keeping the spirit of the country alive. (Rankin and Jamieson, 2002)[14]

After a traditional song, 'Djamku Ngurra', the seriousness of the mood is fractured as train tracks are projected onto the screen and Jamieson and his brothers enact a scene in response to these tracks. They pretend to be Spinifex people confronted by the tracks for the first time and wonder if these are tracks of a serpent or a goanna. After some discussion a train is heard; it begins to travel down the tracks towards the stage. At the same time a toy train crosses the stage just under the screens. They run in fear and one of them says in Pitjantjatjara, which is translated on the screen into English, 'I just #@! My pants'. The other responds: 'You're not supposed to have any pants; you're supposed to be pretending you're naked. Oh well, they can't understand us anyway' (Rankin and Jamieson, 2002). This tongue-in-cheek humour is hilarious and the scene looks like something from a Charlie Chaplin film (and perhaps pays homage to the Lumière brothers). This mini play within the play works well, as it again shifts the mood whilst at the same time conveying the fear and anxiety that must have been experienced by the Spinifex people when they first encountered a train. This sequence is used as a transitional one in order to introduce the train and to discuss its impact on the lives of the community members. According to Cane, when they first encountered the train the Spinifex people thought it was a 'Water snake man (Wati Wanampi) and recall the terror of actually seeing the water snake, streaking across the plains: the Indian-Pacific Express' (Cane, 2002: 172).

Nuclear testing – profound disturbance

The train sequence leads to a discussion of the mission at Oolea in South Australia, and of the movement of people from the desert to the Mission. The documentary is used here to introduce elder, Hughie Windlass, who talks about the people moving from the land to the mission. He explains how the mission land was good land as there was water there and the people enjoyed being there. They had freedom to practice their cultural traditions as well as having access to schooling and the supplies the mission provided. However, in the early 1950s, the people were told to move off the mission.[15] It was here that the British government was going to test 'the bomb'. Windlass explains that the officials left the mission and the people but did not provide transport for the Indigenous people so that they could leave the land. He now sees the land as desolate, and says that even the water snake has left:

And here was a big place, with a snake...
It was underground where the snake was,
Water snake
You wouldn't believe it but there you are
When everything moved out, he moved out, that snake moved out too...
And today, you can't get ground water there today
Now today look here, make me sad now.
(Windlass in Rankin and Jamieson, 2002)

The lack of spectacle or artifice or even drama allows Windlass's alterity and his utter despair at the destruction of the sacred landscape as a result of the nuclear tests to emerge. The fact that the landscape has been destroyed to such an extent that even the sacred spirits have fled makes the devastation wreaked on the Spinifex people as a consequence of the nuclear testing more profound. Windlass does not provide facts and figures. The disjunction between the poetic mode of telling and the seriousness of the story works to disturb spectators. It is at moments such as these that the orders of responsibility collide most profoundly for this spectator at least. I find it immensely difficult to remain seated and quell the desire to respond to the injustices being relayed in Windlass's testimony. This is a feeling that intensifies as the focus on the nuclear testing continues. Dori Laub, in speaking about Holocaust testimony, points out: 'For the listener who enters the contract of the testimony, a journey fraught with dangers lies ahead. There are hazards to the listening to trauma. Trauma – and its impact on the hearer – leaves, indeed, no hiding place intact' (Laub, 1992: 72). There is a sense that there is no place to go, no way of denying or lessening the trauma of the nuclear tests. For Samela Harris these stories also had a profound impact. She says

they tell us the stories of their world as it was and as it became after the atomic testings at Maralinga. They are gut-wrenching stories we must know. They are not just stories of loss of home and culture, but of gross and shameful abuse. (Harris, 2002)

The interview is followed by newsreel footage of the Maralinga tests, showing the scientists at the site and one of the nuclear explosions. Its very objective tone contrasts starkly with the lyrical storytelling style of the elders. The elders tell of the direct impact of the testing on the people through their stories; they share this traumatic event with the audience by describing how they saw the cloud approaching and how it affected them physically. Their storytelling techniques, when juxtaposed with the emotionless, yet upbeat journalistic tone of the official newsreel footage, points to the opposition between the detached account and the lived experiences of the bombs. The voiceover counts down to the explosion and then declares that 'the mighty power of the atom is unleashed, a triumph for British Scientists and the Australian technicians who made possible the tests at Maralinga'. A still image of the mushroom cloud is projected onto the backdrop as the focus shifts to Jamieson, who explains how the community, some of whom were still living in the contaminated zone, responded to the tests.

These shifts in mood – from Windlass's sad yet poetic narrative to the 'objective' news footage and then to Jamieson's explanation of the experiences of some community members who remained within the contaminated zone – create a deep sense of unease amongst the spectators. This can be felt through the tense silence that seems to fall across the space. When the time came to clear the land, Jamieson tells us, 'two native patrol officers were employed to clear an area ten times the size of Japan' (Rankin and Jamieson, 2002). The significance of this fact resonates with the audience, who gasp with shock in response. Jamieson goes on to say that many of the Spinifex people were still on their land:

> Carlene's sister was out in Spinifex, in the prohibited zone, with her family. An army jeep drives up to them. Two army personnel argued about what to do. The junior one said to drive them to Loongana but the senior one said, just give them some rations and tell them to walk. (Rankin and Jamieson, 2002)

The reality of the devastating impact of the tests on the Spinifex people is poignantly reinforced at this moment. Families were separated, relatives were lost, and some individuals died of radiation, yet the officials insisted that the land was empty. For Jeremy Eccles,

> one of the most affecting moments involved Trevor's Auntie
> using language that was barely translated to tell of her parents
> and 2 siblings dying from radiation poisoning and/or the effort
> of walking through unknown desert country to Kalgoorlie, while
> a live camera revealed every emotion. (2002: 5)

Jamieson talks about a newspaper article published in 1986, which his
mother kept. It reported that 'people died out there, they became sick.
When people ate meat and when they drank water they died'. A voice-
over reads this caption as the newspaper is projected onto the screens.
A tribal dance is performed and the community leave the space clapping and chanting. As they are leaving, the footage moves to a current
affairs-style programme in which men involved in the testing are
interviewed. One of them talks about his sense of sadness at the damage done by the tests; the other, a senior British official at the time,
remarks, 'I'm absolutely certain that nobody did suffer'. This statement is repeated and the image is frozen. As Joanne Tompkins writes:

> By the time the mushroom cloud image of Maralinga is screened,
> the play has established a much more detailed understanding of
> the actual region, the history of the people, and a broader interpret-
> ation of the tests than is usually associated with this shot.... The
> specificity that Jamieson has outlined means that his description of
> the precautions taken to clear the supposedly 'empty' and unin-
> habited area become even more chilling. (Tompkins, 2004: 4)

Helen Thomson concurs, she states, 'that official British accounts
assured the media at the time that Maralinga was uninhabited only
adds insult to the damage – to health, culture, kinship groups,
identity – done to the Aborigines' (Thomson, 2002). Once the community have left the stage, Stella Wicker comes on and sings a haunting traditional mission song about Ooldea. She has a beautiful voice
and her song is soulful and heart-wrenching. By the time the song
has finished, amongst the spectators there is a palpable sense of awe,
fear and perhaps disgust at the injustices committed.

There is an eerie calm in the space. At times like this it seems as if
there is no possibility of a response that might ignore or express

resignation about the events. This is a moment of deep shame, and shame, as Levinas explains is 'in the last analysis, an existence that seeks excuses. What shame discovers [*découvre*] is the being who *uncovers* himself [*se* découvre]' (Levinas, 2003: 65). I sit glued to the chair wishing to make amends or to be forgiven, absolved or freed. I feel exactly as Levinas suggests when he describes shame as 'identity's "gnawing away at itself" in remorse' (in Murphy, 2004). I occupy an ambivalent space as I wonder how to respond to this experience. I find myself in the fraught position of proximity and distance outlined at the beginning of this chapter. I feel a deep connection to the community but have no obvious means of contacting them, and I wonder about the validity of any action I might take. Shame will not provide a way out of this position. Instead it opens up the relationship between the subject and the other in a way that is both troubling and potentially productive. This may seem unhelpful, to a reader distanced from the work, and perhaps it is given that as Carol Martin explains, documentary theatre could be read as a 'form of propaganda' that presents

> its text and performances ... not just as a version of what happened but the version of what happened. The intention is to persuade spectators to understand specific events in particular ways. Even when the text is indefinite in its conclusions, audience response may not be. (Martin, 2006: 11)

Perhaps my individual reactions, described above, are testament to the work's skill at manipulation. However if manipulation is what is at play here it is operating at a very intricate level as the responses generated for me, and for Australian spectators and critics such as Harris, Thomson, Eccles, Tompkins and others, reveal that the testimonial sequences (in the context of the larger work) open up questions about the function and limits of any response to this work specifically and to the Spinifex people more generally.

The end, and beyond

The final scene in the performance is a triumphant one: we are told about the granting of native title to the Spinifex people. This was the largest grant of land through title in Australia. Details from Scott Cane's book are projected onto the screen and the significance of the triumph after so much pain is evident. The grant of native title to the Spinifex people means that their rightful ownership of 50,000 square kilometres of land is acknowledged. The documentary explains that the boundaries of the claim were defined by where people were born and where their dreaming was. To celebrate, the cast perform two dances. Firstly the women perform a traditional dance followed by the men who perform an emu dance. Finally elder Roy performs an owl dance and the cast do a curtain call. This is briefly interrupted by Jamieson's final speech, which frames the end of the performance as one of celebration. He says:

> I learned heaps putting this show together but I still have heaps to learn. ... I hope the show acts as a bridge connecting the ancient spiritual world to the black and white world and not to this modern white global village. (Rankin and Jamieson, 2002)

MAMU is a performance that is about recuperating and sharing the stories of the Spinifex people. It is a work that does not preach, confine or present a definitive or mediated portrait of the community; rather, it creates a 'performative' image of a group who are vibrant, culturally complex and who have survived a diverse range of obstacles since colonisation.

The success of the performance lies in the ways in which these stories of survival are performed. The combination of live storytelling, dance, song and documentary footage allows the elders to speak in their own voices, as well as providing spectators with insights into the landscape of the Spinifex people. This results in a performance that is both an important cultural document as well as an engaging theatrical experience.

MAMU raises questions and does not provide easy answers; it unsettles, provokes and entertains. But, most significantly, it explores the power of alterity to create an understanding of the depth of cultural history, knowledge and significance of the Spinifex people and it also, through the intimate sharing of disturbing stories of neglect by successive governments, has the potential to unleash feelings of shame in spectators who are aware of or invested in the context, as Gaita explains. These are feelings that do not necessarily lead to self-flagellation, excuses, blame and then nothingness. As Ann Murphy, drawing on Levinas, remarks, 'shame before another becomes much more than an indictment of self, it becomes a symptom of sensibility. Compassion and responsibility appear as the condition for the possibility of sense at all' (Murphy, 2004).

MAMU, with its messy structure and its intimacy, manages the dual burden outlined at the beginning of this chapter skillfully. In the process it pierces spectators – particularly those who understand the political and social context surrounding the work – it calls them to respond and to consider what to do with this responsibility on leaving the performance space.

4
Sandakan Threnody: Testimony and the Dangers of Polyphony

> The Value of testimony lies essentially in what it lacks; at its center it contains something that cannot be borne witness to and that discharges the survivors of authority. The 'true' witnesses, the 'complete witnesses,' are those who did not bear witness and could not bear witness. (Agamben, 1999: 34)

Sandakan Threnody is an episodic and dream-like performance. It combines a range of artistic vocabularies in order to reveal stories of trauma, torture and loss experienced by the Australian and British Prisoners of War held in Sandakan, Borneo, towards the end of World War II. The work's director, Ong Keng Sen explains that 'ultimately there are three different journeys, which are being woven onstage: the live action, the music and the video. It is my role to pull these three together' (Ong, 2004).[1] The use of testimony and personal documents, as well as a range of different cultural and artistic forms within these three journeys raise important ethical questions about the ways in which the performance draws on its stories, testimonies and its artistic forms to represent or recuperate this event.

Any work dealing with a traumatic event carries a complex burden in terms of how it decides to negotiate the often-horrific events that inform it. There is a negotiation that takes place between the need to tell the tale (or uncover the story) and the dangers (or even impossibility in some cases) of this telling. In *Sandakan Threnody* I read Ong's three journeys as representing the desire to balance the unveiling of the 'conspiracies of silence' (Ong, 2004)[2] that surround the POWs in

Sandakan with a range of artistic vocabularies so that the perform-ance becomes more than a literal re-telling.

'At the crossroads'

Given Ong's international reputation for large scale intercultural works it is interesting to note that *Sandakan Threnody* is not billed as an intercultural performance per se. Nonetheless he states in the pro-gramme notes for the production, that he has 'a concrete responsibil-ity towards the past and the future through working with collaborators from many cultures' (Ong, 2004). One of the focal points of this chapter is to consider how the use of forms, stories and cultures in *Sandakan Threnody* operates in terms of allowing that responsibility to be represented. Ong writes that *Sandakan Threnody* is different from his previous works because,

> it is the first time that the many cultures in my work have signifi-cance in an immediate social, political context. I think it is no longer possible to talk about war through one culture. **Sandakan Threnody** is positioned at the crossroads of Japan, Australia and Borneo/Singapore/Southeast Asia (the site of the war). (Ong, 2004; original emphasis)

As a director, Ong has created several major intercultural and cross-cultural projects as well as facilitating intercultural workshops for artists from Asia and latterly from around the world. Through his work he has contributed significantly to debates about cultural exchange, trans, intra and intercultural processes. He has encour-aged collaboration across art forms and cultures and has supported (and even championed) the work of traditional and contemporary practitioners from a diverse range of cultures.[3] While Ong remains a controversial figure, he plays an important role in the debates sur-rounding the politics and processes of cultural exchange in contem-porary theatre and performance as well as the implications of these within the wider globalised landscape.

Ong has been critiqued for his focus on the aesthetic, as this focus is read by some scholars as one that leads to a lack of recogni-tion of the historical or ideological frameworks surrounding the use of specific artistic forms. Rustom Bharucha, for example, sees him as demonstrating an 'openness' to other cultures. Bharucha argues that this 'openness' 'is less a moral imperative than a creative opportunity to engage and play with the cultures of the world, whose forms, technique and artefacts are available for his creative use' (Bharucha, 2000: 14). While this may appear to be harsh criticism it is a view that is shared by many respondents to Ong's work, and most particularly to his intercultural projects. Yong Li Lan, for example, in her discussion of his trilogy of Shakespearean productions, points out that the 'plurality of Asian performances ... agglomerated an Asia that was presented through fragments dislocated from their social contexts of performance' (Yong, 2004).[4]

It is necessary to acknowledge, at this juncture, that Ong's apparent refusal to contextualise the use of different artistic forms (his 'openness') is not the result of an accident or a lack of consideration on his part. As a skilled director he makes active choices about how he wants the elements employed in his performances to function. While Yong Li Lan comments on the potential for agglomeration, she also explains that in his Shakespearean trilogy, 'this was a deliberate post-modernist strategy, not an inevitable effect of dissonant styles' (Yong, 2004). Ong elaborates on these deliberate choices in an interview with Alette Scavenius about his third intercultural Shakespearean performance *Search: Hamlet,* he states:

> I think very often in my pieces there is a huge challenge or a huge tension. In *Lear,* for instance, the tension was between the traditional performers and the contemporary performers, and very often it was a struggle between how to balance, but that tension actually made the piece – in the same way, *Desdemona* was a tension between audience expectations of the piece after the beautiful exotic *Lear* and our denial of this expectation. (Scavenius, 2002)

In a recently published interview he explains that he prefers to call his work 'transcultural' rather than intercultural. He points out that 'when we work transculturally, it's about both cultures moving into a third space. Both cultures have to lose themselves to find themselves' (Ong in Leverett, 2007: 55). As well as considering the ways in which the work uses its modes and stories to draw attention to the experiences of trauma, loss and pain suffered by those involved in war, this chapter will also explore how the cultures and artistic forms involved in *Sandakan Threnody* both 'lose' and 'find themselves' in the performance's journey to this 'third space'.

The artistic vocabularies employed in the work include contemporary dance (Kota Yamazaki and Tim Harvey), acting and narration (Matthew Crosby and Lok Meng Chue), kabuki (Gojo Masanosuke), contemporary performance (Rizman Putra) and Mills's composition/score. Documentary segments include interviews with the daughter of one of the six survivors, Australian POW William 'Bill' Moxham. Susan Moxham talks about her father's experiences of war's aftermath. Tetsuya Yamamoto, the son of Japanese Captain Shoichi Yamamoto, is interviewed and discusses his understanding of honour, war and responsibility.[5] Footage of the performers travelling to Borneo to experience the environment, to engage with the place and with locals who assisted the POWs, and to visit the memorial is also included, as well as two historical film clips. The first is a propaganda trailer, *This is Japan*, which was originally screened in Australia in the early 1940s and is concerned with mistrust and hatred of the Japanese. The second is a documentary sequence at the beginning of the performance showing prisoners being hanged.

Sandakan the story

Sandakan Threnody is based on the experiences of Australian soldiers who were imprisoned in Borneo in 1945.[6] Of the 2,428 men imprisoned in Sandakan, approximately 1,066 were forced to march across the rugged terrain from Sandakan to Ranau in Sabah. There were three marches in total. These took place in January, May and June of 1945. Most of the POWs were too ill to survive the journey, which was 260km long and took up to a month of trekking barefoot through dense crocodile-and-snake-infested jungle. The pain and suffering endured was, at times, overwhelming and, as Ong points out, 'as they dragged their bodies through the jungle, many of them were crawling like animals. Through the thick tropical jungle, they lost their ability to even stand, due to lack of food and the terrible terrain' (Ong, 2004).[7]

Only six prisoners survived the camps, by escaping into the jungle with the assistance of local anti-Japanese guerrillas. The remaining prisoners died as a result of torture, starvation, disease or execution. Composer Jonathan Mills's father was a medical officer at Sandakan but was transferred to another camp and survived the war. Mills wrote an orchestral piece as a creative response to this horrific event, a response that he hoped might trigger reflection on the devastation caused by war. This orchestral piece was significantly reworked to form the musical score for the performance *Sandakan Threnody*. Mills approached Ong to discuss the possibility of collaborating on a performance project about Sandakan, and after two years the performance work *Sandakan Threnody* emerged.[8] Mills states in the programme notes that 'the title of the work derives from the Greek word threnos, which means grieving, but with an explicit emphasis on a public act of grieving' (Mills, 2004). He goes on to point out that

> it has not been my intention in writing *Sandakan Threnody* to make accusations. No culture or country has a monopoly on righteousness. The rituals of many cultures rely on the representation of a transforming journey, a pilgrimage or a path to enlightenment. By contrast, the marches from Sandakan to Ranau had no purpose and provided no enlightenment. (Mills, 2004)

Mills wants to reveal the pain and trauma experienced at Sandakan, and Ong sees 'several conspiracies of silence in both Australia and Japan' in response to the events that took place there. Consequently, this work then sets out to 'float' stories of 'of trauma and dignity' experienced in and in response to war 'to the surface' (Ong, 2004). According to Lynette Ramsay Silver, in her book *Sandakan: A Conspiracy of Silence*,

> the press, not usually noted for its reticence, entered into a gentlemen's agreement with the Australian Government to reveal nothing but the most scant details. The rationale behind this decision, which was to cause immense grief and torment to the relatives of dead POWs in the years ahead, was that the story of Australians held by the Japanese was too appalling to be disclosed. Consequently, while the entire world knew everything there was to know about atrocities perpetrated by Nazi Germany in Europe, the families of POWs held in Japanese-occupied territory were given no information. (1998: 283)

The lack of awareness of the suffering of these POWs within the wider community meant that they and their families were not afforded the opportunity to grieve or to condemn. And yet, according to Peta Bowden and Emma Rooksby, 'moral condemnation is important to the sustenance of the community, to the articulation of the socio-ethical expectations of its members and to victims' recovery from extreme violations of those expectations' (2006: 247). There is ongoing controversy in Japan about wartime experiences, their representation and memorialisation. Despite the lack of national recognition of the war, individual citizens have undergone personal reflection and there is a strong anti-war movement. But as Peter Eckersall explains, 'many Japanese political elites continue to perpetuate a reading of WW2 in which Japan is positioned as the victim of western imperial aggression' (Grehan, 2007).[9] Because the Japanese have never acknowledged the extent of their brutality during the war nor undergone a period of national reflection, and Ong sees *Sandakan Threnody* as an explicit resistance to the silencing of these stories, it is important to consider the ways in which the performance engages spectators in a process of reflection about conflict in both historical and current contexts.

The known and the unknown tale

Given that a simple sharing of the historical material may, in effect, dilute the power of the story, traumatise spectators, or result in an experience of 'the crudest form of empathy' (Brecht, 1976: 518), Ong must tread a fine line between deconstructing these 'conspiracies' and presenting them in a way that allows spectators to inscribe their own responses onto or within the performance.

James Hatley, writing on witnessing and representation in his book *Suffering Witness*, argues cogently about the complexities involved in representing or responding to horror. Hatley draws on Saul Friedlander's discussion of the 'inadequacy of any representation of the *Shoah*' and the latter's call for history to be reshaped as commentary that 'disrupt[s] the facile linear progression of narration, introduce[s] alternative interpretations, question[s] any partial conclusions, withstand[s] the need for closure' (Friedlander in Hatley 2000: 113). Hatley is of course concerned with the Holocaust, but his suggestion about the ways in which history should be dealt with is significant as, drawing on Levinas, he calls for a process of response that disallows any easy identification (or reduction of the other to the same) for the subject, and in this case the spectator. He emphasises the necessity of uncertainty or ambivalence in response to traumatic stories. Levinas elaborates cogently on this when he says:

> The witness is not reducible to the relationship that leads from an index to the indicated. That would make it a disclosure and a thematization. It is the bottomless passivity of responsibility, and thus, sincerity. It is the meaning of language, before language scatters into words, into themes equal to the words and dissimulating in the said the openness of the saying exposed like a bleeding wound. But the trace of the witness given, the sincerity or glory, is not effaced even in its said. (Levinas, 1998: 151)

This focus on 'disruption' and the desire to avoid 'thematization' seems to reflect the process at work in *Sandakan Threnody*. As with representations of the Shoah, the horrors of the 'death marches' and prison camps in Borneo are such that attempting to develop a performance in response to this material is a complex task. As Martin Buzacott, in his review of the production, remarks:

> History is littered with horrific tales of man's inhumanity to man, but for sheer shock value there's not much that can match the atrocities committed on Australian prisoners of war during World War II's notorious death marches in Borneo. (2004: 9)

Sandakan Threnody juxtaposes the facts and archival material (via testimony and narration) and documentary elements with abstract choreographed sequences. Situating the performance within the context of the current war (on terror), Ong points to the ways in which 'power can be abused'; he wants to use the work to attempt to 'transcend the cultural bigotry which leads to war' (2004). This approach clearly worked for some spectators. As Keith Gallasch in his review of *Sandakan Threnody* points out: the performance 'does not attempt to reproduce the death marches, rather it reflects on their consequences and poses disturbing questions about our ongoing relationship with war, with the maltreatment of prisoners and the clash of loyalty and morality' (Gallasch, 2004).

While the works addressed in this book provoke an experience of participation that is for the most part antithetical to Levinas's understanding of the term; because they rupture any frenzied or singular group response to representation, *Sandakan Threnody* adds another level of complexity to this idea. Some parts of the performance are compelling and they mobilise participation, for a range of spectators, in the sense defined in Chapter 1, as an active, complex and productive process. Other parts of the performance seem to work against this participation. It is not that they generate an experience of a singular non-reflexive group reaction (in the Levinasian sense of the term); rather, they seem by virtue of their isolation or lack of connectedness with other elements of the performance, to detract from the overall coherence of the work. This may, as I have suggested earlier, be a deliberate strategy, however it makes both processes of response and responsibility difficult at times. As Gallasch explains 'Sandakan Threnody is at its best when the weave is tight and the alternation of elements and shifts in patterning are rhythmically insistent. This is mostly in the first half where the totality of the hybrid is most felt as organic' (Gallasch, 2004). And as journalist Rosemary Duffy states in response to the performance:

> There is no denying the potency of *Sandakan Threnody* but at times I felt Ong did not trust the intrinsic power of the story to speak for itself and there was a tendency to overload the dramaturgy. The kabuki scenes were compelling without the overlay of music, which in that context, sounded histrionic and jarring. The twisted tortured choreography became irritating through overuse, and at times seemed quite superfluous. (2004)

It seems as if, in the desire to uncover the 'conspiracies of silence' which the story contains, there is at times a lack of connectedness between the artistic vocabularies employed in the performance. These moments demonstrate that 'openness' can have its limits and that the work, at times, runs the risk of alienating its spectators rather than engaging them to reflect on, or participate in a process of uncovering.

The performance

The performance begins with a gruesome silent black-and-white documentary of soldiers being hanged. This is accompanied by the narrator, Lok Meng Chue's, statement that 'it's all buried somewhere inside'.[10] When the footage finishes the music starts and a dancer comes on to the stage. Lok Meng Chue, seated at a wooden office table with a reading light, reads aloud a letter to Lieutenant Bill Sticpewich. The letter is obviously from an ex-Japanese solider who talks about military prison and his family and life in Japan. The soldier asks Sticpewich if he can introduce him to the (Australian) soldiers stationed in his town so that he can 'increase his customer base'.[11] More footage is shown, this time of war, soldiers, marching and bombs. Lok Meng Chue narrates the marches from Sandakan, detailing the number of miles walked per day, the type and quantity of rations and the numbers of POWs lost along the way.

Three dancers dance or writhe on the stage as if participating in the marches (in an abstract fashion). And the Australian dancer, Tim Harvey, says, speaking of the cast's journey to Sandakan Memorial Park, 'I slept in an extra half-hour...the only reason I'm travelling out to the war memorial today is because I've been told it is worthwhile...to me it seems a dead experience. I just think so what'. This is followed by Lok Meng Chue's narration. She reads from documentation in an emotionless tone: 'mutilated bodies astride the track'. Harvey goes on to say that when he is told that remains are buried near the spot where he is standing, he wonders 'if I am stepping on those remains right now.'

Lok Meng Chue then narrates the story of the march to Ranau, 'first march to Ranau, 455 set off'. Harvey dances slowly as he talks. He goes on: 'The visual impact is very strong, I wish I'd brought my camera with me because the light is very beautiful'. For writer Richard Lord, the apparent lack of understanding exhibited by Harvey resulted in a moment in which performance did not 'escape entirely from the slack jaws of banality: for instance, some of the thoughts of the young Australian...were decidedly trite' (2004). It is unclear why Ong chose to include documentation of the journey to Sandakan undertaken by the cast. The decision to take the cast on the journey is understandable, but its function as an aesthetic, political or artistic artefact within the work is difficult to decipher.

Matthew Crosby comes on and drags one of the dancers to the side of the stage, saying 'we'll put you off the road over here. Maybe a local will come for you. Susan, hello pet, what's that? Snowy your sheep, in the dunny? Snowy who put you in there?' In contrast to

Harvey's responses to the journey, Crosby's spoken segments are mesmerising. He is a skilled performer who manages to present fragments of narrative from a range of characters through a bleak, minimalist performance style – the art of the blank stare is perfected – so that spectators gain some sense of the depth of trauma experienced in the aftermath of war.

He portrays one of the six survivors, the Australian soldier William 'Bill' Moxham, both as he marches through the jungle and on his return to Australia suffering from post-traumatic stress disorder. Some of his most affecting scenes are those in which, as in the quotation above, he performs sequences involving Moxham moving between the reality of the marches and the reality (or trauma) of life on his return home. For example, a little later in the performance he oscillates between attempting to coax another sick POW to the next food drop, a rant about eating the Japanese and raping their wives, and an imaginary discussion with his daughter Susan: 'Susan, come on, pet, daddy wants to play'. His speech is confused and unsettled. He says: 'Susan come out come out wherever you are', come on pet I'm not going to hurt you, I'll bloody murder you'. This is delivered in a style that positions him as a pathetic and lost soul, as he moves from a calm detached almost playful call to a sharp aggressive shout.[12] This portrayal calls to mind Agamben's discussion of the relationship between the human and the inhuman in *Remnants of Auschwitz*. Agamben explains that

> what testimony says is something completely different, which can be formulated in the following theses: 'human beings are human insofar as they are not human' or, more precisely, 'human beings are human insofar as they bear witness to the inhuman'. (Agamben, 1999: 121)

Crosby's portrayal of these points of connection or disconnection between the human and the inhuman in Moxham's story continue throughout the performance and act as a connective fabric to weave some of the diverse elements together. As Dorothy Chansky remarks:

> Moxham is played by the extraordinary Australian actor Matthew Crosby, who manages the physical endurance and suppleness

necessary both to embody his character and to convey his pain artfully as well as providing the world-weariness suitable to a man who has packed what seem like centuries into a few decades of living. (2004)

The strength and significance of Crosby *as* Moxham reciting the monologues becomes even more apparent when they are juxtaposed with the use of documentary footage of the 'real' Susan Moxham talking about her father.

Perhaps somewhat paradoxically, given the need to avoid banalisation and crude empathy, and the necessity that work dealing with such horror engages spectators in a process of response and responsibility, of the journeys in *Sandakan Threnody* the most profound sense of connection and responsibility is engendered for some spectators in response to the documentary footage of Susan Moxham and Tetsuya Yamamoto. This footage punctures the highly stylised modes of performance and dance that surround it. As in *The Career Highlights of the MAMU* the footage is stark. It dominates the performance space and it sits in contrast to the other journeys Ong outlines both in terms of its form and content. It is during this footage that spectators may begin to gain some insight into the personal impact of war on the children of those involved. Feelings of humiliation, shame, honour, trauma and loss are detected in the interviews. These feelings work to create a sense of emotional connectedness with the stories being told. For Duffy, for example, 'the drama was at its most riveting and most moving when the faces and voices of 'real' people were used' (Duffy, 2004).

Because it sits in dramatic contrast to the other aspects of the performance, and because both Moxham and Yamamoto are brutally straightforward (albeit in different ways), their testimonies demand responsibility. They reveal the trauma of war not only on 'survivors' but also on families, on those left behind. The testimonies are pared back, simple and bleak. They are not overlaid with movement, sound or other dialogue and they puncture the flow of the work as well as evoking ethical questions about silence, trauma and responsibility. They generate moments in which the 'saying' interrupts the 'said' and where the significance of the other's call is made manifest both bodily or at a sensory level and intellectually as spectators experience the impacts of these stories. Testimony functions here, not as literal truth (as discussed in Chapter 3), but rather, echoing Agamben, as a space within which the boundaries between the human and the inhuman can emerge.

Susan Moxham and Tetsuya Yamamoto reflect on their experiences of and responses to their fathers and their own experiences as the children of war. These elements of the performance, when combined with the impassioned yet pathetic lines spoken by Matthew Crosby as he performs the persona of William 'Bill' Moxham and also when he performs as Captain Yamamoto, are revealing. As Duffy explains 'the interviews with Susan Moxham...and Tetsuya Yamamoto...speak eloquently of the terrible scars left on the psyches of those indirectly involved' (2004). The significance of these interviews is reinforced through situating them against Lok Meng Chue's authoritative and emotionless performance as an interrogator (at the war crimes trial) of Captain Yamamoto. This interrogation is narrated during the projection of the documentary interview with Yamamoto's son, Tetsuya.

Both Moxham and Yamamoto speak calmly about their understandings of their respective fathers. Moxham, whose interview is projected from a totally dark performance space where her face is the only source of light in the theatre and therefore every expression can be read clearly, makes references to her father's inability to adjust back to the world and relates his responses to those of the character Kurtz in Conrad's *Heart of Darkness* (and its adaptation in *Apocalypse Now*). She talks about the devastation wreaked by war on those who were not there and of the silences.

> My father crossed between what is civilised and what is uncivilised.... Where other people who couldn't go on in the marches were bayoneted they privately made the decision that they couldn't...but in my father's case he had such a zeal for life, he was prepared to put up with ongoing tortures.

She goes on to say 'he made the decision...that there was hope...that there was opportunity...but to survive in that situation means that morals were cast aside. There is no place for morals in a prisoner of war camp...you don't win war by being moral.' Her tone is one of resigned calm. Her approach, tone and story are compelling. She seems determined to deconstruct the 'hero' myth and to explain the demoralising impacts of war on its victims and their families.

Most of the media (and official) representations of Australian soldiers are patriotic, often nostalgic and focus on valorising of their heroism. Yet here is the daughter of a POW explaining that her father 'crossed the line'. This admission has a profound impact on me as an Australian spectator, as there is apparently little tolerance of 'difference' or space for the telling of alternative stories about war in this country. Moxham's ambivalence about her father – in terms of her ability to highlight the difficulties of living with someone who has been damaged (beyond repair) by his experiences – is refreshing and shocking at the same time.[13]

Moxham says that 'to attribute the term hero to someone who survives a place like Sandakan' is very difficult.[14] She moves beyond positioning her father as a hero and acknowledges the destruction war wreaks on individuals. She avoids the rush to sentimentalise or to memorialise, and peels away the artifice of war to reveal the real and painful devastation experienced by all involved. Her testimony as the child of a 'survivor' triggers a host of ethical questions about truth, duty, honour, torture and humanity.

The stark nature of the footage combined with Moxham's honest and emotionally complex story ruptures the flow of the performance in ways that demand a response. Levinas writes that in response to art 'one forgets the priority of the face's susceptibility to suffering and becomes obsessed or fascinated with its image, with an appearing for the sake of appearing' (Hatley, 2000: 115). However, the experience of watching and listening to Moxham, although emotionally charged, does not necessarily result in spectators becoming overwhelmed to the point that they forget to respond or become 'obsessed or fascinated' with her story. Instead, there is, for some spectators at least, a response at a sensory level as the call touches, or has the potential to touch spectators emotionally and viscerally, and at a practical level, by experiencing the desire to revisit preconceived ideas about war, soldiers and suffering.

Documentary and silence

Tetsuya Yamamoto's interview is equally complex. He is asked about his father and loyalty. His replies are often silenced (as the sound is turned off); the replies we do hear are proud and are delivered in a 'matter of fact' style. The projected interview with Yamamoto is combined with interventions by Lok Meng Chue who sits facing the screen and recites 'trial notes' from the trial of Captain Yamamoto at strategic moments during the interview scene. The (documentary) interviewer asks, 'was this a source of shame that your father was a war criminal?' The music rises, a dancer crawls on the stage; Yamamoto answers but we do not hear his answer. Lok Meng Chue says 'trial notes of Captain Yamamoto' and reads his evidence about fairness and support of the prisoners of war as if she were Captain Yamamoto:

> With regard to the handling of prisoners of war this was an international problem and they were to be treated with kindness... all rations, supplies are to be divided equally between Japanese officers and prisoners of war... I further told them that this was a very important task.

It is not clear how spectators are expected to read, or respond to, Shoichi Yamamoto. Was he an honourable soldier? Obviously his trial statements seem to indicate that he was – at least when on trial. But how did so many deaths occur if this were the case? The fusing of the characters of Yamamoto Senior and Junior allows spectators to engage with the legacy of war and the ways in which respect is culturally inscribed. The interviewer remarks that 'some young boys like to talk about their fathers in war... and say "he's a brave soldier and did brave things"'. Yamamoto answers 'if we had won the war we would have talked about it... when I was a boy I wanted to be a soldier'. The interviewer continues: 'as far as Australians are concerned the death marches are considered to be an atrocity... does it concern you that your father is considered to be involved in an atrocity?' No answer.

Lok Meng Chue continues her interrogation and Crosby, acting as Captain Abe (who was under the command of Captain Yamamoto), talks about the survivors and the dangers they pose in terms of the war crimes trials, as well as the sad fact that there was no time to commit suicide before trial. She then asks Crosby another question and he becomes Yamamoto Senior. He talks about war, comradeship, loyalty and marching. Yamamoto Junior says 'I told my son his grandfather was executed as a war criminal but he has to pay respects to his grandfather for the rest of his life'. Later on in the scene, when photographs of Yamamoto Senior and Junior (family photos) are projected, Crosby, performing as Yamamoto Senior, asks his son (from the grave), 'have you studied the ways of the military strategists', and a little later on 'do you stare sometimes at my picture ... do you remember the touch of my hand on your shoulder?'. The photographs are removed and Lok Meng Chue comments, 'interview with Tetsuya Yamamoto son of Shoichi Yamamoto. "Please don't ask me any more about my mother it is quite emotional for me. ... I just imagine my father through photos ... please don't ask me about my mother"'. He explains that his mother did not receive a pension because of his father's conviction.[15]

It is during these moments when the voices are multiple and the pain of the individuals evident that *Sandakan Threnody* demands a generative (and productive) engagement between spectators and the performance. Here the testimonial is used not just as a tool for recuperation, but to disallow singular answers or recordings of the events, and to challenge perceptions of culture, power and representation both past and present and perhaps, as Ong, pointed out, to move both the performers and the story to a 'third space'.

Despite this the silencing of Tetsuya Yamamoto raises some significant questions about cultural differences and how they are represented and about the power of testimony and witnessing. Yamamoto's answers were frequently silenced, and even though spectators could, at certain points, read the subtitles (the questions were delivered in English and the replies in Japanese), they were not always sure of the question he was being asked, nor could they make sense of the replies in full. As Kenneth Kwok writes,

> Ong himself edits and censors the words of the son of a Japanese war criminal. In this vignette, the interviewer's questions come across loud and clear but when the man replies, sometimes there is no sound and you only see his lips moving to stop just in time for the next audible question. Sometimes there is translation and sometimes there is not. It is a disturbing scene that asks powerful questions about the reliability of words, especially answers. (2004)

Perhaps this was a direct political strategy to disallow his voice, to prevent a rejoinder. This strategy seemed to position *Sandakan Threnody* (at least at times) as an anti-Japanese performance that relied on testimony to unveil the brutality of the Japanese soldiers and regime, rather than as a work that attempted to use the (previously hidden) stories to reveal alternative ways of reading war or trauma or torture and ultimately to offer spectators something 'new'. On these grounds the work could be read as ethically flawed and as a performance that closed off rather than opened up possibilities for complex responses. On the other hand, it could also be read as a work that reflects the fact that there is no possibility of an answer that will soothe. This scene and these moments of silence may function as moments of 'disruption' that facilitate an understanding of Yamamoto as the kind of witness described by Levinas earlier in this chapter. The complicated questions raised here can be better understood within the context of Agamben's argument that:

> Testimony thus guarantees not the factual truth of the statement safeguarded in the archive, but rather its unarchivability, its exteriority with respect to the archive – that is, the necessity by which, as the existence of language, it escapes both memory and forgetting. (Agamben, 1999: 158)

If the testimony used in this production is understood as something that exists outside the archive, as an unsettled and unsettling set of fragments then it has the potential to liberate a range of responses that draw attention to the frailty of language and of memory. As Kwok sees it, the interview asks powerful questions about 'the reliability of words'. Yamamoto's apparent passivity may provoke non Japanese spectators to search for a space in which he might condemn his father for his actions, yet he does not (or if he does it is not audible). He states that it is crucial that his own son honour his grandfather. There might be a kind of cultural misunderstanding at work here, where spectators seek explanation from Yamamoto, who is, after all, also a victim of this process. As Pang Khee Teik asks:

> Could his admission of guilt absolve us of ours? I feel this inability to release individuals from the culpability we expect them to inherit from their ancestors is one of the reasons war continues in its vicious cycle of tribal vindication. (2004)

Carol Fisher Sorgenfrei in her book, *Unspeakable Acts*, provides important contextual information that makes Yamamoto's responses more readable. Sorgenfrei explains some of the complexities of Japanese cultural identity post-WWII. She talks about the many books written on the subject and the 'obsessive postwar search for cultural identity' (2005: 104) that occupied Japanese people. She reflects that 'the question of being insiders (unique in a positive way within an isolated culture) or outsiders (unique in a negative way due to difference from the rest of the world) continues to haunt many Japanese' (2005: 104). Perhaps Yamamoto's aloofness can be read as a protection mechanism (as the son of a convicted war criminal) within this fraught cultural landscape. Sorgenfrei explains that

> in traditional Shintō thought, a member of a society could become temporarily polluted, requiring exile from the village or home until purification was obtained. Sources of impurity included the shedding of blood ... exposure to death, loathsome diseases, bestiality, incest and the practice of sorcery or witchcraft, among other things. ... However, after World War II, some Japanese and many non-Japanese refused to accept that those who had been defiled (or who had committed war crimes) could ever be purified. (2005: 104)

This information helps, to some extent, frame Yamamoto's distance.[16] What is also interesting here is the juxtaposing of the words and responses of Moxham and Yamamoto. Moxham moves beyond honouring her father by acknowledging the destruction of war on his mind and emotions. Yamamoto, on the other hand, does not pass any judgement on his father's actions. There is a play between these responses that has the potential to make spectators feel at once involved in the story and estranged by its implications. As Moxham talks about the devastation war wreaks on those who do not (directly) participate, it becomes possible to imagine the implications of her experiences growing up with a father who had been seriously damaged as a result of his participation in war.

For Chansky, Moxham's interview did not have this impact. In fact, in her review, she describes Moxham as demonstrating 'self-assured arrogance', which when measured against the demeanour of Tetsuya Yamamoto, positions Yamamoto's son as 'a study in pained reserve' (Chansky, 2004). Susan Moxham actually replied to Chansky's review (via an online forum) to critique what she felt were some of the mis-interpretations of her interview. She remarks:

> I am alarmed at the following interpretation: 'Moxham's daughter has no interest in visiting Sandakan, can't accept that surviving alone makes one a hero and believes her father "crossed the line" and could never again be civilised. "It's all Heart of Darkness" and "Apocalypse Now," she informs us.' Then I am described as dis-playing 'arrogance.' As a child of a survivor of a war, I would like to remind critics that the suffering and inhumanity of war con-tinues long after the war had ended. It becomes something of an epidemic which infects others, who did not physically participate in the war. (Moxham, 2004)

Regardless of these differences in response, both interviews are affecting. Susan Moxham is sad yet resigned, or perhaps 'self assured' as Chansky reads it. Tetsuya Yamamoto's stiff or potentially affect-less delivery presents a challenge, and reminds spectators that even though they hear the call of the other this does not mean that they can decode this in a way that compartmentalises or reduces the call, or indeed the other, to the same. As Agamben states in the epigraph to this chapter 'the value of testimony lies essentially in what it lacks' (1999: 34). Moxham and Yamamoto do not bear witness to the atro-cities, they instead respond to the traces, fragments and pain that they are left to endure. They are witnesses who are involved in intri-cate ways with Sandakan and they are witnesses who implicate us in to their stories. Their testimony brings unspeakable pain into lan-guage (if haltingly at times), it disrupts, it avoids disclosure (in the Levinasian sense) and it engages us in a process of response and responsibility to Sandakan and its legacy. It is through these frank and provocative interviews as well as the incursions by Lok Meng Chue and the responses of Crosby that we can see revealed the pain and insanity caused by the war and its conspiracies.

Kabuki and 'postmodern'

Towards the end of the performance the dancers exit and the space is bathed in a deep red light. A recording for solo tenor of Randolph Stowe's poem 'Sleep' can be heard and Gojo Masanosuke enters as the kabuki onnagata and dances slowly in a red kimono.[17] Lok Meng Chue, who is seated up stage centre, narrates a passage about the torture of Officer Green by the Japanese soldier, Moritake. Green was nailed to a cross by his hands first and then Moritake:

> Nailed his feet onto a horizontal board. Drove a 20cm nail through his forehead. Took a butcher's knife and cut two pieces of flesh from his abdomen. Moritake slowly donned rubber gloves. Split Green from neck to navel. Removed liver and heart. Cut in two. Sliced more flesh from thighs, arms, abdomen. Left corpse to decompose. Maggots infected remains. Set a light with kerosene. All evidence of appalling crime destroyed.[18]

Masanosuke's geisha dance continues and the singing resumes. Lok Meng Chue gets up and walks behind Masanosuke; the latter removes the red kimono. The geisha is now dressed in white, the colour of mourning. Masanosuke's movements are slow, meditative and evoke a sense of sorrow and loss. For Ong this represents the fact that the 'woman is finally transformed into a bird, a symbol of hope for humanity', and that the 'kabuki presence' represents 'a gold thread through the tapestry of war and pain' (Ong, 2004). Just as spectators are lulled into this haunting vignette the 'Hairy Midget' (a performer dressed in a spiky black outfit who could be seen as a representation of contemporary dance in sculptural form) comes on and dances as if in parallel to Masanosuke, or as if they are slowly involved in a stand-off. Ong says that the Hairy Midget 'danced a duet with the bird of hope' (Ong, 2004). For some spectators the dancers do not seem to connect, and while Masanosuke's performance, and the ideas of hope, grief and loss that the onnagata represents, are understandable and potentially profound, the interventions of the Hairy Midget are difficult to read or respond to in any significant way.

For Richard Lord, who confesses 'a profound ignorance of kabuki rituals' this scene was 'very effective'. He points out that this 'stark sequence did convey a compelling sense of exorcism' (Lord, 2004). For Pang Kee Teik however, the scene raised more disturbing questions. He states that

> at some level, this hyper sense of surreal was beautiful – the grief reduced to a couple of twitches. It was like defining horror, an

exercise defying any articulation. Yet this inarticulation wasn't completely silent. It resounded with the performers' attempt at pontificating their own inarticulation about war. (2004)

The inability or refusal of the performers to communicate here is critical in terms of the ways in which it reflects on Ong's potential 'openness' as well as his interest in transculturalism as an approach, and in relation to the ways in which a work can 'find' and 'lose' cultural forms. In this regard it is also important to consider the choice of kabuki and particularly the onnagata role for this scene. This role is always feminised, and as Brian Powell explains, '*kabuki* developed the art of portraying symbolic femininity to a high degree' (Powell, 2002: xxviii).[19] The onnagata was often placed in a position of sacrifice for the nation (particularly in the wartime plays). It is curious to see this trope employed here as it is could be read as making links to orientalist notions of Asianness as feminine.[20]

Ong describes the scene as follows: 'A male dancer impersonates a woman (the onnagata role). This is a symbolic role of an old woman ravaged by memory; time flashes back into a past life where there is the joy of love and the tragedy of death' (Ong, 2004). Perhaps there is a desire here to consider the role of mothers in Japan after the war (and a link to Yamamoto's sensitivity about his mother), or an attempt to reflect on the sacrifices made by women in giving their sons to war?

Despite Ong's explanation it is not all that clear why the onnagata was chosen and this means that the question of what is being represented here is very complicated. It is also unclear how this dance is shaped (or framed) by the performance in a way that challenges or disrupts its traditional links in order that it might be read as offering the 'hope' Ong outlines, rather than a series of fragmented and confusing images.

Obviously for spectators such as Lord, who are not familiar with the history of kabuki, the scene is provocative and important, but for others it becomes 'alienating' (Buzacott, 2004), or as Pang Khee Teik points out, it can be read as both significant and solipsistic. Ong's comments about a 'gold thread' do not really help in terms of my own response to this scene as my engagement with this dance is overlaid with a concern about what the kabuki is representing. This concern is reinforced by the apparent inability of the dancers to communicate. The lack of connection echoes back to Ong's production *Lear*, in which as I have explained, each artistic form was presented almost in insolation, and the work was charged with the exoticisation of Asian traditions.

The final scenes of the performance are perplexing. The stage is suddenly lit with bright light and the performance approaches its climax. The pace quickens and there are many fragmented vignettes with the Hairy Midget, dancing both behind and in front of the projection screen, and Crosby as Moxham, talking in a lost, abstract fashion. He says, for example, 'within this darkness I see no flower petals... just half dead spirits who sit and watch us... somewhere along the way I lost my name.' Lok Meng Chue then talks about 'lice balls, little flakes of skin like after sunburn, peeling off... the whole thing lined with puss... terrible aching feet.' Crosby dances and the other performers run on and off performing abstract movement sequences. This continues for a time and nobody seems to be connecting with anybody else. Ong says that the performers in the last scene are 'like the tragic clowns of Beckett's **Waiting for Godot** – waiting for war wounds to finally come to rest. For perhaps we are still infected by the invisible virus of hatred and fear' (Ong, 2004; original emphasis). Richard Lord speaks of this scene and describes the Hairy Midget as 'a creature... in a costume suggesting a porcupine-needled tinsel toy' (2004). He goes on to explain that although the programme notes describe this 'enigma' as the 'Hairy Midget'

> I was unable to discern any of this, any more than I was able to note that the Kabuki dancer from earlier symbolised 'an old woman ravaged by memory' who is then transformed into a bird as 'a symbol of home for humanity'. I did admire the beauty of the Kabuki to which Keng Sen refers, but the wider purpose it was meant to signify? Sorry, I was caught up in the beauty of the dance and also trying to digest what had come before it. (Lord, 2004)

Ong's aim here is admirable, and the desire to move beyond hatred is a significant one. However it seems that for Lord, and other spectators, this scene remains disconnected. Rather than being read as absurdist, it is experienced, in the context of the larger work, as a set of isolated moments.

Gradually the light fades to darkness. Lok Meng Chue sits in the spotlight and the names of some of the soldiers who died are read out as their photos flash before us in the darkness. The performance ends; there is silence amongst the audience and finally, hesitantly, someone begins to clap.

In the end

The performance presents a range of stories, fragments and symbols about war and its aftermath as it attempts to deconstruct the 'conspiracies of silence' that surround Sandakan. It contains moments of beauty, ugliness and pain and allows spectators to engage in a process of reflection and response that raises ethical questions about the impacts of war on those who survive and those who are left behind.

Sandakan Threnody does not engender an experience of participation in which spectators engage uncritically because they are overburdened with empathy (in any simplistic sense), or that results in the kind of passive participation Levinas abhors. Instead, they have the opportunity to participate in a complicated process of consideration and reflection in response (particularly) to the documentary sequences with Susan Moxham and Tetsuya Yamamoto, as well as to the performed interventions in Yamamoto's testimony by both Lok Meng Chue and Matthew Crosby. These scenes strip away artifice and demand a reaction to the literal, embodied wounds inflicted by war. It is when they are considered alongside the kabuki scenes that the importance of the work emerges.

The performance reveals, for spectators, the ways in which testimony can unveil and hide, rupture and highlight the real bodily impacts of war on those who endure its impacts, either directly or indirectly. Despite this statement however, there is also the possibility that in the co-location of culturally and artistically diverse bodies and performance codes the work runs the risk, at times, of ahistoricising both bodies and codes and therefore of detracting from the processes of remembering and overturning conspiracies of silence.

It seems as if Ong's 'openness' and his desire to weave the three journeys together leads the production on its own difficult journey particularly in terms of the function and role of the more abstract vocabularies used, as well as in the choice to foreground kabuki and the onnagata role. It is as if there are moments in which the vocabularies and stories – much like the cultures Ong talks about – both 'lose' and 'find' themselves in the journey to the 'third space' he envisages. Whether this experience of confusion is deliberate or not, it results, for spectators, in a host of conflicting and productive ethical questions about both the potential and the difficulty of recuperating traumatic history; the function memory, the role of testimony and the idea (and limits) of 'transcultural' performance, more broadly.

5

'The Refugee', Empathy and Participation: Ariane Mnouchkine and Théâtre du Soleil's *Le Dernier Caravansérail (Odyssées)*

> The fact remains that viewing suffering is especially problematic when the object of suffering is presumed to be real...when the spectacle of the unfortunate and his suffering is conveyed to a distant and sheltered spectator there is a greater likelihood of this spectacle being apprehended in a fictional mode the more the horizon of action recedes into the distance. (Boltanski, 1999: 23)

Le Dernier Caravansérail is a spectacular epic performance work. Its stories describe some of the hardships and challenges faced by desperate people – refugees from Central Asia and the Middle East, countries such as Kurdistan, Iran, Georgia, Afghanistan, Pakistan, and Russia (amongst others). The performers speak in a range of languages, including Farsi, French, Russian and Bulgarian to tell these stories. There are a small number of recurring stories; however, the majority of the vignettes or scenes stand alone as simple tales depicting experiences such as escapes, torture, clandestine love, refugee camps, tribunals and sweat shops.

The performance invites spectators to witness the odysseys[1] of a range of people fleeing horror, poverty and war. The stories reflect the journeys undertaken by refugees and asylum seekers and draw attention to the corruption, manipulation and control they are subjected to at the hands of traffickers and officials. *Le Dernier Caravansérail* is a devised work that is informed by a two-year development phase and a series of interviews with refugees.[2] Ariane Mnouchkine's long-time collaborator, Hélène Cixous, in the notes for the French production asks, 'how can one put one-self as close as possible to the Other's place without appropriating it?' (Wehle, 2005: 82). The six-hour performance sets out to answer this question by representing multiple stories about the dangers of being rootless and the politics and pain involved in attempting to find a safe haven.

Complexities and contradictions

The work layers story upon story of people seeking refuge, and these stories not only give voice to those fleeing terror, they also raise questions about the figure of the camp, the idea of rootlessness and the issues of power and corruption involved in fleeing and in trafficking. In Brian Singleton's words:

> The play, often performed in dumbshow in simple and appalling scenes, holds up the west as culpable of inflicting suffering as the so-called axis-of-evil states. It provides no answers for the problems faced by countless refugees, for whom the term 'diaspora' means a scattering in a literal sense, but also for whom a realignment and resettlement is an impossibility. For Sangatte, read Woomera, read the Norwegian cargo ship, Tampa. (Singleton, 2003: 228)

Both the 'impossibility' of return and the elusiveness of belonging that Singleton alludes to are starkly revealed as the work unfolds. His point about culpability is also important. In a cultural context in which blame is so easily ascribed to the other (whoever that other might be), and rarely owned, this work manages not only to highlight the culpability of the West as an abstract governing body, but to locate that culpability within the body of the audience. *Le Dernier Caravansérail* is performed internationally at a time when the 'war on terror' (and the media coverage it receives) vividly demonstrates the ways in which refugee camps have been (and continue to be) used as zones of torture.[3] Considering this context, it is a performance that has the potential to mobilise debates about torture, control and terror in significant ways. It also has the potential to engender responsibility on the part of spectators who may already be experiencing a sense of unease at the treatment of others in the name of protection. The programme notes point out that

> at the origin of this adventure, there was the promise made to those whose stories are told here: to give them a voice. To *bear witness* to those who never leave a trace, whose cries and murmurs are never heard. Those who are silenced always. (Théâtre du Soleil, 2005; my emphasis)

What does 'bearing witness' entail for both performers and spectators in the context of this work? This chapter considers the complexities of both the culpability Singleton sees the play revealing and the insulation Boltanski refers to in the epigraph to this chapter – where by virtue of our insulation and distance – we read the suffering as mere fictional spectacle. In view of Cixous's claim that 'spectacle first strikes, seduces, carries away, charms us, in such a way that we can forget that it's the golden and magnificent costume clothing terrible massacres. It's a paradox, but it's made to be one' (Cixous in Franke and Chazal, 1999: 158) I explore the use of spectacle to 'seduce', 'clothe' and to reveal the difficult and painful experiences of refugees. In the process questions are raised about the limits of emotional responsiveness or empathy and the ways in which this responsiveness might translate into responsibility in the ontological realm. I also consider how the performance positions the self other relationship and how spectators are implicated in this relationship, as well as the challenge this positioning poses to the idea of participation in both the Levinasian sense (as something that is passive, and potentially uncritical) and as I define it in Chapter 1 (as an active and critical process of response and responsibility).

The act of negotiating relationships between the self and the other was one that was not limited to the experience of spectatorship at this performance. It is also something that had to be considered by both Mnouchkine and Cixous as they balanced the need to tell these stories with their own creative input in the performance. As William McEvoy sees it:

> The wish to inscribe a hospitality-based ethics in their performance by 'hosting' these other voices became more important than

anti-realistic principles, and in fact such moments of realism entered into a complex dialogue with the production's overt theatricality and use of images. (McEvoy, 2006: 217)

In the end they made the decision that 'the alterity of the migrant others...had to take precedence over the staging of the ethically aware creative self' (McEvoy, 2006: 218). In what could be read as a Levinasian move, they insist that the focus in this production is on the other and the other's stories. There is a desire to uncover the saying by rupturing the said, to allow the call of the other to impact on spectators, in the Levinasian sense, as something which can wound, something that is experienced corporeally by spectators (Levinas, 1998: 15). As a result of the emotional resonance and depth of these stories, this 'hospitality-based ethics' stimulates a range of complicated and wide-ranging responses for spectators.

Julie Salverson's approach to her work with refugees in Canada seems to both echo and challenge the decisions made by Mnouchkine, Cixous and Théâtre du Soleil in this production. Salverson explains that 'if our theatre is to bear witness to the "saying" of refugee stories, we must take care not to reduce testimony to the interpretive frame' (Salverson, 1999). In their decision to tell these stories with as little interference as possible Mnouchkine and her collaborators attempt to provide a space in which there is no reduction of the stories to a point where their power is either lost or they become tokenistic. This is a difficult process as there are dangers in seeking 'truth' in representation. As Salverson continues, speaking of her own project:

If our play invites an audience to step into the shoes of the refugee, to empathize with her 'as if,' then the refugee becomes an object of spectacle and the audience member – and, by extension playwright, director and actors – offstage voyeurs. Both are less secure, less able to listen and respond within the encounter. It is possible that both even disappear. (Salverson, 1999)

As an experienced director Mnouchkine understands the risks involved in foregrounding the stories of the refugees. Nonetheless, she explains that 'theatre isn't there to deal with abstract ideas or to defend ideologies. I was not in search of ideologies. I was in search of lives' (Mnouchkine in Héliot, 2005). It seems, then, that for Mnouchkine the need to share these stories is so important that it outweighs any risk of voyeurism.[4]

The refugee and the camp

In *Means Without End*, Giorgio Agamben talks about the need to build political philosophy anew, and to position the refugee at the core of this process. In fact, Agamben argues that the refugee poses the fundamental ethical challenge of our age. He writes:

> Given the by now unstoppable decline of the nation-state and the general corrosion of traditional political-juridical categories, the refugee is perhaps the only thinkable figure for the people of our time and the only category in which one may see today...the forms and limits of a coming political community. It is even possible that, if we want to be equal to the absolutely new tasks ahead, we will have to abandon decidedly, without reservation, the fundamental concepts through which we have so far represented the subjects of the political (Man, the Citizen...the sovereign people, the worker, and so forth) and build our political philosophy anew, starting from the one and only figure of the refugee. (Agamben, 2000: 15)

Agamben's theorisation of the refugee as *the* figure of the contemporary age, a figure who poses a challenge to existing notions of citizenship, justice and sovereignty, is a significant one. It questions the ways in which relations among and between people might operate. When this theorisation is combined with his understanding of the refugee camp it highlights the need for spaces within which the refugee crisis and the ways in which it is managed and conceived by governments, societies (and more broadly) non-refugees, can be re-imagined. Of the camp, Agamben suggests that

> one ought to reflect on the paradoxical status of the camp as a space of exception: the camp is a piece of territory that is placed outside the normal juridical order; for all that, however, it is not simply an external space. According to the etymological meaning

of the term *exception* (*ex-capere*), what is being excluded in the camp is *captured outside,* that is, it is included by virtue of its very exclusion. (2000: 40; original emphasis)

While inhabitants of the camp are not considered to have any legitimate (or as yet proven) legal claim to citizenship within the nation state, they are, as Suvendrini Perera (following Agamben) explains, 'brought even more firmly under its control by virtue of their exclusion from its laws' (Perera, 2002). Despite efforts by governments to tighten control over borders and to implement zones of exclusion (as in Australia, for example) the flow of human traffic across borders continues.

The arrival of refugees and asylum seekers generates complex responses from residents and citizens of the destination states about the ways in which the camps are controlled and the refugees are treated. Notwithstanding the fact that many of the camps are rendered invisible for reasons of political expediency or as a result of deliberate positioning in geographical isolation, they are, as Agamben makes clear, positioned in an unstable space of 'exception' within nations: a space that threatens to erupt at any moment. Some citizens respond to a media-assisted (or media generated) fear of the unknown other by reinforcing stereotypes or adopting racist positions. Others experience a profound sense of unease about the act of confining or containing refugees and asylum seekers (particularly children) and the methods employed to do so.

Mnouchkine and Théâtre du Soleil's decision to document the experiences of refugees and asylum seekers sits alongside the work of other artists (such as Salverson) concerned with the plight of those seeking refuge, and at the same time attempting to broaden the parameters of debate on this crucial political, social and cultural issue.[5] As Agamben points out,

> inasmuch as the refugee unhinges the old trinity of state/nation/territory – this apparently marginal figure deserves rather to be considered the central figure of our political history. It would be well not to forget that the first camps in Europe were built as places to control refugees, and that the progression – internment camps, concentration camps, extermination camps – represents a perfectly real filiation. (n.d.)

Agamben is proposing a fundamental shift in the balance of moral power in societies so that the refugee becomes the central icon of any relationship, rather than a victim or an object to be responded to or managed. This shift has implications for notions of responsibility and for subjectivity. If it is to work it will require serious reconsideration of how both response and responsibility might operate in such a changed environment. There is no doubt that this is exciting material, particularly when linked to Levinasian philosophy, and my discussions about globalisation, mobility and poverty (following Bauman and Kapuscinski) in Chapter 1. It is possible to read Mnouchkine's painstaking process of interviewing and documenting the experiences of refugees as one that attempts to take up Agamben's challenge and begin the process of transforming the figure of the refugee.

The company, the objectives, the performance

Ariane Mnouchkine and ten other artists formed *Le Société Coopérative Ouvrière de Production* (The Theatre of the Sun, workers' production cooperative) in 1964. Since that time she and the collective have worked tirelessly to create large-scale theatrical productions that engage with significant political issues, to reveal hidden stories and histories, to generate a speaking space for the other, and to stimulate reflection on the part of spectators. Mnouchkine is devoutly committed to challenging injustice, and this commitment frames her life and her art. In turn, this adds depth to any reading of *Le Dernier Caravansérail* because it positions the work as one that is informed by a deep ethico-political commitment to the subjects and histories represented.[6]

Armelle Héliot in her interview with Mnouchkine in the programme notes tells us that 'Ariane Mnouchkine and her collaborators employed the poetics of the theatre in order to interrogate the responsibilities of a world where disadvantaged people are marginalised and ignored' (Théâtre du Soleil, 2005). In order to create this space for considering 'responsibilities' the production uses 42 vignettes depicting the difficulties and dangers faced by oppressed people, as they exist in homelands in which they are persecuted or marginalised, as they attempt to flee, or as they negotiate a new place. The performance is in two parts. Part I 'Le Fleuve cruel' (The Cruel River) 'recounts the departures, the exoduses', and Part II – 'Origines et destins' (Origins and Destinies) 'explores the reasons for these departures' (Théâtre du Soleil, 2005).

As spectators enter the performance space they become aware that the company is trying to remove the theatrical frame, to allow the audience to gain a full sense of the performance-as-process. At the Melbourne production the dressing rooms are in the open space of the Royal Exhibition Building, and are in full view.[7] The actors sit and prepare as audience members casually wander around and observe. Food can be purchased and consumed and tables are set up with information on refugees, asylum and various support groups. The stage resembles a grand tent with ramps on both sides and a partly see-through scrim that separates the musicians who perform to the side of the stage. According to Judith Miller, the performance space 'englobes the production's dazzling paradoxes: a feeling of sumptuousness and emptiness, of extreme stylisation (including the balletic quality of the set changes) and of almost television realism' (2006: 214).

Each scene takes place on a small platform or box (caravans, small houses, etc.). The performers either wheel themselves or are wheeled on and off the stage. They play multiple roles and no performer ever touches the ground while performing a scene. The fact that they never set foot on the stage acts as a poignant metaphor for the idea of rootlessness. There is a constant frenzy of activity in the space as performers run on and off stage between scenes. Trolleys, props and sets are moved at speed. When not in a scene, the performers help with the sets and effects so the process of generating the spectacle is always made visible. The programme notes state that, 'each platform that appears is like a fragment of the world, and as the platforms appear, one after the other, they end up peopling the stage and transforming it into a planisphere' (Théâtre du Soleil, 2005). There is exquisite attention to detail in every aspect of the staging. The sets are beautifully constructed, the music evocative and the costumes symbolic.

Representing testimony

The performance relies heavily on the testimony of those interviewed by Mnouchkine. She writes, 'little by little, I began to collect their words. Then it suddenly seemed necessary for them to tell me everything. I recorded 100 hours of interviews. They all asked me to tell what had happened, to them, to their families' (Mnouchkine in Héliot, 2005). Indeed, the performance is described, in the 'Melbourne International Arts Festival' brochure as a work which 'combines an intricate mosaic of voices of asylum seekers lamenting cultures and countries left behind with evocative sounds and vivid imagery to give a human face to the plight of those forced to leave their homes in search of a better life' (2005: 24). The programme notes explain that the performance is 'an ocean of odysseys, sometimes heroic, sometimes banal, but always dramatic and traumatic' (2005). The stories are told in a straightforward fashion without meta-commentary or analysis of the political or social context within which they take place, and without any discussion about why and how the world came to be in this terrible state. Mnouchkine points out that in her interviews with detainees she told them 'that I unfortunately couldn't do anything for them, that I didn't have any power, but that what I could do was make theatre, and that [Théâtre du Soleil] wanted to tell their stories' (Mnouchkine in Héliot, 2005). During the intensive rehearsal period the cast work collaboratively to generate images and fragments that reflect the complexity of the experiences of those seeking refuge in more 'moderate' countries.

The decision to tell so many stories means that characters are symbolic rather than fully fleshed out. As Singleton explains, 'the piece is a consciously naïve recounting of testimonies by dozens of refugees/asylum seekers' (Singleton, 2003: 227). The desire, on behalf of the company, to represent the diversity of experiences (to share the testimony) adequately and to avoid appropriating the other's pain led to this decision to represent as many stories as possible. In the notes for the French production, Cixous asks, 'how can we avoid appropriating other people's anguish when we use it to make theatre?' (McEvoy, 2006: 219). This is an admirable and significant concern, particularly considering the vulnerability of the people in question.

At this juncture it is worth reflecting on the use of testimony in the other productions addressed in this book. In *The Career Highlights of the MAMU* (Chapter 3) the testimony (via filmed interviews with the elders) worked to jolt spectators out of the intimacy and warmth of the live performance into a position where they had the potential to experience the absolute alterity of the other who spoke of land, culture and loss from their 'country', without artifice. In *Sandakan Threnody* (Chapter 4), the testimonial narrative fractured the more abstract sequences of the performance and facilitated an emotional connection with the children of those directly involved in war. In this production, however, the testimony works and is experienced in a different way. There is no filmic documentary footage and there is very little spoken text in the performance. Each vignette is a discrete testimonial in itself. Because they are gathered from painstaking interviews the entire performance becomes a testimonial to the experiences of those who are fleeing. Nevertheless these are performed testimonies; therefore, while Mnouchkine and her collaborators are careful to foreground the literal stories, there is an intricate layering of representations involved. The performed testimonies are combined with oral testimonies (directly recorded from the interview process) that are, as Béatrice Picon-Vallin writes,

> present at the very heart of the performance, in their original languages, with their specific sounds and qualities, and emotions, which make the interviewees' voices break. As they are being broadcast, they are simultaneously being translated on screen. (Picon-Vallin, 2006: 86–87)

The projected translations are used as a connective web throughout the work. They attest to the at times unbearable pain experienced by people fleeing or caught in the zone of exclusion, or 'captured outside' as Agamben describes it. These testimonies are brief, symbolic, simple and almost allegorical, as they represent the multiple kinds of trauma that might be experienced in the process of fleeing or attempting to flee. They punctuate the performance, reminding audiences of the 'lives' Mnouchkine is sharing with us.[8]

Visibility and empathy

Part I begins with a letter from Mnouchkine addressed to Nadereh. The letter is projected in beautiful cursive script onto the backdrop. It tells stories of loss and talks about those who are stranded. It also celebrates the fact that the play has been written: 'we have finally created the play that we promised nearly a year ago…a few instants out of all they told us...on the island of Lombok.'[9] This first letter also reminds spectators that the performance is based on interviews and that it is attempting to enact a conversation both with the refugees and the spectators about the 'real' experiences of people fleeing terror. Alison Croggon, who was so moved by the work that she wrote her review in the form of a letter to Mnouchkine, points out that this first letter signals

> both intention and refusal. The intention was to expose the genesis of this work, the reality of the people whose stories were turned into this work of theatre by you and your company. The refusal was of the betrayal of art, which so easily exploits the suffering of others to make a beautiful object. (2005)

Croggon goes on to explain that her experience of the performance was one of inclusion and emotional involvement. She found empowering the way in which the dressing rooms were visible and the performance leached into the space, rather than remaining contained on the stage. It allowed her to feel that the strict boundaries between the artwork and the spectators were being broken down. Croggon believes in the work, in its ability to present so many different stories of 'human beings in exile' and in its ability to reflect the complexity of the refugee experience, by showing us that 'as well as being full of grief and love and generosity, human beings can be murderous, cruel, weak, ignorant and stupid' (Croggon, 2005). She goes on to explain that although 'they might be cruel or stupid [this] doesn't mean that they might not be also victims of forces beyond their control' (2005). It seems that for Croggon the decision to present so many stories allowed *Le Dernier Caravansérail* to move beyond binaries and to present a rich portrait of the difficult and competing forces that shape the experiences of the dispossessed.

These competing forces begin to emerge in the spectacular and arresting opening scene of Part I as it depicts refugees attempting to cross an angry river. They are standing on the bank waiting to cross, using a flimsy boat and an overhead rope to prevent them and the boat from being washed away. Large sheets of grey fabric that billow across the entire stage represent the river. This billowing effect is achieved by the performers (who are not involved in this scene) standing at the sides of the stage and shaking the fabric. Jean-Jacques

Lemêtre's musical composition is loud and evocative; it creates intensity in the space as spectators strain to hear the negotiations taking place between the refugees and the smugglers. Even though some of the negotiations are explained via the surtitles, from the action taking place, the desperation of the people attempting to make it to the other side of the treacherous river is obvious. The combination of loud music and the vivid portrayal of the 'angry' river as well as the deep anxiety of those attempting to cross is, as Owen Richardson writes, poignant, and it captures our attention immediately:

> The sound of wind and water almost drowning out the actors' voices, the transition from low light to bright, the realistic physicality of the performers, all these combine to thrilling effect. Straight away you are on the edge of your seat, for the first of many times over the next three hours. (Richardson, 2005: 30)

There is something about this dramatic opening that generates a deep emotional engagement in audiences. The spectacle is captivating. As a spectator, I find that the visual rendering of this story – a story I know well – has the ability to provoke in ways that simple re-telling does not. I wish for the safe return of the ferryman, and like Richardson, I too am moved by the drama of the scene. Croggon's responses also reflect this experience. She sees the work as generating stories of the refugees and the traffickers, which acknowledge, through the depiction of the interactions between the 'vulnerable' refugees and the 'ruthless' traffickers, the ways in which greed, power, desperation and money can impact on and perhaps curtail one's humanity. This facilitates, for Croggon, via the generation of empathy, an engagement with the work. She believes that the performance allows spectators to reflect on the experiences of the other and she points out, quoting John Berger, 'that it affirms the idea that 'the naming of the intolerable is itself the hope' (2005). In fact, she goes to great lengths to argue against reading *Le Dernier Caravansérail* as a sentimental work that 'exploits the suffering of other to make a beautiful object that is nothing more than a plaything of the privileged' (2005).

These responses are detailed and they interrogate the ways in which the performance engenders more than empathy in any singular or uncritical sense via a consideration of how it reaches 'into the intimate and complex spaces of our own lives' as Croggon describes it. There is, however, the potential that this level of emotional investment might, for some spectators, alter the focus of responses away from the other and towards the self – to reciprocity instead of 'being for' – as Levinasian ethics demands. This view is expressed by Ong Keng Sen who remarks that:

> Perhaps, I feel that it's [*Le Dernier Caravansérail*] still concerned too much with human stories. Part of my problem with it is that it is very manipulative emotionally. It's very French-humanistic – very, very human stories. Working with or talking with a lot of French directors, I have found that they are not concerned about politics; they feel that that's another thing. They say, 'I want to talk about the human stories; I want to talk about the stories of individuals.' I feel that the piece contained very little social-political discussion; it was really stories of individuals who were in very dire circumstances. (Leverett, 2007: 56)

For Ong the work may not have been open enough. It elicited particular kinds of emotional responses, instead of raising questions. Of course it could be argued that the scenes generate empathy for a reason. And that empathy is necessary in the context of a world where the refugee and the camp are often isolated, excluded or vilified. And obviously despite (or perhaps because of) her emotional involvement Croggon's responses were both rich and nuanced. The risk, however, that such a heavy reliance on emotional reactions will return the focus to spectators, instead of hearing and responding to the call of the other, remains. Kalina Stefanova's experience makes this clear, she explains that: 'After the end of Mnoushkin's show one feels like one has experienced the other people's pain with one's own body, having wept the other people's sorrows with one's own tears' (Stefanova, 2004). Such a response deconstructs or has the potential to deconstruct Agamben's call to position the refugee at the centre of a new philosophy as well as the potential for a Levinasian ethics. As the work unfolds spectators are confronted with myriad scenes of hardship and pain and these scenes result in a range of at times contradictory responses from spectators and critics.

In 'An Afghan Love' a story is told in three parts that are subtitled 'The Bird', 'Starry Night' and 'The End'. It depicts two young innocents attempting to share their love without attracting the oppressive gaze (and associated punishment) of the Taliban. In the first of these three scenes, 'The Bird', we see the lovers giggling, talking and the boy's attempt to kiss the girl as they sit outside a little house. A member of the Taliban arrives and the girl hides. The Taliban soldier demands American cigarettes and when he is asked to pay for these he shows his weapon ominously. When he leaves the girl emerges from her hiding spot and is visibly traumatised by the close call. The Taliban soldier returns and he demands tea; the girl, who is fully covered in a burka, sits nervously behind him as he drinks his tea. The boy tries to pretend that she is his sister. The soldiers harass the young man for his lack of beard and they forcibly cut his hair and hold it up to his face. Then they give him a present. When he unwraps it the body of a smashed bird is revealed. In 'Starry Night' the young couple are in a cabin embracing; they appear very nervous. The cabin is rotated on the stage and we see the Taliban soldiers peering in. They strike and the man is beaten. The young woman is taken away; he is beaten some more and spat on. A voiceover states 'it is decreed that all non-Islamic statues be destroyed. Allah is the only true sanctuary. (The Ministry for the Promotion of Virtue and the Rejection of Vice).' In 'The End', the young man arrives clandestinely to see his love. She is locked up and barricaded in a cabin. He sobs. The Taliban come out. Someone in a burka is taken to the front and beaten but it is not the girl, it is a man in disguise. The cabin is rotated and we see her hanging by the neck, dead. These three scenes reflect the issues of brutality and manipulation that the work reveals. They are shocking and, in their simplicity, provide some idea of the kinds of torture and trauma faced by Afghani people under the Taliban regime.

As well as the story of the Afghan lovers there are several scenes set on the rail tracks of the cavernous Eurotunnel. Mnouchkine conducted many interviews at the Sangatte refugee camp near Calais, and these interviews and the stories she gathered are reflected in the Eurotunnel scenes.[10] These stories of desperate people who pass through a hole in the chain-link fence deep inside the tunnel and then attempt to cling on to moving trains are harrowing. They also depict the ruthlessness of the smugglers and the way in which a desire for monetary gain overrides any interest in, or compassion for, the physical or emotional well being of asylum seekers. In her review, Marilyn Stasio suggests that the scenes set in the Eurotunnel with its ominous black fence represent 'a kind of purgatory for desperate people at the mercy of smugglers who rob them blind, or exact harsher terms of sexual slavery of pretty young women...who dare the perilous journey alone' (2005). The work does not shy away from melodrama and contains scenes of brutality, gore and violence. While the scenes are simple they still manage to illustrate the multiple and at times conflicting roles people play. This means that, for Narelle Sullivan, at least,

> Mnoushkine is careful to offer a humanity that is complex and contradictory: the sinister, leather clad people smuggler is also a father who sings lullabies to his young child via his mobile phone; not all refugees are simply presented as victims – many take advantage of others to make their way. (Sullivan, 2006)

In contrast to this response Helen Gilbert and Jacqueline Lo express concern about the use of stark and evocative images or 'snapshots' and they argue that:

> The show's visual appeal, much lauded by critics, turns on a collocation of images that infuse the harrowing traumas communicated by the refugee stories with the aesthetic pleasures of orientalism. Particularly resonant in this respect are the snapshots of Afghanistan: elusive women in full, pale-blue burqas; a starkly beautiful burnt-out hut; the cruel Taliban, both mysterious and immediately recognizable beneath black beards and turbans. (Gilbert and Lo, 2007: 205)

The question of orientalism is a difficult one. If the work evokes orientalist 'pleasures' then its focus rests primarily with the subject and not with the other, and therefore it again calls the ideas of both Agamben and Levinas into question. If, however, as Brian Singleton argues, Mnouchkine 'circumvented the charge of Orientalism in a range of ways' (2007: 29) then the relationship can be read as one in which the refugee is central and the call of the other is responded to. Singleton explains that this circumvention occurs because, 'subjects were only represented momentarily. The effect of this was that we were unable to identify with them and therefore challenge their representation by others' (2007: 30). He goes on to suggest that 'by far the greatest means of escape from representing otherness in an objectified way was to be found in the text of the play' (Singleton, 2007: 30). This is a cogent point and it seems that the content of the stories, their impact and the fact that they are based on 'real' experiences (and that these are carefully threaded through the performance via the voiceovers) counterbalances, for some spectators, the 'aesthetic pleasures of orientalism' that Gilbert and Lo see operating in the work.

Yet concern remains that the repetition of stories of hardship, brutality and loss result in, or have the potential to result in, a flattening out of the stories (and those they represent) so that any detailed understanding of the experiences of refugees and asylum seekers on an emotional physical or even geographical level becomes almost impossible. For Gilbert and Lo this results in a situation whereby:

> the audience as collective witness to the verbatim testimonies – often projected in exquisite (foreign) handwriting – thus recedes from visibility while the conditions of ethical responsiveness are subordinated to the imperatives of voyeurism. (Gilbert and Lo, 2007: 205)

While the audience, at times, recedes from visibility, there is also a risk that the other will recede, as spectators become concerned with consumption and not with the 'ethical responsiveness' that, as Gilbert and Lo make clear, is 'subordinated'. This is the danger (outlined earlier) involved in attempting to balance the need to give refugees a voice and at the same time to create a performance work that actively engages spectators.

Given these diverse and contradictory readings of the work it is necessary to return to a consideration of the idea of participation. Is the performance, by virtue of its positioning of the audience (at times) as voyeurs generating the kind of participation that Levinas saw as occurring for spectators in response to art (that of passive or unthinking acceptance)? A kind of participation that sits in opposition to an actively aware and engaged spectatorship as advocated in this book? Do spectators, as Gilbert and Lo argue, recede or become uncritical or unreflexive as scene after scene unfolds before them? If so then what might the value of the work be? I think that while there are moments when this kind of spectatorship is experienced (that the work overwhelms spectators in such a way that they might feel Boltanski's 'isolation' or Gilbert and Lo's 'voyeurism' or indeed an emotional over-identification with the refugee stories), these are also countered by other moments of deep politically charged involvement (and participation in the active sense as outlined in Chapter 1) for a range of spectators.

Participation and shame

The performance is long, complicated and spectacular and it does not elicit a singular set of responses, instead it involves spectators in a multilayered emotional and intellectual response process that includes moments of participation in both senses of the term.

Politically inflected involvement occurs, at the Australian performance, in response to the opening of Part II 'Origins and Destinies', where spectators become answerable in the sense outlined by Levinas when he talks about our 'exposure' to the other and our inability to refuse. It is also during this scene that the spectacle reveals its 'terrible massacres' in the way Cixous proposes, when she talks about the function of spectacle. As a spectator I experience more than the culpability Singleton describes, in fact I experience a feeling of shame that provokes a raft of difficult and interesting questions about responsibility and proximity. I again draw on Levinas's understanding of shame here, as something beyond guilt, a 'guiltless responsibility' (Levinas, 1989: 83) that is inescapable and infinite, rather than guilt which would perhaps, as Anne Murphy explains, 'imply the finitude of responsibility, or a specific breach of contract' (Murphy, 2004). Interestingly, Gilbert and Lo make the point that 'the sense of shame that has permeated responses to most asylum theatre in Australia was noticeably absent' (Gilbert and Lo, 2007: 205) from this performance. While this reading is informed primarily by the reviews the production received in Australia, my own response to this scene does not conform and I think this illustrates the difficulty of reading this work in any definitive way.

As Part II begins we see a boat in distress and about to sink as it attempts to stay afloat on the angry grey ocean. We hear a helicopter and believe the refuges will be saved. Suddenly performers dressed as Australian Special Air Service (SAS) soldiers descend from ropes (hooked to the roof of the Royal Exhibition building) as if to rescue the refugees. The refugees clamour and shout and, as they do so, the soldiers say, through a megaphone, 'you have entered Australian territorial waters you must turn your boat around'.[11] Despite this rejection the refugees try desperately to escape their vessel, which is now burning. They stand with outstretched arms frantically waving and crying out for help. The boat is dilapidated and does not look seaworthy. It is fragile and leaking, overburdened by the weight of those who desperately cling to it as they precariously navigate the huge swells. The ocean – an ocean represented by rivers of rippling grey silk – is so furious that it obscures the boat at times and we wonder if it has actually succumbed to the angry waters, only to see it rise again in the lee of the waves.

The refugees, who are desperate to be rescued and to find a safe haven, plead with the SAS soldiers only to realise that they are being rejected and told to turn around, despite the fact that the boat is now on fire. 'Go back to where you came from. Australia does not accept you.' This statement 'Australia does not accept you' is left on the screen as the ocean recedes and as it does so it reveals a naked, drowned man lying on a trolley. It would be consoling to believe that this scene represented pure fantasy, that it was an exaggerated portrayal (for dramatic effect) of what can happen to those who attempt to 'arrive' in Australia by boat; however, it is not exaggerated, it accurately reflects what has occurred. As Suvendrini Perera points out:

> The boarding of the Tampa by armed SAS troops was also the prelude to drastic new legislation which (among other things) authorised the navy to forcibly intercept and 'push off' asylum seekers from Australian waters (Kelly 2001; Marr 2001). One such instance, the HMAS Adelaide's decision to open warning fire on, and then board, a boat carrying asylum seekers, was the cause of the boat's sinking and the children thrown into the sea allegations. A few days later two women asylum seekers drowned, the first fatalities directly attributable to the new 'push off' policy, as a fire broke out on yet another boat boarded by the Australian navy. Once again earlier sensationalised allegations by politicians that asylum seekers had deliberately set fire to their own boat were later challenged and quietly allowed to subside. (Garran and Saunders 2001: MacCallum 2002) (Perera, 2002: 9)

The cruelty inherent in refusing people on a burning boat sanctuary is powerfully represented in this scene. It is embarrassing to watch. Even though the Australian audience, for the most part, know about this policy and are aware of the 'children overboard affair' seeing it rendered theatrically and in such a stark fashion, moves us beyond mere recognition of the act as the psychological, physical and emotional impacts of such a policy become apparent through the performance. This is, for some spectators, a moment of deep shame. Miriam Cosic in her review of the Australian production points out that in response to this scene, 'not a sigh escaped the audience ... it was as though we were all holding our breath. No sense of "That's right" reverberated around the cavernous theatre space, despite the clear sympathy of the crowd; rather a sense of "My god, what do we do"' (Cosic, 2005: 16). While I cannot claim that this was necessarily a moment of collective shame, I think the production, as with *The Career Highlights of the MAMU* stimulates questions about how one lives in a country that behaves (via the democratically elected government) in such an inhuman fashion. At this point in the performance I, and perhaps those spectators Cosic alludes to, feel compelled to respond, to act on a feeling of responsibility for the situation. It seems that a combination of the visual rendering (in spectacular fashion) of the experience of refugees as they are pushed off, and the proximity of the story, given that it focuses on and names the Australian government and people ('Australia doesn't want you'), operate together to implicate the audience in an ethical exchange with the ideas generated by this scene. It is at this moment in the performance that as an individual spectator, I feel responsible for both the other and for my own actions and responses to the other.

Responsibility operates here in the Levinasian sense: 'responsibility is what is incumbent on me exclusively, and what, *humanly,* I cannot refuse' (Levinas, 1985: 101). My humanity is called into question as I try to negotiate my way through the ethical issues this scene raises. I try to reflect on what I have done, or could have done to prevent this. I frantically recall protest marches, petitions and then wonder about the absurdity of my response and my desire to avoid being implicated or held responsible for such atrocities. Martin Ball finds that the 'scenes relating to Australia are dramatic, intense, and disturbing, not the least in the way Mnouchkine undercuts our moral outrage by acknowledging the dissembling strategies of bureaucrats and asylum-seekers' (Ball, 2005: 16). My response reflects Ball's statement. This scene works to powerful effect not only to engage me responsibly but also to push me to interrogate what responsibility must signify for it to be more than an empty gesture, or an act of acknowledgment. Perhaps for a French spectator a sense of culpability or even shame might emerge in response to the Sangatte scenes?

There is something complicated, open or wounding about shame and it is at work here. Spectators who experience this shame feel directly called upon by the other to account for themselves. They are not asked to empathise or to feel sorry for the other; instead, to justify their position. Could this be an example of Agamben's reformulated political philosophy in action? In order to work through these responses I again turn to Levinas and his writings about shame. As discussed in Chapter 3, Levinas makes clear that shame exposes us; when we experience shame we try to prevent its sting but we know that there is no possibility of escape. We cannot escape because it is part of us, of our experience and our sense of self (2003: 64). This is not a point at which the work meets the emotional needs of an audience; rather, it is a point where each spectator's responsibility for the other (in the pre-ontological realm) has the potential to translate into something practical. It is a moment where Cosic's 'what do we do' becomes an urgent question.

Making 'political change'

While the language of the programme notes suggests that the company wants to use the testimonies gathered to inform the work and generate a space for the recognition of the plight of refugees, it also hints that they are striving for more than this: that perhaps they are attempting to move from spectators' recognition of the stories of the silenced and oppressed to a sense of responsibility that is motivation for action, or that they are repositioning the refugee in terms similar to those outlined by Agamben. As the programme notes point out: 'Ariane Mnouchkine and her collaborators employed the poetics of the theatre in order to interrogate the *responsibilities* of a world where disadvantaged people are marginalised and ignored' (Héliot, 2005; my emphasis). In Melbourne, the audience response to *Le Dernier*

Caravansérail was so overwhelming and demand for the performance so great, that despite a six-day season in a theatre of 600 seats, the run was extended by two days at a cost of A$160,000, which was underwritten by the State Government of Victoria.[12]

When the decision to extend the season was announced by the Director of the Melbourne International Arts Festival, Kristy Edmonds, at the end of the performance I attended, the audience, who were already on their feet for a long ovation, were delighted, and they vigorously applauded the decision.[13] Edmonds said that the show would be extended for another two nights and that the extension demonstrated how 'theatre can play a role in making political changes...we can be listened to.'[14] In fact the decision by the government to underwrite the extra performances in Melbourne, is according to Béatrice Picon-Vallin, a marker of *Théâtre du Soleil*'s success because this was a production in which 'Soleil is not exactly kind to Australia' (Picon-Vallin). This view is complicated by Gilbert and Lo's argument that 'shame' was not present in response to the work. They read the performance, instead, as functioning 'quite differently in relation to its interpretative community, seeming to confirm the nation's visibility in the global (dis)order' (Gilbert and Lo, 2007: 206). Whether the responses indicate an experience of shame, responsibility, empathy or a desire to be a member of a globally disordered community, it seems that the performance impacted on its audiences. In Australia it was, for example, hailed as the 'stand-out hit' of the Melbourne Festival by critic Raymond Gill (2005).

It is, nonetheless important to return to the questions asked at the outset of the chapter about the space the performance provides for careful and detailed responses to the global refugee crisis. Does the spectacle of *Le Dernier Caravansérail* (as a whole) override the individual moments of ethical engagement? Does the work, with its focus on visibility and remaining truthful to the stories of the oppressed, become an anodyne for the comfortable classes who – within the Australian context, for example – may feel that by attending they have contributed to the debates, that they have demonstrated – safely – their objections to the Australian government's reductive, harmful and racist policies of exclusion? Does the reliance on multiple stories of hardship, through spectacle generate a kind of awe and brief sadness that can be talked about on leaving the theatre but then set aside?

As an individual spectator the performance engendered moments of voyeurism for me, via the deep emotional responses I had to a number of scenes but it also effectively punctured this mood in other scenes, and images from those arresting vignettes remain with me. Philippa Wehle's response accords with this experience, focussing on the ways in which the work impacts on spectators in a practical sense, as it leaves them with a desire to search for answers to the global refugee crisis (Wehle, 2005: 85). This desire to find answers reflects the notion of responsibility I see the production generating. There is a need, for some spectators, to do something about all of the suffering the work shares, to move beyond empathy into action of some kind. For other spectators the vignettes effect a kind of surface engagement where spectators are, or have the potential to be, positioned as 'voyeurs' or tourists who are collectors of aesthetic experiences, (Bauman, 1998: 94) in the sense outlined by Bauman in Chapter 1. Charles Isherwood, in his review of the New York performance believes that:

> It's our ingrained indifference – the natural human impulse to observe from afar the miseries of others, to be moved to pity and then look away – that Ms. Mnouchkine is seeking to confront and challenge. This deeply socially engaged artist insists that we keep looking, until at last we see and feel. (Isherwood, 2005)

What Mnouchkine is trying to do here, it seems to me, is to bring the images up close, to use symbolism, spectacle and storytelling to fracture the distance or 'ingrained indifference' and engage spectators on an emotional level with the experiences of refugees and asylum seekers. This is a difficult task as a reliance on 'snapshots' and the desire for visibility or the generation of a space for representation does not always allow spectators to see the other's face and to adopt an active position in which responsibility is enabled; however it is a risk the company felt they must take.

In the end *Le Dernier Caravansérail* has the potential to offer a challenge to Levinasian notions of responsibility, specifically in terms of its mobilisation of participation. Spectators experience a number of emotional, visceral and intellectual states when they witness the multiple stories of pain, trauma and hardship the performance presents. As a result of this witnessing they leave the performance with a range of complicated and at times contradictory responses that might include a sense of culpability or insulation, empathy and emotional disturbance as well as the desire to respond to and mobilise responsibility for the other. Ultimately these difficult and at times conflicting responses also mean that at least for some spectators the work begins Agamben's process of repositioning the refugee as *the* figure of the twenty-first century.

6
Otherness and Responsibility in *Three Tales* by Steve Reich and Beryl Korot and *Nature's Little Helpers* by Patricia Piccinini

> There was a time when it must have seemed highly improbable that machines should learn to make their wants known by sound, even through the ears of man; may we not conceive, then, that a day will come when those ears will be no longer needed, and the hearing will be done by the delicacy of the machine's own construction? – when its language shall have been developed from the cry of animals to a speech as intricate as our own? (Butler, [1872] 1965: 195)

It seems as if we may be approaching the time, imagined by Samuel Butler in 1872, in which machines might speak in a form that is 'as intricate as our own'. A time where robots can follow instructions, and a time where we can 'make' life forms in a laboratory. In this context it is important to return to two of the key terms in this book, the other and responsibility, and to ask questions about the relevance of these terms (particularly in the Levinasian sense) in light of contemporary technological developments. This final chapter challenges the ideas explored throughout this book because it asks about the limits or usefulness of these key terms by exploring how they are made manifest in, and in response to, two significant, and yet considerably different, creative works.

The works chosen are the digital opera, *Three Tales* (2002), by Steve Reich and Beryl Korot, and the installation/photography work,

Nature's Little Helpers (2004), by Patricia Piccinini. Both works engage spectators on a range of levels and elicit complex responses about technology, power and the limits of the human, as it is currently understood. As the chapter progresses, the discussion considers the 'face' of the other and the fact of recognition and it asks how spectators might recognise the call of the other in the silent colonised subject or the posthuman/clone/cyborg in the first instance, and then what they might do if the other appeared in their bedroom in the second.

In *Three Tales* and *Nature's Little Helpers* there is an anxiety about the other as posthuman that echoes the ideas of Butler and the concerns of writers such as Isaac Asimov, Philip K. Dick and Arthur C. Clarke in the 1950s and 1960s.[1] What both *Three Tales* and *Nature's Little Helpers* uncover is a desire, in advanced technological societies, to play with otherness and ideas of the human and to worry about the implications of this playing later on.[2] In the process of exploring these issues the works also raise questions about power and control and the precariousness of our position at the top of the evolutionary perch. As a species, it seems that in general we are happy to invent, toy with, and mix elements to generate 'new' forms; however, both works question the implications of this process. It is both threatening and exciting to imagine the end of the human and realise the desire to play and remain safe at the same time. But, if the posthuman is understood as

> a category or classification of life that goes beyond essentialist thinking and the traditional binary oppositions by which the human has historically been defined. Its paragon, the cyborg, is a hybrid rather than pure being, for whom the technological is elemental rather than optional. Less a terminal event (the end of the human), the cyborg has evolved, *theoretically*, as a transitional evocation of what the human is becoming in the informatic age. (Jonson, Tofts and Cavallaro, 2003: 8; my emphasis)[3]

Then perhaps anxiety about the end of the human may be unfounded. Nonetheless, both works provoke spectators to reflect on the *literal* development of superior machines or objects and the implications of these for the human, as it is currently understood. The works also challenge both Levinasian ethics and the possibility of practical responsibility, via their questioning of the significance and meaning of responsibility and otherness in the twenty-first century.

There is much debate in performance studies about the role and function of technology and about relationships between bodies and machines, liveness and representation. Exploring the limits of the body and the ways in which it can be mined for theatrical representation is, of course, not new. However the concerns about erasure and marginalisation that technology raises – particularly for the body of the performer – continue to garner significant interest and debate. From Yuri Annenkov's 1921 manifesto *The Theatre to the End* where he argues that:

> The master of the new theatre will have a conception of the theatre completely different from that of the contemporary playwright, director, stage designer. Only the mechanical and the electric will be the creative ones in the new liberated theatre. (in Dixon, 2007: 54)

To Patrice Pavis's 2003 essay where he writes that:

> When certain directors escape into new technology, from the inside to the outside of theatrical performance, they no longer consider themselves as the central subject, artist or aesthetic subject, but simply as an organiser of functioning, a functionary of meaning. ... But it is necessary to pick out, amongst the machines, videos, technology and other computers, some fragments of body and some scraps of text. (Pavis, 2003: 191)

As Pavis's essay demonstrates these concerns remain and relationships between the use of 'live' bodies and technology within a theatrical context are often fraught. Instead of focusing on the role of bodies in theatre or performance specifically, *Three Tales* and *Nature's Little Helpers* extend the debate by using technology to consider the functioning of bodies within the world more broadly. Rather than pushing the limits of performance they use installation art and digital opera to probe the limits of the human. The works align with Steve Dixon's discussions of cyborg and robot performances, which he terms 'metal performance', in his groundbreaking work *Digital*

Performance. Dixon remarks that:

> Metal performance belies deep-seated fears and fascinations asso-
> ciated with machinic embodiments, and [] these are explored by
> artists in relation to two distinct themes: the humanization of
> machines and the dehumanization (or 'machinization') of humans.
> (Dixon, 2007: 272)

Both *Three Tales* and *Nature's Little Helpers* explore issues of 'humanization' and 'dehumanization' yet they do so in a way that disallows
any easy responses or categorisations of their themes and ideas in
binary terms. In fact both works blur the boundaries between the
human and the machine and as a result they open up the possibility
for nuanced and disturbing responses on the part of spectators.

In *Three Tales* Reich and Korot use the trope of technology to take
spectators on a journey from a consideration of the kinds of responsibility elicited for the other as a dispossessed, disempowered human
(in this case the inhabitants of Bikini Atoll, for example) to a consideration of how responsibility might work when subjects engage with
a much more complicated conceptualisation of the other: as posthuman and potentially either an extension of the self or as something
entirely other (or potentially unrecognisable).[4] This other (the posthuman) is an other who has the potential to exist beyond the
Levinasian understanding of the other as one whose otherness is
'determined as the absence of a common trait, essence, or form'
(Wyschogrod, 2004: 126). Thinking about the other in a posthuman
context is both important and challenging. While for Wyschogrod this
other may be beyond the known, for Matthew Causey it is necessary to ask the following question: 'If we are approaching the posthuman condition, will we need or desire the appearance of the flesh
of the Other? Wouldn't a posthuman be at home in the simulacrum
without referentials?' (Causey, 2006: 54). This provocative question
echoes the key issues this chapter seeks to address. If the other is
unrecognisable or perhaps even, as Causey suggests, unnecessary,
what happens to responsibility?

While *Three Tales* introduces the idea of the posthuman, Piccinini's
Nature's Little Helpers takes the question of responsibility in a slightly
different direction by actually manifesting the other (or rendering
'it' artistically), and using installation and photography to project 'it'

into the private or 'safe' sphere of the domestic space. This means that questions about responsibility, the other and the posthuman are no longer abstract or *'theoretical'* constructs; rather, they demand a consideration of the limits of individual responsibility in response to the posthuman, the post-animal or clone. Piccinini is interested in emotion, and her work triggers consideration about ethics, politics and responsibility through the development of an emotional invest-ment, connectedness or response on the part of audiences. She explores the implications of making things, and of experimenting with forms. In her 'Artist's Statement' for *Nature's Little Helpers* she points out that

> anyone who thinks that they can maintain control of the things that they create is fooling themselves. Whether it is genetically modified canola, the cane toad, a work on the secondary market or an image on the internet, once the thing leaves our hands all we can do is watch. (Piccinini)

When I am confronted with the installation 'Undivided' of a little boy in bed with a 'surrogate', I wonder about the limits of care and responsibility as I understand them. While the 'surrogate' – a hybrid creature that bears some resemblance to a wombat but is almost hair-less and slightly reptilian – looks benevolent, it is a creature that exists outside the frame of the known and therefore it challenges my response. As it lies snuggled up with the boy, I ask myself questions about what responsibility might really mean in the context of such a scenario. Also, when I see 'The Embrace', an installation depicting a woman with a creature clinging on to her face, I am not sure how to read this 'embrace'. Is the contact welcome? Who is frightened here? And what might the 'release' of creatures into the environment do to questions of containment, control and power? Imogen Neale describes her response to the exhibition in Wellington:

> The pieces combine to leave you with a very curious taste in your mouth – something that stays with you and haunts you through-out the day – that rolls everything you come upon around in a residue of its own questioning. Neither a blatant protest for or against genetic engineering, [it] serves to generate some pertinent questions that address the ways and methods we are going to use,

if at all (and if so, when) to prepare for our future: humans, animals and nature's little helpers. (Neale, 2006)

The work is beautifully crafted and it asks sophisticated questions by
involving spectators emotionally and viscerally in a process of considering their own very personal limits. It thus extends or challenges
the idea of practical responsibility to the point that 'real' questions
need to be asked about care, 'containment' and the limits of our relationship with the posthuman or post-animal other.

The three tales

Three Tales is a digital opera that uses three different stories to probe
the relationships between technology and humans in the twentieth
century. The opera score, composed by Steve Reich, is performed live
by *Steve Reich Ensemble* and *Synergy Vocals*. The singers are positioned
on the stage in front of a very large video screen and they perform
alongside (or in front of) Beryl Korot's video footage, using techniques of looping and repetition to sing statements that are either
projected on the screen in print (for example newspaper headlines),
or statements made by interviewees in the video footage.

The first story, 'Hindenburg', deals with the crash by the Hindenburg
zeppelin in the sky above Lakehurst, New Jersey in 1937. It explores
peoples' faith in technology and their dismay at the crash. The
second, 'Bikini' presents footage of the residents of Bikini, Atoll being
moved off their homeland in 1946 by US forces in order that they
might use the atoll to test the hydrogen bomb. The 167 displaced
islanders may never return to this contaminated land and this story
reflects on questions of dispossession and power. The third story,
'Dolly', explores issues of cloning and the posthuman. Drawing on
the cloning of Dolly the sheep in 1997, it takes the form of a documentary or lecture. 'Dolly' comprises a range of interviews with leading thinkers who provide their views on cloning, cyborgs, robots and
immortality. This story uses looping, repetition and the juxtaposing
of statements or positions to avoid didacticism and to open up a
space in which spectators might consider the fragility and limits of
the concept 'human'.

While *Three Tales* is concerned with interrelationships between
technology and the human, in its depiction of these tales it engages

spectators in a complicated process of negotiation about questions of otherness and responsibility. I explore this process by drawing on Levinas's work to think through the possibility (as outlined earlier) of applying Levinasian ethics to discussions about the posthuman other. The journey through otherness in *Three Tales* is prefaced by the first tale, 'Hindenburg', which establishes the relationship between humans and technology (in the 1930s) as one of fascination and trust. By focusing on this and the two following stories, it becomes clear that this work presents a multifaceted picture of the ways in which technology has 'advanced' in the twentieth century and of the costs of this advancement.

In many respects it is apt to discuss *Three Tales* here, as its themes and focus draw together some of the key ideas related to the other works addressed in earlier chapters. There are particular resonances with *The Career Highlights of the MAMU* (Chapter 3) in terms of the impact of the nuclear tests on the residents of Bikini Atoll, and with *Genesi: from the museum of sleep* (Chapter 2) in terms of the focus on the function and use of technology by the human, and the use of the Book of Genesis. Extracts from the Book of Genesis are used in both 'Bikini' and 'Dolly'. These extracts act as an anchor or perhaps as a voice of reason or morality against which the discussions about technology are positioned. In this regard I read *Three Tales* as charting a trajectory from the 'beginning' to the contemporary moment, and in the process juxtaposing 'God's' ideas about human life with those currently held. It also reflects on the relationships between 'creation', as presented in the Bible, and scientific understandings of evolution and technology.

In an interview with David Allenby, Reich and Korot point out that there are two stories of creation in Genesis. The first story 'describing how G-d created Man and Woman at the same time and gave them dominion over the birds and the beasts and everything on the face of the earth.' In the second story 'man is made from the dust of the earth, woman from his rib. They are placed in the Garden of Eden "to serve it and to keep it"' making him, according to Korot 'a more humble type of human being'. However, she goes on to explain that in Bikini in 1946 'the man of dominion came upon the humble man and asked (or rather told) him to make a sacrifice of their homeland for the sake of all mankind (sic)' (Allenby, 2003: 8). Reich makes the point that this story tells us that 'we do have dominion, and therefore responsibility' (Allenby, 2003: 8). It is interesting to think, then, about how it is that *Three Tales* engages this responsibility. While the issues of dispossession as outlined in 'Bikini' and cloning in 'Dolly' might, on the surface seem quite distinct, they are joined through the lens of technology and the question of responsibility.

The performance asks spectators to consider how they might respond to the dispossession of one group of people for the comfort and reassurance of others. It also asks them to consider how they might fashion their responsibility to the question of the posthuman: the clone, the robot or the cyborg. By including the views of a range of leading scientists, philosophers and other thinkers, the third tale, 'Dolly', takes on an added depth. Through the manipulation of sound within the lecture format 'Dolly' avoids replaying the sensationalist and potentially shallow anxieties of various power groups, which promoted pro- and anti-cloning positions in the wake of Dolly's birth (or re-birth, as Rebecca Schneider put it) in 1997. As Schneider explains:

> Thirty hours after the news of Dolly hit the media, New York State legislator John Marchi announced a bill to make human cloning illegal and conservative ministers, rabbis, bishops, and columnists rallied in support. Anticipating the uproar around the clone, a pro-clone action group sprang up composed of members of gay and lesbian communities in New York, calling themselves the Clone Rights United Front. (Schneider 2001, 97–98)[5]

Rather than focus on the responses of stakeholders or interest groups, this tale triggers reflection on the genesis of life, the very stuff of humanity. It is not an essentialist rant; instead, it invites spectators, via the interviews, which are strategically merged and juxtaposed to present a range of viewpoints, to experience the fear and tension associated with imagining what might lie beyond the (human) map. Reich suggests the complexity of the work in the programme notes: 'if I wanted to send a message, I'd send you an email. ... If any work of art can be boiled down to an email, then it's trash. Period' (Reich, 2003).

Three Tales generates an open and nuanced exchange between spectators and the performance. While the content might seem to suggest that this digital opera takes on the form of a polemic, the work refuses this function and stimulates ethical questioning through the use of layered and often oblique content coupled with a range of musical and visual techniques. This is a production that works on the senses. Jem Kelly argues that, 'in forging connections between visual representations and rhythmical, melodic and sung forms, the spectator of *Three Tales* is addressed synaesthetically' (Kelly, 2005: 234). In fact, Reich and Korot's manipulation of sound and image to build both the soundscape and the visuals for the opera can be interpreted as an attempt to re-sensitise the senses through techniques such as repetition and looping as well as 'slow motion sound'. Reich uses 'slow motion sound' (a technique he developed) to allow him to 'slow down a speaker or sound without changing pitch or timbre'. He also uses a technique that allows him to generate a 'kind of audible vapor trail' by 'making an extension of a single vowel in time'. He comments that this is 'equivalent to freeze frame in film' (Allenby, 2003: 8). These techniques, coupled with Korot's layering of still images and film footage and her use of a painterly technique with some of the images in 'Bikini', work together to create a rich tapestry of sound and image.[6] As Fred Cohn describes it,

> instead of a traditional stage setting, *Three Tales* makes use of a huge video screen, displaying Korot's dizzying assemblage of computer-altered film footage, photos and graphics. A small band of musicians and a five-voice chorus perform onstage underneath the screen. The singers' movement is minimal; they're onstage to offer Greek-chorus-like commentary. (Cohn, 2003: 50)

Hindenburg

The first of the three tales, 'Hindenburg' combines newspaper head-lines, reports from announcers and onlookers, and an interview with Freya von Moltke.[7] The shock experienced by the media covering the story is evident in the recordings. For example, the radio announcer, Herb Morrison, who witnessed the explosion, reports: 'it flashed, it flashed and it's crashing, it's crashing terrible. It burst, it burst into flame. Get this Scotty! Get this Scotty! It flashed, it flashed and it's crashing' (Reich and Korot, 2003: 1). The power of this statement is augmented by its repetition. The Hindenburg was, according to Reich, 'the first major disaster captured on film' (Allenby, 2003: 6), and the filmic sequences are used to demonstrate the esteem with which the craft was regarded, as well as the incredulity of reporters and onlookers as it exploded. The statement 'it could not have been a technical matter' is repeatedly typed on the screen (as if arriving by telegram) and is sung by three tenors, as the visuals show the giant dirigible bursting into flames and crashing to the ground and people running for their lives to escape the flames. Kelly writes that the repetition of this phrase throughout 'Hindenberg' is important: 'A consequence of this heavy repetition of the same phrase is to make the listener dwell upon the significance of each word in relation to the words around it and to the music that accompanies it' (Kelly, 2005: 226).

The combination of visual images of the explosion and voiceovers from the reporters at the scene reflect the thwarted desire of society at that time to maintain its faith in technology and the associated advancement it represented, as well as the belief that the explosion was motivated by an act of sabotage rather than the result of a technical failure (see Figure 6.1). As the Newsreel announcer states:

> The Hindenburg has gone. Her tragedy will not halt the march of progress. From her ashes will arise the knowledge, from her fate, the lesson, that will lead to a greater and a better means of mastering the air. If so, her dead will not have died in vain. (Reich and Korot, 2003: 1)

This first tale sets the tone and structure for the opera. 'Hindenburg' acts as a cautionary tale about technology and trust. For Kelly, it had a destabilising effect. He explains that the

> inter-*play* of imposing images, repetitive melodic music and song is structured in such a way that the presence of the actual incident of the Hindenburg is questioned, foregrounding that the disaster remains perpetually inaccessible except through the remnants of its representations and mediated forms. (Kelly, 2005: 227; original emphasis)

Hindenburg' ends leaving spectators such as Kelly with the eerie sense that technology can explode, vanish and at the same time capture 'remnants'.

Figure 6.1 Images of The Hindenburg, by Beryl Korot, *Three Tales,* 2002. (Photograph courtesy Beryl Korot)

Bikini

The second story is the story of Bikini Atoll located in the Republic of the Marshall Islands, in the central Pacific. It documents the removal of the Bikinians in preparation for the nuclear explosions on the atoll conducted by the American Government in 1946.[8] The narrative elements are compiled from documents filed by journalists and reporters who witnessed the bombing, as well as extracts from the Book of Genesis. The Genesis text is woven with the other material to punctuate the (visual) narrative flow and to raise questions about how humans might 'multiply... fill the earth... and subdue it'. In fact, what the story shows spectators is the way in which one group 'subdue' another in the search for advanced power. As a British radio announcer observes: 'small and remote, it's just the place... for the next atom bomb... [to] turn this great destructive power into something for the benefit of all mankind (sic)' (Reich and Korot, 2003: 3). Korot explains that the extracts from Genesis '... are typed out, white letters against black, whereas other texts within the piece appear as part of a collaged image and are often in the form of headlines' (Allenby, 2003: 8). The video images are diverse and combine archival material from the US Naval Science Photographic Lab as well as a range of other (mostly newsreel) sources (see Figure 6.2).

'Bikini' plays with ideas of power and empowerment in ways that reflect the dangers of human experimentation with technology. Although the story of nuclear testing is related in a very different manner than it is in *The Career Highlights of the MAMU* (Chapter 3), many of the issues resonate. While in *MAMU* the use of the documentary footage of the elders speaking from their country adds depth to the performance, in *Three Tales* the Islanders seem to be absolutely othered by being rendered voiceless and silent. This is a powerful technique, and it works effectively to demonstrate, as the visuals do, the dominance of the Americans over the Bikinians.

The Islanders are moved off the land for the benefit of 'mankind', and they are shown packing up their possessions and boarding navy vessels. They do not have a voice in this story, apart from King Judah's statement 'it's all changed. It's not the same' (Reich and Korot, 2003: 4), which is a headline from the *New York Times* and is sung by two sopranos and three tenors as part of the 'Coda'

Figure 6.2 Images of Bikini Atoll, by Beryl Korot, *Three Tales*, 2002. (Photograph courtesy Beryl Korot)

to 'Bikini'. This story is rich and complicated both visually and musically. For Fred Cohn,

> 'Bikini' takes the form of a grim countdown, leading not to the familiar mushroom-cloud imagery, but to a visualization of what the former tropical paradise might have looked like from within the blast. (Cohn, 2003: 51)

Korot uses 'techniques to create distance from the documentary source material' of the story. She does this by turning 'the live film footage of the islanders into photographic stills'. She made these stills 'painterly and then animated them at a different rate from the usual 30 frames per second' (Allenby, 2003: 7–8). The effect is of Impressionist paintings, or black-and-white versions of some of Gauguin's Tahitian paintings. She wants to create a 'different feeling', and in using this technique she achieves this difference. The painterly images seem less 'real' and perhaps more romantic, creating a temporary schism between the 'reality' or the implications of the events unfolding in the story and their images. For Kelly this effect connotes 'a literalist mode of seeing that suggests a phenomenological existence outside western conventions' (2005: 232). This is emblematic of the entire story, where layering, looping and juxtaposing are used to liberate a set of often-contradictory responses from spectators as this story of domination, suppression, silence and sacrifice demands. While the footage is pointed in its depiction of the Islanders' dispossession, their positioning as silent or voiceless others along with the techniques of sound and image gives this tale an openness that subverts a polemical or didactic representation of the story. Kelly goes on to explain that,

> this strategy of filtration conveys a sense of an imaginary, pre-industrial, primordial mode of existence no longer readily accessible, and as such the treated images of the islanders become metonymic of pre-technologized primitive cultures, past and remotely present. Alternatively, the images can also be read as an idealization, a romanticized and nostalgic evocation of a lifestyle that never existed. (Kelly, 2005: 232)

'Bikini' generates a curiosity, rather than an anger or sense of failure. This curiosity is productive as it leads spectators to ask questions about the Islanders and their frame of mind at the time of the evacuation and, by extension, about the implications of this move on their culture and identity as a nation.

The fact that the Islanders do not speak, or that they are not permitted a voice, is important. This is not a work in which identifiable performers or personae mobilise stories or fragments of ideas, but it isn't a documentary work either. There is a lack that operates here: the lack of performer as embodied participant in the process. In other works addressed in this book, ethical questions have been liberated in response to the ideas generated by the performance and the performers, or in certain cases, particularly in *The Career Highlights of the MAMU* (Chapter 3) and *Sandakan Threnody* (Chapter 4), via the testimony of interviewees within the performance. In this work, by contrast, there is an absence or silence at play. This lack connects back to Pavis's concern about the absence of bodies in technologically driven work and the need to 'pick out some fragments'. In response to *Three Tales*, and particularly, Bikini there is a feeling of being deliberately kept at a distance: separated from the Islanders and placed in a potentially helpless or voyeuristic position regarding their plight. No real connection is engendered, or perhaps allowed, as we witness them being loaded onto ships. Because the voices heard are either those of the journalists or the US military, spectators do not gain any insight into the feelings of the residents on their (forced) departure. However, they do, by virtue of the use of voiceovers from military personnel and documentary footage, gain a sense of the complete suppression of the residents' own feelings and individual responses to their plight.

Footage shows the community, seated on the sandy beach, being lectured to, or advised by a US Naval Officer about the use of the island for the greater good. He says, 'Now, then James, Now then James, tell them please' and this scenario is repeated throughout this story, a few words added each time, until the whole sentence unfolds: 'that the United States Government, wants to take this great destructive power... turn this great destructive power into something for the benefit of all mankind (Reich and Korot, 2003: 3).[9] The footage shows the Bikinians packing and preparing to leave. It also shows their animals being packed in crates, dragged and herded onto ships. The herding of the animals is evocative of the Book of Genesis and the story of Noah's Ark, as well as metaphorically reflecting the experience of the residents as they are dispossessed of their lands and also herded (although not so literally) onto ships for departure.

The combination of singing – which in this tale is primarily the singing of news reports, material from the US navy archives and British radio sequences – and video imagery and voices of military personnel does not invite spectators in to any kind of direct emotional relationship with the soon-to-be former residents of Bikini Atoll. In fact, the Islanders and their animals are treated in the same way, as objects or obstacles to be removed. While the impacts of the testing are made clear through the montage of video elements and the use of the vivid (almost blinding) yellow wash or haze that the island becomes as a result of the blast (the view from inside which Cohn mentions), the silencing of the Islanders is a strategy that effectively distances spectators. However, despite or perhaps because of this deliberate separation and silencing, spectators may find themselves eager to know how to respond to the call or face of the other (in a practical sense). This denial or silencing of their voices and stories does not mean that we turn away and refuse (or are unable) to engage with the other's plight; rather, the denial compels us to act. Levinas writes that:

> I am not at all sure that the face is a phenomenon. A phenomenon is what appears. Appearance is not the mode of being of the face. The face is, from the start, the demand.... It is the frailty of the one who needs you, who is counting on you. (in Wright, Hughes and Ainley, 1988: 171)

While the residents do not speak in the realm of the 'said', the footage and the act of recording and transmitting this allows their 'saying' to be heard as the visual images rupture the 'said' and demonstrate the power of the realm of the 'saying'. Perhaps the face operates here in its silence. Levinas continues:

> I think that the beginning of language is in the face. In a certain way, in its silence, it calls you. Your reaction to the face is a response. Not just a response, but a responsibility. These two words [*réponse, responsabilité*] are closely related. (in Wright, Hughes and Ainley, 1988: 169)

There is a sense of sadness at the dispossession unfolding on the screen, the simplicity of their possessions, the unsentimental loading of cargo (both human and animal) onto ships. The Islanders' lack of struggle, response or voice is moving. The final footage of some of the Islanders visiting the atoll many years later and finding it still uninhabitable is unsettling. I am left with a sense of responsibility but am uncertain what I can do with it. I want, in this context, more than just a response or a responsibility in the pre-ontological realm; I want a response that is linked to action of some kind. I feel that Levinas's notion of responsibility needs to be extended. I wish for some kind of moral guidance on how to act, only to remind myself of Bauman's argument about the *'pluralism* of rules' (Bauman, 1993: 20) and the impossibility of guidance on how to act ethically in the postmodern world. For Kelly, the sense of both distance and closeness to 'Bikini' and its residents is achieved through the 'use of iconic and temporally displaced indexical sound and image'. It is one that also results in unsettlement. He writes that:

> By positioning the spectator in an ambivalent relation to the explosion of the bomb, s/he is at once complicit with the historiographical process that is taking place and also is engaged in an anticipatory sense with the explosion.... The spectator is both critically distanced from the information presented and engaged emotionally through a sense of anticipation developed by sound. (Kelly, 2005: 230)

The relationship between sound and image, and I would add the Islanders' lack of voice, generates a complicated and contradictory set of responses for spectators, to this tale.

Dolly

The issue of responsibility and the face is further complicated in the third tale, 'Dolly'. In 'Bikini' the other is silenced by both the coloniser and by the creative choices made by Reich and Korot. Despite, or perhaps because of this the relationship between spectators and the other emerges from a need to transcend this silencing. In 'Dolly' the issues of responsibility and the other become even more complicated as the parameters for the other expand and the issue of recognition comes to the fore. Discussions of the posthuman or potentially non-human other, as I have explained, present a challenge to Levinasian ethics and therefore to the possibility of response and of responsibility. In 'Questions to Emmanuel Levinas' Luce Irigaray teases out the problem of identifying the other:

> Who is the other, the Other (*l'auture, autrui*), etc.? How can the other be defined? Levinas speaks of 'the Other' (*autrui*), of 'respect for the Other' (*respect d'autrui*), of the 'face of the Other' (*visage d'autrui*), etc. But how to define this Other which seems so self-evident to him, and which I see as a postulate, the projection or the remnant of a system, a hermeneutic locus of crystallization of meaning, etc.? (Irigaray, 1991: 112; original emphasis)

These are important questions. While Irigaray uses them to problematise Levinas's approach to sexuality and religion (among other things), I want to use responses to 'Dolly' to ask how the concept of the other functions, or might function, in a technologically advanced landscape where the boundaries of the human are constantly being expanded and interrogated. Reich points out that:

> Cloning is emblematic of the many biological procedures and digital devices by which we are now beginning to manipulate the human body. The possibilities are endless and the question arises whether we are the right beings for the job. As we step into remaking our own species, we cross a line never crossed before. We encounter opportunities and dangers we've never contemplated. Dolly meditates on this and the religious background from which we came. (Allenby, 2003: 10)

In this regard, 'Dolly' moves spectators from an experience of observation of the dispossession of people in 1946 for the 'greater good' of 'mankind' into the present and to questions about what constitutes humanity, how we might understand the rapid changes that are taking place, and how the whole concept of responsibility might work in this charged environment. While there are no performers in 'Bikini' there are a myriad in 'Dolly': from Dolly herself, who says 'Baaa', to scientists and thinkers who are leading the discussion, reflection and experimentation with cellular and non-cellular materials. 'Dolly' is divided into four sections: 'Cloning Technique', 'Human Body as Machine', 'Darwin', and 'Robots/Cyborgs/Immortality.' It is interesting to note that the Genesis extracts in this story are about God's advice to Adam not to eat from the 'Tree of Knowledge' and I read this as reflecting the potential hubris involved in our becoming too confident with genetic experimentation. While the creation of a clone in Dolly the sheep may seem a significant advance in technology and in our understanding of the human and its limits, it also signifies a precipice over the edge of which the future is uncertain and potentially lethal.

This tale begins with Kismet the robot quoting from the Book of Genesis about God placing Adam in the Garden of Eden. Kismet is a machine with big red rubber lips, large blue eyes with lids, brows and lashes, and pink ears that look as if they are pieces of pink paper stuck in the side of 'his/her' 'head' (see Figure 6.3).

> Kismet is the robot created by Cynthia Breazeal at MIT, designed for interactions with humans. Ms. Breazeal writes, 'a new range of applications (domestic, entertainment, health care, etc.) is driving the development of robots that can interact and cooperate with people, and play a part in their daily lives.' Kismet has aroused media interest worldwide. (Reich and Korot, 2002)

While Kismet looks comical, the idea of the robot as an intelligent machine plays a key role in this story, and it is positioned both alongside and against the human as we currently understand it. At this point it is worth returning to Dixon's analysis of 'metal performance' as his discussion of robots could be applied to the comical Kismet. He argues that 'the artificiality of robot movement mirrors the artificiality of camp' (Dixon, 2007: 274) although it is Kismet's face and voice rather than awkward movements per se that generate humour, the point remains a valid one. On a somewhat more serious note though, Dixon continues, 'although robots may not yet be self-aware, they are quintessentially self-conscious entities, calculating and computing their every move' (Dixon, 2007: 274). So while Kismet looks funny, we should not be lured into thinking that he is not capable of having a particular kind of intelligence. Kismet's initial statement is followed by projection of a discussion on the process of cloning. Interview footage of Ruth Deech, Richard Dawkins,

Figure 6.3   Images of Kismet the Robot, Rodney Brooks and Cynthia Breazeal, by Beryl Korot, *Three Tales*. 2002. (Photograph courtesy Beryl Korot)

James D. Watson and Gina Kolata is interspersed as they explain how cloning works.[10] 'We, and all other animals, are machines created by our genes. Machines, machines, are machines (looped)' (Reich and Korot, 2003: 4). In this section of the performance, Kismet asks, 'would you like to be cloned?' And this is followed by what appear to be responses from Stephen J. Gould, Richard Dawkins and Jason Lanier.[11] Each has a different response and thus begins the complex journey, embarked upon by spectators, through this story.

Richard Dawkins makes the claim that we are 'machines' and that he doesn't think that 'there's anything that we are, that is in principle, deeply different from what computers are'. His remarks are interspersed with comments by Rodney Brooks who while also celebrating the relationships between our brains and technology, argues that this position 'leaves out a whole lot of stuff that we do with one another...we look at each other in the eye...we smile' (Reich and Korot, 2003: 6).[12] The word 'machines' is repeated endlessly during this part of the story (as a backdrop or soundscape) and it becomes a rhythm that frames the rest of the commentary. Brooks's position may be reassuring, as the repeated claims by Dawkins generate a sense of unease because they seem to negate emotion, connectedness and social relationships. Of course, unease may also triggered by the desire to make a claim for the uniqueness of human life, as the idea that we are the same as machines makes us less crucial, somehow. While Dawkins goes on to say, 'I have no sense of guilt pulling the plug on any machine', Adin Steinsaltz complicates matters further by asking: 'it's a machine or not a machine. The real question would be: Are you responsible or not responsible for anything' (Reich and Korot, 2003: 6).[13] This is an interesting point, as it is not clear here whether Steinsaltz is asking about the responsibility of the subject or the other.

It is in 'Dolly' that Dixon's theorisation of metal performance becomes most pertinent. Dixon draws on Hans Moravec's proposition that humans can either 'adopt the fabulous mechanisms of robots, thus becoming robots themselves, or they can retire into obscurity' (in Dixon, 2007: 277), to explain that:

> Metal performance reflects this techno-zeitgeist, which senses a gradual but inevitable merging of flesh and metal. There are thus two routes to the robot, which are perceived as operating

simultaneously: one via AI, building artificial intelligence, sentient beings; the other through cyborgism, adopting the human form to a supposedly superior robotic and computational physiognomy. (Dixon, 2007: 277–278)

These routes are addressed 'simultaneously' in 'Dolly' as the views of a range of thinkers are presented via fragmentation and looping in ways that refuse to allow a singular mode or voice to emerge as the correct one. Instead what emerges, as Steinsaltz explains above, is the question of responsibility and how it might, if at all, operate in such a changed environment.

The posthuman and the issue of recognition

This question continues as the tale unfolds. In the section 'Robots/ Cyborg/Immortality' Sherry Turkle relates the following story:

> One 10 year old said to me
> The robots are like Pinocchio
> not like real boys
> They're sort of alive
> sort of alive
> doesn't have a mother
> doesn't have siblings
> doesn't know its gonna die (sic)

This is immediately followed by Ray Kurzweil's statement, 'we're going to be thrown from our perch of evolutionary superiority' (Reich and Korot, 2003: 7). There are several issues that arise from these statements. The first and most obvious is the lack of attachment or emotional life of the robot (or the idea of the robot) being discussed by the ten-year-old. What would life without 'emotional' life mean or be like? This is an old question, but it becomes startlingly 'real' in the context of this performance where spectators are introduced to Dolly the sheep, Kismet the robot and an array of scientists/scholars who bombard them with stories about the 'reality' or inevitability of the robot or newly imagined (or as yet unimagined) 'human'.

Questions swirl around as we grapple with myriad positions. What does it take to be a human? Does this discussion return us to a desire for essentialist ideas or, alternatively, to a freedom from emotional baggage that we can currently only dream of? Or does it, in fact, point to the lack of an originary moment, a celebration of the multiplicity, of the repeat, the loop or the copy?[14] As Dixon's discussion of metal performance reveals, a shift occurred with the cloning of Dolly the sheep, when questions about the 'us' and 'them' nature of machines and humans became further complicated by the figure of the clone. As anxiety reached its peak, Rebecca Schneider asked some cogent questions:

> How can clones scare us when we are ourselves clones? We have been telling ourselves since Genesis and Plato that we are ourselves already the very stuff of copies, the meat of inauthenticity, mere inappropriate clones of Original Fathers or Foundational Ideas. ... While postmodernists may claim that the culture of the copy has reached fevered pitch, that 'pitch' is a habit of Western identity formation ... Due to this, the trouble with the double, the *truly* inauthentic, the 'aper' the actor, or the clown has always been that in the very 'outness' of its inauthenticity it is more genuine than we. (Schneider, 2001: 110)

Of course Schneider is right, we shouldn't be scared of the 'clone' (or the posthuman however it manifests itself) because we are, as she points out, 'the meat of inauthenticity'. Nonetheless, the concept of the clone or the robot, the cyborg, or the posthuman as something that might 'throw us from our perch', and as something that is potentially so radically other that we may not identify it, is, at the very least, unsettling. The idea of being 'thrown from our perch of evolutionary superiority' is quite dramatic and it links back to Dixon's argument about metal performance and the option of the 'machinization' of humans (2007: 272). It suggests more radical evolutionary changes than we might imagine if we agree with much of the research indicating that these changes are likely to be gradual and that, rather than being thrown, we will become (evolve into) the next thing. Or it suggests that we are, to varying degrees, already clones, as Schneider argues (and in this regard echoing Dixon's other option 'the humanization of machines' (2007: 272)). The idea of being thrown is also interesting here as it implies violence or rupture, which indicates, perhaps, that our own inauthenticity will be revealed.

'Dolly' in its negotiation of these fractured and looped responses to technology and bodies proposes both humanization and machinization in ways that trigger what Dixon, drawing on the cyborg performance of Julie Wilson, calls 'a "something other" that is uncertain of its current ontology but senses its future becoming' (Dixon, 2007: 305).

Because of the ambivalence the work generates about technology, the human and attachment to these ideas, it can be read as a performance that opens up space within which spectators can reflect on the limits of their own ethical responsibility.

The other in the bedroom: Patricia Piccinini's *Nature's Little Helpers*[15]

The issue of responsibility and its limits is an ongoing theme in the work of Australian artist, Patricia Piccinini.[16] While *Three Tales* presents spectators with Dolly the sheep and Kismet the robot, Piccinini takes this one step further and develops 'beings' that are not as easily categorisable as either robot or animal, human or post human. As she points out, her work is not

> dry, cool and rational; it is wet, warm and emotional. Much of the context that underpins my work is medical or environmental; many of the technologies that I comment upon are aimed at saving lives, easing suffering, protecting biodiversity. It is one thing to calmly opine on ethics but another to cling desperately to their possibilities as you see something or somebody close slipping away. (Piccinini, 2006)

As stated at the outset of this chapter, Piccinini's work appeals on an emotional level as much as it does on an ethical or political one. She uses her figures to draw spectators in, to engender a connection and to probe, and at times to explore, the limits of intimacy. Her recent series of works, entitled *Nature's Little Helpers*, was presented at the Robert Miller Gallery in New York. Of this work there are two installations that link in significant ways to the issues already raised in this chapter. The first, *The Embrace*, depicts a woman (remarkably like Piccinini) made from silicone, fibreglass, human hair, plywood, leather and clothing who is standing aghast in the gallery space with a creature clinging on to her face. The creature resembles a combination of existing animals but is not identifiable as any particular species. Piccinini's face is obscured as the creature latches on to her. It is as if the creature has leapt from its cocoon on the wall to embrace (the title of this aspect of the installation) her. The obscuring of the face is interesting and raises questions about the call of the other and our inability to avoid that call. It could, in fact, be read as a humorous affront to Levinas's philosophy.

This work deconstructs any boundaries around the relationship between the 'human' and the other and situates them in direct contact with one another. While the creature has the potential to make spectators squirm, particularly when they see it clinging to Piccinini's face, the humour of the piece allows it to resonate beyond the polemic.

The second installation in the series that is important (in the context of this book) comprises the following materials: 'silicone, fiberglass, human hair, teddy, bed and linen'. It is titled 'Undivided' and depicts a small boy with ginger hair sleeping peacefully on a single bed. There is also another figure in the bed and this is one of Piccinini's creatures. Lying with its arm around the boy it is protecting or comforting the young child. From the side of the bed, where we see the child, this picture evokes a warmth and sense of emotional connection with both the child and his protector. As pointed out at the outset of this chapter, the creature ('surrogate') is hairless and difficult to categorise: it doesn't look like anything else we might know (echoing concerns raised earlier about the unknown/unknowable other) it seems benign and caring. However, when we look at it from the other side of the bed, we see baby creatures emerging from the surrogate's back. The first of these creatures does indeed look like a wombat and has a coat of greyish or brown fur. Its nose and paws or claws are evident, as if it is about to emerge from a circular opening in a pouch in the 'surrogate's' lower back (see Figure 6.4).

The second, which is about half-way up the back, a much smaller wombat-like animal (which may be another surrogate), is hairless and resting as if it finds sleeping more comfortable both within and outside of the pouch. The third is just a swollen pouch with some pink flesh inside it. These animals or objects alter our engagement with the work significantly. While there is the potential for an emotional connection with the surrogate as we watch it cradle and protect

Figure 6.4   Patricia Piccinini, Undivided, 2004. Silicon, fibreglass, clothing, human hair, bed, dimensions variable. (Photograph: Graham Baring, courtesy Patricia Piccinini)

the young child, the vision of other animals emerging from it generates a visceral response. We may squirm and want to take a step back, or want to separate ourselves from this figure or mutant, and begin to reconsider its relationship to the sleeping child. The surrogate is unsettling. While a portrait on the wall of a small child and the surrogate nestled happily together may provide some reassurance, the installation ultimately generates a sense of unease. As Imogen Neale, in response to the drawings that accompanied the work at the Wellington exhibition, expresses

> it is the four graphite drawings that best capture the essence of what Piccinini is trying to get at. Perhaps this is because the drawings place a child – the penultimate human jewel – and a creature – the penultimate human anxiety – in very close proximity. Looking at the drawings you want to find the child's guardian and ask; 'do you know this animal? Is it safe? Will the child be okay?' Or, alternatively, you want to remove the child from the drawing, lift it away from this creature that you can't help but feel very wary of. (Neale, 2006)

This is, I would argue, what Piccinini wants to evoke. Unease encourages us to consider the ethical issues involved in cloning and how these relate to both the motivations for cloning – the desire to do good by creating a species to assist another that is under threat – and also the issue of responsibility for the 'clone' once it is made. This is perplexing terrain and serious consideration of all of the political, ethical and social (not to mention environmental) concerns reveals that easy solutions or moral positions quickly come unstuck in response to the issues involved. Questions that might be considered include: are these creatures going to live in my house, to sleep cradling my child? Who is going to 'take care of them'? Instead of generating a feeling of ambivalence that is linked to the end of the species as it is currently understood (as in *Three Tales*), Piccinini's installation opens up a host of ethical questions about responsibility as it might literally operate.

Matthew Causey in his discussion of Eduardo Kac's work (notably the GFP bunny) considers the limits of responsibility when 'new' biological beings are made. His argument can be usefully applied to Piccinini's work. Causey states:

> As Dr. Frankenstein learned, that which we create deserves our care and responsibility. We are animals, and our machines are our extensions, supplementing and sometimes displacing ourselves.

> *Transgenic art* is a process for the manufacturing of monsters and machines, and thereby the artist must become the *care-taker* of these other beings. Without a concerned *care-taking*, these monsters and machines will return with desires and demands no posthuman can supply. (Causey, 2006: 149; original emphasis)

While Causey sees it as the artist's responsibility to care for the 'products' of transgenic art, Piccinini's project is less clear-cut as her creatures are situated outside the lab and in the world. A Levinasian notion of responsibility is not going to assist (in terms of Piccinini's creatures particularly) with these concerns, as the creatures in question are not even sentient and therefore they cannot have a 'face'. In effect Kac's 'products' and Piccinini's 'helpers' act as metaphors or cautionary figurations that stimulate ethical reflection about the limits of responsibility and the implications of cloning or developing new (hybrid) species. As Suzanne Anker and Dorothy Nelkin suggest:

> Transgenic techniques have to a great extent been employed on the farm. Bioengineers have created sheep-goat chimeras, known colloquially as 'geeps,' and transgenic pigs that produce low-cholesterol meat. More recently, scientists are implanting human genes into animals so that they become, in effect, biological factories for the production of body substances, therapeutic materials, or pharmaceutical products. ... As part of the war on terrorism, cows are also engineered to produce antibodies to botulism, and human genes are added to assure they can be safely used in human vaccinations in the event of terrorist attacks. (2004: 90)

Taking these ideas into account, then, Piccinini's work has extra resonance as it introduces an emotional element into the debate. She wants us to confront the implication (however hazy) of cloning and technological advancement. She attempts to engage spectators in an emotional play by provoking responses of care, love, fear and anxiety to generate reflection on complex ethical questions about responsibility. These questions include, as Jacqueline Millner points out, 'what are our responsibilities towards life created through other than biological reproduction? Should our ethical responsibilities depend on the means of life's creation?' (Millner, 2001). Or should they depend on the humanness of the face of the other? By infiltrating the domestic sphere (by implication) through this work, Piccinini reinforces the question and limits of practical responsibility. Despite the fact that this work does not sit easily (or perhaps at all?) within a Levinasian ethical frame, it does have the potential to evoke responses from spectators about their ethical positions regarding the posthuman, the animal (or even the post-animal) and the clone.

Responsibility, recognition and the 'face'[17]

If the robot, cyborg or posthuman is an other devoid of human life (as we currently understand it) or is perhaps (part-) animal can Levinasian notions of responsibility be found useful? Alternatively, if, the robot, posthuman or cyborg is an entity that is us or that we are becoming, then how does responsibility for the other work in this context? While I draw on Levinas here, it is interesting to see how these works, and particularly 'Dolly', challenge or probe the limits of his philosophy. It is clear that Levinas's ethics extends primarily (or perhaps solely) towards the human other. In the following interview excerpt he explains that:

> I cannot say at what moment you have the right to be called 'face'. The human face is completely different and only afterwards do we discover the face of an animal. I don't know if a snake has a face…I do not know at what moment the human appears, but what I want to emphasize is that the human breaks with pure being, which is always a persistence in being… [W]ith the appearance of the human – and this is my entire philosophy – there is something more important than my life, and that is the life of the other. (in Wright, Hughes and Ainley, 1988: 171–172)

It is not only the appearance of the other (the human face) that is important for Levinas; it is the other's call to us, as through this call the other engages our responsibility. As Susan Benso points out,

> Levinas's ethics retains anthropologocentric features in its reading life still in terms of an opposition between human and non-human, where the human *logos* of ethics is the defining factor

whereas the nonhuman is understood merely as the derivative
negation of humanity. (Benso, 2000: 43)[18]

Notwithstanding the fact that, as stated earlier, the other can call
through silence, it seems that there is no place for Dolly in Levinas's
ethics. The sheep does not have a face and therefore, according to
Levinas, it cannot call me into an ethical relationship. However, the
position of the cyborg, 'surrogate', posthuman or robot is more complicated, as it may indeed have a face, and may then be able to call
me. This is an interesting dilemma: where do we situate Kismet in
this regard? Is it a thing? Levinas states that 'things are those which
never present themselves personally, and, in the end, they have no
identity. ... Things offer themselves to be grasped, they do not offer a
face. They are beings without faces' (in Benso, 2000: 46). Benso goes
on to say that

> the facial absence legitimates the proscription of things from eth-
> ics and their condemnation to the realm of ontology, to the point
> that, according to Levinas, 'ontology is a relation with things
> which manifests things'. (Benso, 2000: 46)

Perhaps, then, despite the difficulties of knowing how to activate
practical responsibility for (or in response to) the posthuman, cyborg,
robot or 'surrogate', it is only this kind of responsibility, which operates in the ontological realm, that is available.

In an important discussion of Levinas's 'humanism', Simon
Critchley considers Levinas's famous encounter with 'Bobby' the
dog. He reminds us that it was Bobby 'who alone recognized Levinas
and his fellow Jewish prisoners of war as human beings during their
time in the camps in Germany' (Critchley, 1992: 181). Levinas, in
fact, makes the statement that 'the dog was the last Kantian in Nazi
Germany, without the brain needed to universalize maxims and
drives' (Levinas, 1990: 153). This implies, according to John Llewelyn,
that 'he [Bobby] is too stupid, *trop bête*. Bobby is without *logos* and
that is why he is without ethics' (Llewelyn, 1991: 236; original
emphasis). So although the dog was kind to Levinas and his fellow
prisoners (and he recognised them), Bobby cannot be afforded an
ethical response or responsibility because he is without language. If
this is the case, then, responsibility (in Levinasian terms) does not

seem to extend beyond the realm of the human.[19] Llewelyn goes on to explain that:

> Just as Kant maintains that I can have obligations only to a being that has, or (to cover the infantile and the senile) is of the kind that can have, obligations, so Levinas seems to imply that I can have responsibilities only toward beings capable of having responsibilities. (Llewelyn, 1991: 237)

The situation becomes even more fraught if we consider Todd May's critical essay on the limitations of Levinasian philosophy. May uses Levinas's apparent refusal to extend his ethics beyond the human to the nonhuman to point out that this move implies that

> only those beings sufficiently like me – beings of whom I can say that there is something it is to be like them in the relevant sense – can elicit in me the ethical experience. But with that restriction, we are removed from the realm of the infinitely other to the realm of the finitely other. The ethical experience is elicited in me by beings that are not so foreign to me as to be normatively incapable of eliciting in me the ethical experience. (May, 1997: 145)

Jill Robbins would disagree with May on this issue. She points out that it is in fact central to Levinas's ethics to argue against the suppression of 'alterity.' Robbins explains that 'interpreting the other as a necessary moment of the same, that is, in an all too dalectizable manner ... would reduce the absolutely other to the other *of* the same' (Robbins, 1999: xiii). Either way, this causes a further problem for the cyborg or the posthuman. If the cyborg has the potential to be me, in that we are all 'machines', an argument put forward in *Three Tales*, and if it also has the potential to be something that is, as Joanna Zylinska suggests, 'incalculably different', (Zylinska, 2002: 234)[20] then both of these options call Levinasian ethics into question. In the first there is no other to call me (linking to Causey's concern outlined at the outset of this chapter), and in the second I may not recognise the face or understand the language. There may also be other forms of otherness that remain as yet unimagined.

In spite of these serious limitations, if the crucial concept of responsibility is to be of use in the twenty-first century then there is a need to extend Levinasian ethics and particularly to extend the parameters of the other so that it can incorporate the idea of the other beyond something that is solely the domain of the human.

I believe that for this important ethics to remain useful, it must be adapted to acknowledge that the other is a concept or figure that might be differently imagined and experienced in the contemporary moment. Levinas's focus on the other as that which is not me, that which calls me to act and that which compels me to move beyond my own self-interested ideas, is crucial in the atomised world in which we live. In the current world order, with its 'war on terror', futures (biological and other) are uncertain, the idea of the other must be broadened out to include those others, both cellular, part, and absolutely other, which we come into contact with. If the function of Levinasian philosophy is to take responsibility for the other, then, at this moment, the concept of the other must include those others that are more than posthuman or even 'post' posthuman – in the form of assemblages, machines and figurations that have not yet been imagined.

As a caution, however, at the end of this tale, it is worth reflecting on Vivian Sobchack's critique of the 'millennial discourses that would decontextualize our flesh into insensate sign or digitize it into bits of information in cyberspace' (2004: 170). Sobchack warns that the idea of the cyborg, the prosthesis and/or the robot has been extended to such a radical degree that we are in danger of obfuscating the importance of the material body in our rush towards this 'hybrid being'. The lived materiality of the body, Sobchack reminds us, must not be ignored. Drawing on her own experiences of her prosthetic leg, she asks us

> to recognize and make explicit the deep and dangerous ambivalence that informs the reversible relations we, as lived bodies, have with our tools and their function of enabling us to transcend many of our physical limitations. (2004: 170)

This caution is a significant one, and it reminds us that it is often from the position of privilege that we celebrate or appropriate the latest 'trick' in the theoretical toolbox. Sobchack encourages us to think about bodies that need or rely on prosthetics or other forms of technological intervention to survive or live more easily, and to use this information to inform our discussions, lest we get 'carried away' (2004: 170).[21] This concern also causes reflection on the relationship between the posthuman and the millions of people around the world (outside laboratories and universities) who do not have the necessary access to money, time or technology, which imagining or developing a posthuman body demands.

While discussions of cloning and the posthuman have decreased in recent years, as if they are now a fait accompli, (and so 'nineties), the challenges as well as the opportunities these technologies present to our experience of the lived body (as it is currently formulated or understood) is something that both *Three Tales* and *Nature's Little Helpers* make startlingly real. The 'dangerous ambivalence' that Sobchack highlights is reinforced for audiences as they are bombarded with statements about the human as machine, as redundant and perhaps even as obsolete. Yet the ambivalence these works generate about the human and its 'posts' also has the potential to urge spectators to test the limits of responsibility in both its Levinasian and practical senses in order to explore how far responsibility can be developed as an idea *and* as a practice.

Afterword

> The condition of witnessing what one did not (and perhaps cannot) see is the condition of whatever age we are now entering. Whether we call this period 'the postmodern age' or 'the age of terrorism,' it is characterized both by an intimate reawakening to the fragility of life and a more general sense of connection to one another that exceeds simple geophysical, ideological or cultural proximity. (Phelan, 2004: 577)

Peggy Phelan is of course right when she talks about the changed world in which we live and also right in her reflection on the 'reawakening to the fragility of life'. However, what is most interesting is her assertion that there is a 'more general sense of connection to one another'. In concluding this book, I would like to raise a series of questions that explore whether a 'reawakening' necessarily leads to the 'sense of connection' Phelan proposes. If this is the case then what might this 'sense of connection' actually mean, and how might it be made manifest between and among spectators in technologically advanced societies? If, on the other hand societies are becoming more atomised, what might be done about this? My focus is not on providing answers but on thinking about the limits and the potential of practical responsibility both within and beyond the performance space.

This book has explored the kinds of ethical questions performance might raise for spectators. It has reflected on what spectators might do with those questions, which often emerge in the form of provocations, anxieties or a sense of ambivalence once spectators leave the theatre. They may experience a desire to act in response to the ideas raised and the political and social issues discussed within a work but, apart from engaging in dialogue about them or changing their attitudes towards a particular concept or event, they are often unclear about what, if any, other practical action they might take. Perhaps it is through debating and sharing responses and reactions with others that spectators actually do intervene and, as a result, have the potential to experience the connectedness to which Phelan refers.

To explore this issue a little further I consider a recent incident, which did not occur within the context of a performance but in response to a public speech. Given that I am interested in how spectators mobilise practical responsibility in, and in response to, performance (both within and beyond the theatre), I think it is fair to discuss the action or inaction of spectators in response to this incident as it clearly illustrates some perplexing and important questions about the definition and limits of responsibility in the contemporary moment.

On 17 September 2007 a University of Florida student was Tasered[1] by security guards at a town hall forum presented by Senator John Kerry. During question time, the student, Andrew Meyer, stepped up to the microphone after Kerry's presentation and began to ask questions. He felt that he needed to provide background information about his first question (which was ostensibly about why Kerry conceded defeat in the 2004 United States Presidential election, given the alleged rigging of the result). The question and background was delivered in a rambling and, at times, slightly aggressive style, and Meyer was asked to focus. He then posed two questions, the first about why Kerry conceded defeat, and the second about whether Kerry was in a secret society during his undergraduate days. Before the second question was finished, the microphone was unplugged and Meyer was escorted to the back of the room by security guards. Initially it seemed as if his removal provided relief to the audience (some people clapped); however, he was vocal in his protest against his removal. He shouted (and later screamed), 'Help, help' repeatedly and kept asking, 'What did I do?' Eventually, after a struggle with a number of security guards dressed in black uniforms, he was pinned down on the floor, at the back of the hall, surrounded and Tasered in the chest. While this was occurring Senator Kerry attempted to restore order to the proceedings.[2]

What is significant about this incident is the kinds of responses it elicited. While one audience member can be heard screaming, 'What are you doing, leave him alone' (once he was Tasered), the remainder of the audience either stayed seated (and seemed to be either unaware or to deliberately ignore the disturbance) or they took the opportunity to capture the incident as it unfolded on their mobile telephones.

It is difficult to watch the film of this incident, which as a result of the recording by spectators, is available on *YouTube*, without feeling anxious. The painful screams of Meyer as he is Tasered resonate. The lack of physical intervention by individuals or the audience collectively seems incomprehensible to me, albeit from the safe distance beyond the screen. However, as the censoring, or silencing of Meyer while he was asking his question indicates, the incident took place within a highly surveilled forum. In this context, then, perhaps the act of capturing the incident on a phone replaced the need for or possibility of embodied intervention? Did spectators feel that by filming the subduing of this man they were taking responsibility? Is this what responsibility entails in the twenty-first century and, if so, have we passed the era of bodily or physical intervention? And in the context of this incident would some form of physical intervention actually represent an act of responsibility? For example, the lack of embodied response may have occurred out of respect for, or consideration of, Meyer's plight. Spectators may have felt that intervention would inflame the situation even further and that this would not assist Meyer. They may also have been fearful of being Tasered themselves. Would being subdued alongside Meyer achieve anything anyway?

The broader questions that arise here surround the movement from responsibility in the pre-ontological realm, where we are compelled to respond to the 'call of the other' as Levinas argues, into some form of action in the ontological realm. Given the apparent emotional intensity of the scene how might spectators meaningfully respond in practical terms?

By witnessing the incident and disseminating it via a mobile telephone to fora such as *YouTube*, spectators are perhaps taking forms of action that are, in the contemporary space, more strategically productive, acts that can be interpreted as representing political resistance. The fact that my own responses to the event come from my experience of the incident on *YouTube* means that the incident was widely shared, commented on and responded to. It should also be noted that students staged a protest the following day, and these acts may all be read as examples of practical responsibility, and may represent the connection to which Phelan alludes.[3]

Situations such as this one are important because they uncover significant questions about the idea and function of responsibility in situated contexts, and they ask spectators individually and as a community to consider the limits of their ability or willingness to act. I would argue that this incident and the responses to it show Bauman's 'postmodern ethics' (1993) in action. In a society where we have so many rules, so many decisions to make, and so little moral guidance, we must develop new ways (however contingent) of responding. While the incident is disturbing, perhaps it is a symbol of both the complexities of any response and the ways in which the act of responding has changed in a technologically driven environment.

Phelan's sense of connection does not emerge automatically. It requires commitment and involvement. To maintain this connection means that spectators must respond and participate, not in a group frenzy or as automatons (the sense abhorred by Levinas), but rather in the sense proposed in this book: as active, questioning, at times resistant and at others willing participants in a meaning-making process. When this happens, as responses to the Meyer incident demonstrate, practical responsibility has valiance and the power to both generate and sustain, at least momentarily, this sense of connection. It might also begin a process of ethical reflection about both response and responsibility and the significance of these for individual spectators and for audiences more broadly.

Ultimately this incident, along with the works addressed in this book challenge spectators to consider a host of difficult and often contradictory ethical questions about the importance of a commitment to response and responsibility and how such a commitment might be activated and sustained.

Notes

Introduction

1. Or, as John Bell also suggests, 'the idea of performance offers concepts, means of analysis, and methods of action which can help us figure out where we are and what we ought to do' (2003: 67).
2. Although *Genesi: from the museum of sleep* premiered in 1999, it subsequently toured a range of cities on the international festival circuit and I attended a performance of this work at His Majesty's Theatre, Perth, Western Australia on Thursday, 30 January 2003.

Chapter 1

1. Martha Nussbaum addresses many similar issues to Bauman in her paper 'Compassion & Terror' (2003).
2. It is important to distinguish between morality and ethics at this juncture. For Bauman, the moral is the overarching code by which one is judged. Moral systems include the justice system, the legal system (etc.). Ethics, on the other hand, is the process by which individual subjects make sense of these systems and how they apply them to their own lives. I follow Bauman's understanding of these terms. For more information, see *Postmodern Ethics* (1993).
3. Justice is understood here as defined by Levinas, 'Justice is necessary, that is, comparison, coexistence, contemporaneousness, assembling, order, thematization, the *visibility* of faces, and thus intentionality and the intellect, and in intentionality and the intellect, the intelligibility of a system, and thence also a copresence on an equal footing as before a court of justice' (1998: 157; original emphasis).
4. As Robert Gibbs points out, 'despite the semblance, the face is not itself the other person's face, but is a facing by the other, a being questioned or called to account for myself' (2003: 109).
5. Jill Robbins states that 'the Saying and the Said is a correlative relation (exceeding correlation) that marks the difference between a conative speech, oriented toward its addressee, interlocutionary and ethical, and a speech oriented toward the referent, more like a speaking *about* than a speaking *to* the other' (1999: 144; original emphasis).
6. As Janelle Reinelt writes
   > I still tear up unashamedly when I'm moved in the theatre, and I still want something more substantive than my emotions to be engaged.... I still want to profess that it is worthwhile to link artistic experience to the political and ethical issues of our time. (Reinelt, 2003: 391–392)

7. For a detailed discussion of 'the third party' see *Otherwise than Being*, pp. 156–62.
8. In fact, it is the political dimension of ethics which Levinas's project promotes that makes it more appropriate to my own theorisation of the subject than Derrida's deconstruction. As Simon Critchley points out 'Derridian deconstruction has a horizon of responsibility or ethical significance, *provided that* ethics is understood in the Levinasian sense' (1992: 236; my emphasis).
9. Kelly Oliver explores the concept of recognition and its limitations in her book *Witnessing: Beyond Recognition* (2001).
10. Jon Erikson provides an interesting counterpoint to this statement when he explains

    I remain interested in what the possibility of examining what an ethical relation to the Other can mean in performance, knowing that the Other can mean racial other, sexual other, gender other, and performative other, even as it always points most directly to the Other within, something with more exteriority to it than we may realise. (Erikson, 1999: 20)

11. See also Paul Ricoeur (1992); Adrian Theodor Peperzak (1997).
12. This is a difficult giving to accomplish and one that both Derrida and Lyotard have written about. For more information see Jill Robbins, 1999.
13. For more details on the complexities of Levinas's relationship to art, see the authors already cited here: Robbins, Eaglestone, and also Edith Wyschogrod (1995, 2002) and Bernard Waldenfels (2002).
14. Robert Eaglestone discusses the contradictions and complexities of Levinas's engagement with the aesthetic, particularly in *Otherwise than Being*, where Levinas appeals to art as having the ability to surpass the 'logocentric constrictions of the said' but then argues that the 'saying' 'cannot be achieved by art' (1997: 160).
15. Jill Robbins talks in detail of the origin of Levinas's use of the word 'participation' and explains the relationship between Levinas's use of the term and Lucien Lévy-Bruhl's work (1999: 86).
16. It is interesting to compare Levinas's concern about participation with Brecht's. According to Jean-Paul Sartre 'Brecht felt that the distance between actors and audience was not great enough, that one tried much too much to *move* the audience, to touch them, and not enough to *show* them; in other words, too many participational relationships, too many images, not enough objectivity' (Sartre, 2000: 52).
17. As Edith Wyschogrod argues:

    The unleashing of a flood of images may lead to expressions of frenzied affect that for Levinas are manifested as paganism, a term he associates with a range of meanings from the exaltation of nature as impersonal fecundity which he identifies with Heidegger's ontology…to the participation in mystical reality he attributes to nonliterate societies as depicted by Levy-Bruhl. (2002: 198)

18. Levinas's fear of art links to a broader fear of relaxation. This fear of relaxation is also discussed in terms of the café: 'In the café, there are no themes.... You relax completely to the point of not being obligated to anyone or anything; and it is because it is possible to go and relax in a café that one tolerates the horrors and injustices of a world without a soul' (1990: 112).

Chapter 2

1. Socìetas Raffaello Sanzio was founded in Cesena, Emilia-Romagna, Italy in 1981 by Romeo Castellucci, Claudia Castellucci, Paolo Guidi and Chiara Guidi.
2. Adapted from Gabriella Giannachi and Nick Kaye, 2002.
3. The core members of Socìetas Raffaello Sanzio are Romeo Castellucci, director, Claudia Castellucci, writer, and Chiara Guidi, dramaturg.
4. Levinas does not extend the concept of the face to animals: The face can only be human in his philosophy. This is a problem I explore in detail in Chapter 6.
5. *Genesi: from the museum of sleep* toured international festivals in numerous European cities, including Amsterdam, Zurich, Berlin, Strasbourg, Paris and Orléans as well as to Australia for *The Perth International Arts Festival* in 2003.
6. I am using the term spectacle here to denote something more dramatic than the act of performing/performance itself. That is it is related to the idea of the spectacular: something that is lavish and amazing. This is the kind of spectacle utilised by Castellucci in *Genesi*.
7. Unpublished notes taken by Peter Eckersall at a forum with Romeo Castellucci in Melbourne, October 2006.
8. The most detailed discussion about the influence of Artaud on Socìetas Raffaello Sanzio's work (apart from comments by Castellucci) can, I believe, be found in Giannachi and Kaye's writing.
9. Masaccio (Tommaso di Ser Giovanni di Simone Guidi Cassai, 1401–1428) was a very significant early Renaissance painter. He worked with Masolini da Panicale (1383–1440) on frescoes in the Brancacci Chapel in Florence. His frescoes are considered masterpieces and they demonstrate his skill with perspective, the use of light, and an ability to generate a psychological intensity in the figures he painted.
10. See also Lisa Vinebaum, who cites Marianne Hirsch on the idea of 'postmemory' 'to characterise the experiences of children of Holocaust survivors, whose memories and experiences are shaped by traumatic events that they did not experience, and which cannot be understood' (Vinebaum, 2001).
11. See Vinebaum for more information on this issue (2001).
12. It is also possible to use Georgio Agamben's work *Remnants of Auschwitz: The Witness and the Archive* (1999) to help frame a response to the work of *Socìetas Raffaello Sanzio* and particularly *Genesi* and *Tragedia Endogonidia*.

This is an approach that has been taken by theorists such as Joe Kelleher (2002, 2006) for example.

13. In fact, Castellucci has stated that *Genesi* 'constitutes the background' to the 11 episodes of *Tragedia* (Peter Eckersall, see note 7).

14. I attended a performance of this work at the Melbourne International Arts Festival in October 2006.

Chapter 3

1.
> The Mamu is the Pitjantjatjara word for a bad spirit or an evil shadow. When the elders saw the black smoke from the south towering above them, they thought it was the Mamu, angry and powerful. From then on the Pitjantjatjara Aborigines called this place Maralinga, meaning 'field of thunder'. (Black Swan Theatre, 2002)

Hereafter I will refer to the production as *MAMU*.

2. Reviewers focussed on the humour of the work, its ability to generate laughter and its authenticity. *MAMU* was reviewed in *Hamburger Abendblatt, Hamburger* (26 August 2002), *Morgenpost* (26 August 2002), *Die Tageszeitung* (26 August 2002), *Die Welt* (26 and 27 August 2002), and *Kieler Nachrichten* (27 August 2002).

3. See (NACCHO and Oxfam, 2007).

4. For information on the history wars or the culture wars as this period is variously known see for example: Keith Windschuttle, 2002, Robert Manne, 2003, Henry Reynolds, 2001, Raimond Gaita, 1999. It must be noted that the first act of the newly elected Labor government in 2008 was to make a formal apology in parliament to Indigenous Australians.

5. The term 'stolen generations' refers to those Indigenous Australians who were forcibly removed from their families by governmental officials, welfare or religious organisations between 1909 and 1969 when the practice was terminated. Children who were removed were brought up in institutions or were fostered out to white families. They often had little or no contact with family members once they were removed from their families and communities. The 1997 *Bringing Them Home Report* by the Human Rights and Equal Opportunities Commission, which investigated the forced removal of Aboriginal children from their families found that the forcible separation 'constituted genocide within the terms of the 1948 Convention on the Prevention and Punishment of the Crime of Genocide' (Hughes d'Aeth, 2002).

6. Country is a term used by Indigenous people to describe a sense of belonging to a particular place. It suggests a deep connection to the landscape that is not just about living on the land but about belonging to or existing within the landscape.

7. The precise geographical boundaries of Spinifex country are unclear, as marking territory in this way stems from a colonial or European process.

The ownership of land or the delineation of territory for the Spinifex people is achieved through stories of connectedness to particular sites and knowledge of the mythical significance of the land, rather than through the creation of boundaries and maps.

8. For more information see The Australian Government National Archives of Australia 'Fact Sheet 129' 'British Nuclear Tests' at: http://www.naa.gov.au/fsheets/fs129.html. See also 'Maralinga – Our Shame' http://www.sea-us.org.au/thunder/britsbombingus.html for photographs of some of the explosions.

9. The National Native Title Tribunal describes Native title as follows: 'Native title is the recognition in Australian law that some Indigenous people continue to hold rights to their lands and waters, which come from their traditional laws and customs' (2006).

10. The centre at Tjuntjuntjara has been built and is being used by the community. The process of telling the story of the Spinifex people is also continuing. As discussed here, through *Ngapartji Ngapartji* Scott Rankin and Trevor Jamieson are extending the work done on *MAMU*. Rankin is a founder of *Big hART*, a multi-disciplinary arts organisation, which generates art in collaboration with communities and groups. It combines performance (and other art forms), political lobbying and contributions to social policy and debate, with outreach educational programmes created for (and with) community members. Rankin and Jamieson, in collaboration with *Big hART*, have developed various programmes for the Spinifex community and have extended the reach and significance of their work beyond the confines of the performance space.

11. It is important to be clear here that the material presented (via documentary footage) in *MAMU* and in *Sandakan Threnody* (as I will discuss in Chapter 4) is not widely known or acknowledged by audiences. While there may be some knowledge of the events there is very little actual understanding of the ramifications of these events on 'survivors' and in this case on the land, traditions and cultures involved. Hans Thies Lehmann talks about documentary theatre of the 1960s in his book *Postdramatic Theatre*. He explains the difficulty this kind of theatre faced because of the fact that the material was already in the public domain (the political or social issues that were the subject of the documentary) and therefore it needed to be reenergised within the theatre. In the case of the works addressed in Chapters 3 and 4 the fact that they are largely unknown and that they allow previously silenced voices to emerge means that they work differently. That they are situated within a larger performance and that their efficacy (in this chapter particularly) emerges via the play of elements also needs to be kept in mind.

12. Projection at the beginning of the performance adapted slightly from Scott Cane's book *Pila Nguru: The Spinifex People*. Scott Rankin and Trevor Jamieson wrote *The Career Highlights of the MAMU*. It premiered at the Adelaide Festival in 2002. It was, however, reworked by Andrew Ross and script consultant Richard Mellick, for performances at The Perth International Arts Festival in 2002. It is this reworked version of the

script that I am using. (All quotes from the performance are taken from the unpublished script). I attended a performance of the work at The Perth International Arts Festival in 2002.

13. Family lines are very specific and a child could be considered Jamieson's uncle. This illustrates the difference between Indigenous and non-Indigenous family systems. Since family is crucial in Aboriginal culture, many performances comprise a segment where family relationships are explained for the audience (this was the case in both *Ningali* by Ningali Lawford, Robyn Archer and Angela Chaplin and *The 7 Stages of Grieving* by Wesley Enoch and Deborah Mailman).

14. Tjukurrpa is a complex term that does not easily translate into English. According to Scott Cane, Tjukurrpa is typically interpreted by Spinifex people, to mean 'The law'. Cane explains that 'this equation of the Tjukurrpa with "law" conveys something more than Europeans might associate with conventional legislation. The Spinifex perception of law incorporates elements of fear, power, complexity, reason and authority but also conveys something universal and metaphysical. It is, in both practice and content, more spiritual than judicial' (2002: 81).

15. Missions were designated communities set up by the government to contain Indigenous populations. They are similar to reservations in North America.

Chapter 4

1. Ong Keng Sen won the Cultural Medallion in 2003 for his outstanding contribution to the arts in Singapore.

2. *Sandakan: A Conspiracy of Silence* is the title of Lynette Ramsay Silver's (1998) book on Sandakan.

3. For example, his 1997 work, *Lear,* took William Shakespeare's *King Lear* as a starting point for an interrogation of 'roots, identity and tradition' through the collaboration of artists from six Asian countries. In this production, Ong attempted to present an intercultural work that focused on a sharing of cultural differences rather than through an 'amalgam which would reduce their difference' (Ong, 1999). However, *Lear* was interpreted as being too concerned with aesthetics and not adequately engaged in the politics of exchange. It was seen as reinforcing the exoticisation of Asia rather than as a project that advanced knowledges or ideas about 'new Asia', as Ong had hoped. In response to this feedback and continued workshops Ong's second Shakespearean adaptation, a reworking of Othello called *Desdemona,* was more process-orientated. As Ong points out:

> After *Lear,* also written by Rio Kishida, I had become dissatisfied with simply directing an Asian production that juxtaposed many different languages and many different traditional expressions. I felt that I had to take a more critical reflexive look at the process that I was engaging in. What was behind the mask of the impeccable precision of the *Lear*

that I had directed. How do I allow the intercultural process to delib-erately peep through at the seams of a new work? (Ong, 2000: 5)

In *Desdemona* the artistic processes were not hidden. They were laid bare and the work became incredibly complex. The performance included video art, installation, slide animations, Kudiyattum, projected email correspondence, Myanmar puppeteering, Indonesian dance and con-temporary performance techniques. It was signalled as a key event at the Adelaide Festival in Australia (where it premiered in 2000), yet once per-formed it was greeted with a resounding silence. Nobody wanted to talk about it because it didn't seem to work. *Desdemona* contained so many different elements that it appeared impossible to read. As Ong moved from 'not enough' process in *Lear* to 'too much' process in *Desdemona* he was again critiqued. Since *Desdemona* Ong has produced a number of performance works and proclaims that his interest is no longer on 'inter-cultural exchange but rather on individual exchange' (personal notes taken by the author at Ong's presentation at the *psi* Conference in Singapore, 2004).

4. There is a substantial body of writing on Ong's work. As well as those cited here, see for example: Bharucha (2004); Peterson (2001); de Reuck (2000); Lee (2004); Wee (2004); and my own writing on his intercultural projects (2000a, 2001, 2004).

5. This footage is from the documentary *Return to Sandakan*, Film Australia (directed by Raymond Quint), 1995.

6. The choice of nations, forms and cultural practices represented in *Sandakan Threnody* has attracted responses that raise questions about the artistic decisions made and the ethical questions that result for spectators. Pang Kee Teik, for example, is concerned about the lack of involvement of the British in this project. He asks:

since this was supposed to be a cross-national project, I am puzzled why the British were left out. Did their not surviving the march com-pletely mean they were less heroic or worthy of representing? I am also equally chaffed that Malaysian artistic inputs were left out. For Sabahans, many of their ancestors had helped the POWs – at great risk to their own lives. (2004)

7. It is worth noting that there is a lot of confusion about the death marches. Many commentators believe that all of the prisoners of war marched from Sandakan to Ranau on the three marches; however, Lynette Ramsay Silver points out that fewer than half of the prisoners participated in the marches. In the performance the focus seems to be, via William 'Bill' Moxham's 'character', on the marches rather than on life – more broadly – at the camps. There is also a conflation of Sandakan (the camp) and the marches, in the Programme Notes. It was not until I read Ramsay Silver's book on Sandakan that I became clear about this. For more information see Ramsay Silver (1998).

8. I attended two performances of this work: the first at Victoria Theatre in Singapore in June 2004 (the world première), and the second in Melbourne in October 2004 as part of the Melbourne International Arts Festival.

9. (Personal email correspondence with me, 21 October 2007). There are numerous examples of this amnesia, such as official denials, textbook omissions and debates about the role of Yasukuni shrine where the souls of Japanese soldiers, including war criminals, are interned. For more information, see Tessa Morris-Suzuki (2005) and Yoshikuni Igarashi (2000).

10. All quotations from the performance are from my notes and a video of the performance given to me by *TheatreWorks*.

11. Sticpewich was one of the six survivors of Sandakan and he was not highly regarded by the other survivors for his ruthlessness and his liaisons with the Japanese. For more information see Ramsay Silver, 1998.

12. Moxham's documentary forms the core of much of the performance as the character of William 'Bill' Moxham is performed by Matthew Crosby. He talks in an abstract/distant/fragmented way to his little 'Susan' throughout the work. The material used to inform this 'character' was drawn from the interview with Susan Moxham, as well as a range of other sources, including diaries. William 'Bill' Moxham committed suicide in 1961. Susan Moxham was not invited to the performance and only found out about it after the season had finished.

13. In an email discussion with me, Sue Moxham explains the difficulties surrounding her interview for the Film Australia documentary. She states:

> I was subjected to a lot of pressure not to do the interview for Film Australia by representatives of the RSL and POW representatives. Pressure was even applied to the producer not to interview me. It is hard for ex soldiers to confront the truth about what really happens when soldiers return from a war. The Returned Servicemens League and other lobby groups cling to words like 'hero' to describe returned and fallen soldiers and cannot help but glorify the war. The other tactic is to say that men like my father were abusers before the war and are not representative of the average soldier. I found it a very hard interview to do and I was emotionally exhausted afterwards. Other families of the POW survivors of Sandakan have had a difficult time.... In a strange twist of fate, I consider the families of the survivors to have undergone more long term suffering that the families of the fallen. (personal email correspondence with Grehan, 1 September 2005)

14. I am reminded here of Primo Levi's comments about the 'Gray Zone' as discussed with reference to *Genesi: From the Museum of Sleep* (Chapter 2).

15. It is important to note that there was a 'renewed interest in mothers in the postwar period', according to Carol Fisher Sorgenfrei, which is
> suggested by the discredited patriarchy represented by the emperor and his deflated military. During the early postwar years, some Japanese turned to mothers as possible saviors; others, however, saw

mothers as part of the prewar problem, because they had been willing to train their sons for sacrifice to the war machine. (2005: 9)

16. This is quite a complicated issue, which raises a host of ethical questions. As Peter Eckersall points out:

> While there is a cultural precedent for silence, it is also problematic to the extent that it perhaps over-emphasises the cultural-essentialist perspective. People ultimately have a choice in these matters and confronting the past horrors might be cast in a different light for different audiences. These silences can be read as a sign of respect for the dead because any attempt to reflect publicly might be considered as an insignificant gesture. On the other hand, Japan has a history of denying its complicity in the war. At the same time, a confessional tone, as is often evident in western culture, might also be considered undignified. (personal email correspondence with me, 21 October 2007)

17. 'Sleep' is sung by Jamie Allen.
18. It seems as if this information is from Ramsay Silver's book. She names the prisoner as 'Honcho' and adds some extra details not mentioned here, see pp. 235–236.
19. In his book *Japan's Modern Theatre: A Century of Continuity and Change*, Powell explains that:

> *Kabuki* had developed at about the same time as *bunraku*, in the second half of the seventeenth century. The spectators' attention was focused on the performers from the first, partly as artists and partly as possible sexual partners. It was the linking of dancing and acting in simple dramatic sketches with first female then male prostitution that led the authorities to ban performers of *kabuki* – or *risqué* turns, as the term originally meant – who might be thought attractive to those wanting to pay for sexual services. Thus from the early 1650s onwards *kabuki* was performed by male actors over the age of seventeen. Liaisons between handsome young actors and fans did not cease by any means, but this and other government regulations helped to ensure that the primary objective of a *kabuki* performance was not prostitution but a display of acting talent. (2002: xxviii; original emphasis)

For a detailed feminist reading of the onnagata see, *Beautiful Boys/Outlaw Bodies: Devising Kabuki Female-Likeness*. Katherine Mezur (2005).

20. During WWII theatre, and kabuki specifically, became deeply connected with wartime propaganda. As Powell makes clear,

> the government was convinced of the potential subversive qualities of theatre, it also viewed theatre as something that could contribute positively to the social changes that were necessary in a time of war. The persuasive powers of theatre could be channeled to raising and maintaining morale. (Powell, 2002: 115)

He goes on to talk about the specific role kabuki played in this process, see particularly the section entitled: '*Kabuki* encouraged and used', pp. 122–125.

Chapter 5

1. The production is in part inspired by Homer, and in the programme notes for the Melbourne season Hélène Cixous, links contemporary wars and their effects on 'fugitives' to both *The Iliad* and *The Odyssey* (Théâtre du Soleil, 2005).

2. The programme notes also state that 'the stories were collected by Ariane Mnouchkine, assisted by Shaghayegh Beheshti, in Sangatte (France) between May 2001 and December 2002; in Villawood Detention Centre (Sydney, Australia) in January 2002; and in Auckland (New Zealand) and Mataram (Lombok Island, Indonesia) in February 2002' (Théâtre du Soleil, 2005).

3. For an important discussion of torture, the camp (Guantanamo Bay) and photography see Susan Sontag's essay 'Regarding the Torture of Others' (2004).

4. As Béatrice Picon-Vallin points out:
   Mnouchkine imbues those with whom she collaborates with her great faith in the theater. 'Only art tells the truth,' she said in January 2004. Her poetic theater is also political, and prefers to show rather than to denounce, so that the conscience can be captured more completely. (Picon-Vallin, 2006: 84)

5. Ariane Mnouchkine is not alone in generating work about refugees/asylum seekers; many other writers, disturbed by the current global situation and the political climate have also created performance works in response. These include Peter Sellars, Ping Chong, Tony Kushner and, in Australia, 'Version 1.0', 'Sidetrack Performance Group' and Nigel Jamieson, to name a few. Philippa Wehle briefly discusses a number of key projects in her article on *Le Dernier Caravansérail* cited in this chapter.

6. Mnouchkine's commitment is evident in her passion about her work and the subjects she represents as well as through acts she personally carries out to effect political change, or to make a statement. An important example is her 'Avignon Declaration' in 1995 when she and Olivier Py, François Tanguy, Emmanuel de Véricourt, Maguy Martin and George Guérin went on hunger strike 'in protest at the inaction of Europe and the USA in relation to Bosnia' (Williams, 1999: 230).

7. The production premiered in 2003 at Théâtre du Soleil's base Cartoucherie de Vincennes in the outskirts of Paris. It was performed for just over two years in Paris and on the international festival circuit. I attended a performance of both parts of *Le Dernier Caravansérail* at The Royal Exhibition Centre in Melbourne, on Sunday 16 October 2005. The performance was co-produced by Théâtre du Soleil and Ruhrtriennale and the Australian tour was supported by Républic Française (Ambassade de France en Australie), the Association Française d'Action Artistique (AFAA) and *SBS* radio.

8. For Brian Singleton 'the written word thus was embodied and came to stand for the body which was no longer visible or which could not be represented'. He adds that, 'one of the performers was an asylum seeker whose application for refugee status has been granted, and he provided a very important sense of "authenticity" to the verbatim testimonies' (2007: 30).

9. Personal notes transcribed by the author at the performance.
10. The Centre for Urgent Humanitarian Care and Shelter of the French Red Cross (CHAUH) was created at Sangatte in 1999. Sangatte (as it was known) was located near the Eurotunnel and as a consequence of the fact that refugees attempted to use the tunnel to enter the UK 'illegally' it was 'finally closed on 30 December 2002', at the 'insistence of the British authorities' (Programme Notes, Théâtre du Soleil, 2005).
11. Personal notes taken by the author at the performance.
12. Victorian Arts Minister Mary Delahunty said that
    Théâtre du Soleil had agreed to forgo its fees for the two extra shows, the Melbourne Museum would forgo rental of the Exhibition Building, and the Government would cover the $60,000 cost of extending the show (which will be offset by the sale of 1,200 tickets at $56.25 to $75.00).
    Ms Delahunty also stated that 'this is astounding and absolutely profound theatre, and it's the quality of theatre and the content of the theatre that's important, but it's got to be high art first' (Gill, 2005).
13. As Judith G. Miller points out: 'Mnouchkine is taking the work to Australia in the fall of 2005. The audiences there might well react with hostility to the piece's condemnation of Australian immigration policy' (2006: 218). In fact, the opposite occurred: audiences were delighted that this oppressive policy was challenged by the work. The overwhelmingly positive and enthusiastic response and the extended run reflected this reception.
14. Personal notes taken by the author at the performance.

Chapter 6

1. Examples include, 'The Three Laws of Robotics' printed at the front of Asimov's *I Robot*. These are:
   1 A robot may not injure a human being, or, through inaction, allow a human being to come to harm.
   2 A robot must obey the orders given it by human beings except where such orders would conflict with the First Law.
   3 A robot must protect its own existence as long as such protection does not conflict with the First or Second Law. 'Handbook of Robotics, 56th Edition, 2058 A.D.' (Asimov, 1950). These laws seem to want to ensure that the robot is developed in a way that means it cannot overtake the human. Robots are welcome but only insofar as they are controllable.
   See also, *Do Androids Dream of Electric Sheep?* by Dick, which was adapted for the 1982 film *Blade Runner,* and Clarke's *The City and the Stars*. In this book set one billion years into the future a computer runs the city, and machines create the people and store their memories when they die.

2. *Three Tales* premiered at the Vienna Music Festival in 2002. It was then performed at the Brooklyn Academy of Music, and subsequently toured many countries, including The Netherlands, Italy, the United Kingdom, Germany, France, Portugal and Australia (amongst others). I attended a performance of *Three Tales* in 2003 at the *Perth International Arts Festival*. The opera was developed with support from The Rockefeller Foundation, The Mary Flagler Cary Charitable Trust, Betty Freeman and National Endowment for the Arts. *Nature's Little Helpers* (2004) is a series of sculptures, photographs and drawings. Patricia Piccinini presented this work in a solo exhibition at the Robert Miller Gallery, New York in 2005. For more information see Patricia Piccinini's excellent website: <www. patriciapiccinini.net>.

3. Ihab Hassan first used the term 'posthumanism' in his keynote speech at the *International Symposium on Post-Modern Performance* in 1976. According to Steve Dixon 'Hassan debates whether posthumanism constitutes a "sudden mutation of the times" or the continuation of a process begun in the prehistoric firelight of the caves of Lascaux' (Dixon, 2007: 150). This understanding clearly links with the definition put forward by Jonson, Tofts and Cavallaro.

4. Reich explains that when asked if he and Korot would consider doing a piece about the twentieth century he felt that

> one of the things that came to mind very quickly was that the twentieth century had been more touched and driven by technology than almost any other human endeavor...we needed some events, some signposts from the early, middle and late parts of the century that would be emblematic of the period and its technology.

It was this search that led to the decision to use the three stories (Hindenburg, Bikini and Dolly) in *Three Tales* (Allenby, 2003: 6).

5. Schneider makes some important points about cloning in relation to concerns about time and repetition in this essay. See Rebecca Schneider (2001).

6. The performance does not work for everyone. Indeed some of my students found the techniques of repetition and looping of concepts and statements difficult to connect with. However, other students readily engaged with the ideas and allowed the combination of looping technology, musical score and profound statements mesmerising, challenging and provocative.

7.

> Freya von Moltke is the widow of Helmuth James von Moltke, the German aristocrat who served in the Abwehr or German Intelligence Service in World War 11 where he worked to undermine Hitler. He was found out and hung in 1944. Freya lived in Germany during World War 1, through Hindenburg's presidency and Hitler's rise to power. She now lives in Hanover, New Hampshire. (Reich and Korot, 2003: 2)

8. Two explosions were carried out on Bikini Atoll in 1946, and both were about the size of the bombs dropped on Nagasaki. Three islands were vapourised as a result. According to Jack Niedenthal, as the Islanders were leaving 'some 24 naval ships, 156 aircraft, 25,000 radiation recording

devices and the navy's 4,000 experimental rats, goats and pigs soon began to arrive for the tests. Over 42,000 US military and civilian personnel were involved in the testing programme at Bikini.' For more information see 'A Short History of the People of Bikini Atoll' at the official Bikini Atoll site: <http: www.bikiniatoll.com>.

9. On the Bikiniatoll website, Jack Niedenthal quotes Commodore Ben H. Wyatt, who asked the residents of Bikini to leave 'temporarily for the good of mankind and to end all world wars'. It is therefore possible that the footage shown in *Three Tales* is of this meeting.

10.

> Ruth Deech is chair of the U.K. Human Fertilisation & Embryology Authority.... Richard Dawkins is the first Charles Simonyi Professor of Public Understanding of Science at Oxford University.... James D. Watson along with Francis Crick and Maurice Wilkins, received the Nobel Prize in Physiology or Medicine in 1962.... Gina Kolata has been writing about science for the *New York Times* for over a decade. (Reich and Korot, 2002)

11. 'Stephen J. Gould was Alexander Agassiz Professor of Zoology at Harvard, curator of invertebrate paleontology at that university's Museum of Comparative Zoology, and Vincent Astor Visiting Professor of Biology at New York University, until his death in May 2002.... Jaron Lanier coined the term "Virtual Reality"' (Reich and Korot, 2002).

12. 'Rodney Brooks is director of the MIT Artificial Intelligence Laboratory, and is the Fujitsu Professor of Computer Science' (Reich and Korot, 2002). Dixon refers to Brooks in *Digital Performance* and says that although the predictions of Brooks (and Moravec and Warwick) 'are commonly dismissed as paranoid science fiction fantasy ... we would note that these individuals .... are scientific researchers who are leading the very development of those futures, at the forefront of practice in cybernetics, robotics and artificial intelligence' (Dixon, 2007: 311).

13.

> Adin Steinsaltz is internationally regarded as one of the leading rabbis of the century.... Sherry Turkle is professor of the sociology of science at MIT and a clinical psychologist.... Ray Kurzweil's inventions include reading machines for the blind, music synthesizers for Stevie Wonder and many others, and speech recognition technology. (Reich and Korot, 2002)

14. It is important to situate this discussion within a framework that acknowledges that evolutionary anxiety is not new and that it initially emerged as a theme in science fantasy writing in the time of Darwin. Samuel Butler, for example, quoted in this chapter's epigraph, raised many similar questions about technology and its implications (or potential implications) in his book *Erewhon*. He pondered:

> But who can say that the vapour engine has not a kind of consciousness? Where does consciousness begin, and where end? Who can draw the line? Who can draw any line? Is not everything interwoven with everything? Is not machinery linked with animal life in an infinite variety of ways? (Butler, 1965: 191)

Butler's 'The Book of the Machines' in *Erewhon* contains many of the key questions about the ethics of evolutionary struggle that continue to circulate in the twenty-first century. In fact these concerns are also echoed in works such as *I, Robot*, where Asimov describes the inhuman reaction of society to a robot that becomes more perfect than humans:

'But you are telling me, Susan, that the "Society for Humanity" is right; and that Mankind *has* lost its own say in its future.' 'It never had any, really.... Now the Machines understand them; and no one can stop them, since the Machines will deal with them as they are dealing with the Society...' 'How horrible!' (Asimov, 1950: 218; original emphasis)

15. As Piccinini points out:

With the sculptures, I have been able to present my creature ideas in a fashion that is direct and strangely believable. People are fascinated by the tiny details, the moles and wrinkles, which almost forces them to accept the possibility of their existing. I also deliberately steer clear of too much sci-fi or horror in my creatures. They stay rooted in the possibilities of real animals. These creatures are almost too easy to accept the real animal world is just as weird anyway. Like the extraordinary bio-geno-tech discoveries that these creatures relate to, the bizarre and unbelievable becomes the obvious and commonplace almost instantly. (Piccinini)

16. Of course, Piccinini is not alone in her interrogation of other life forms (and attendant issues) in her artwork. There are many artists who explore this terrain. For an excellent discussion of a range of such artists, see Suzanne Anker and Dorothy Nelkin (2004).

17. It is also useful to consider the ways in which these issues are being dealt with in the popular imagination. Films such as *I, Robot* and *Blade Runner* both show scenes of the main character watching his face (*I, Robot*) or his eyes (*Blade Runner*) being made. This dramatizes a separation of the subject from its body and allows it the opportunity to reflect on its construction from the position of the other.

18. For more information on this point, see Jeffrey T. Nealon (1998), Jennifer Parker-Starbuck (2006), Edith Wyschogrod (2004) and Christian Diehm (2000).

19. It is interesting at this point to return to Butler who states that

the potato says these things by doing them, which is the best of languages. What is consciousness if this is not consciousness? We find it difficult to sympathize with the emotions of a potato; so we do with those of an oyster. Neither of these things makes a noise on being boiled or opened, and noise appeals to us more strongly than anything else because we make so much about our won sufferings. (Butler, 1965: 193)

20. As Zylinska astutely explains:

The prosthetic ethics of welcome cannot thus be learned in advance, because an encounter with alterity (which we can supplement – even if not substitute – here with prosthecity or monstrosity) is always singular and irreplaceable. But its uncertain occurrence and unpredictable form do not diminish our responsibility to respond to what shows itself as incalculably different. As this alterity transcends our discursive mastery, the ethical moment of being faced with incalculable difference, with 'a species for which we do not yet have a name,' presents itself as inevitable. (2002: 233–234)

21. Indeed, she draws on the work of Donna Haraway, who also cautions us about the 'God trick' and the ways in which the cyborg has been utilised in 'discourses of disembodiment' (Haraway in Sobchack, 2004: 170).

Afterword

1. According to the website *wiseGEEK,* a Taser is 'a non-lethal self-defense weapon that uses compressed nitrogen to shoot two tethered needle-like probes at an assailant in order to deliver an electric shock.' For more information see: www.wisegeek.com/what-is-a-taser.htm.
2. There are several versions of this incident on *YouTube.* The versions I refer to are http://www.youtube.com/watch?v=6bVa6jn4rpE by Kyle Mitchell and http://www.youtube.com/watch?v=IATPoHdpak0&feature=related by GainsvilleSun.
3. Documentary footage of the protest can be seen on *YouTube*: see for example: <http://www.youtube.com/watch?v=UVRMkUWOzJE> and http://www.youtube.com/watch?v=g5YTmAEr_Qk.

Bibliography

Adorno, Theodor. (1967). *Prisms*. Trans. Samuel and Shierry Weber. Neville Spearman: London.

Adorno, Theodor. (1978). 'Commitment.' In *The Essential Frankfurt School Reader*. Ed. Andrew Arato and Eike Gebhardt. Blackwell: Oxford, pp. 300–318.

Agamben, Giorgio. (1999). *Remnants of Auschwitz: The Witness and the Archive*. Trans. Daniel Heller-Roazen. Zone Books: New York.

—— (2000). *Means Without End: Notes on Politics*. Trans. Vincenzo Binetti and Cesare Casarino. University of Minnesota Press: Minneapolis.

—— (n.d.). 'We Refugees.' Trans. Michael Rocke. <http://www.egs.edu/faculty/agamben/agamben-we-refugees.html> (accessed 22 May 2006).

Allenby, David. (2003). 'Steve Reich and Beryl Korot on *Three Tales*.' Program Notes, Perth International Arts Festival, pp. 6–11.

Anker, Suzanne and Nelkin, Dorothy. (2004). *The Molecular Gaze; Art in the Genetic Age*. Cold Spring Harbor Laboratory Press: New York.

Artaud, Antonin. (1993). *The Theatre and its Double*. Trans. Victor Corti. Calder Publications: London.

Asimov, Isaac. (1950). *I, Robot*. Dennis Dobson: London.

Australianpolitics.com (2002). <http://www.australianpolitics.com/news/2002/12/02-12-27.shtml> (accessed 20 January 2006).

Baker, Steve. (2000). *The Postmodern Animal*. Reaktion Books: London.

Ball, Martin. (2005). 'Odysseys of Pain and Poetry.' *The Australian*, 14 October: 16.

Barthes, Roland. (1981). *Camera Lucida: Reflections on Photography*. Trans. Richard Howard. Vintage: London.

Bauman, Zygmunt. (1993). *Postmodern Ethics*. Blackwell: Oxford.

—— (1998). *Globalization: The Human Consequences*. Polity Press: Cambridge.

—— (1999). 'The World Inhospitable to Lévinas.' *Philosophy Today*, 43.2: 151–167.

Beeman, William. O. (1993). 'The Anthropology of Theater and Spectacle.' *Annual Review of Anthropology*, 22: 369–393.

Bell, John. (2003). 'Performance Studies in an Age of Terror.' *TDR*, 47.2: 6–7.

Benso, Syliva. (2000). *The Face of Things: A Different Side of Ethics*. State University of New York Press: Albany.

Bernstein, Michael André. (1994). *Foregone Conclusions: Against Apocalyptic History*. University of California Press: Berkeley.

Bharucha, Rustom. (2000). *The Politics of Cultural Practice: Thinking Through Theatre in an Age of Globalization*. Athlone Press: London.

—— (2000). 'Consumed in Singapore: The Intercultural Spectacle of Lear.' Centre for Advanced Studies Research Paper No. 21. National University of Singapore: Singapore.

Bharucha, Rustom. (2004). 'Foreign Asia/Foreign Shakespeare: Dissenting Voices on New Asian Interculturality, Postcoloniality and Recolonization.' *Theatre Journal,* 56.1: 1–28.

Black Swan Theatre. (2002). *The Career Highlights of the MAMU.* Program Notes. Perth International Arts Festival.

Boltanski, Luc. (1999). *Distant Suffering.* Trans. Braham Burchell. Cambridge University Press: Cambridge.

Borradori, Giovanna. (2003). *Philosophy in a Time of Terror: Dialogues with Jürgen Habermas and Jacques Derrida.* University of Chicago Press: Chicago.

Bowden, Peta and Emma Rooksby. (2006). 'Understanding Condemnation: A Plea for Appropriate Judgement.' In *Judging and Understanding: Essays on Free Will, Narrative, Meaning and the Ethical Limits of Condemnation.* Ed. Pedro Alexis Tabensky. Ashgate: Aldershot and Burlington, pp. 241–256.

Boym, Svetlana. (2001). *The Future of Nostalgia.* Basic Books: New York.

Bramwell, Murray. (2002). 'Devilish Toll of Nuclear Testing.' *The Australian,* 4 March: 15.

Brecht, Bertolt. (1976). 'A Short Organum for the Theatre.' *Avant-Garde Drama: a Casebook 1919–1939.* Eds. Bernard F. Dukore and Daniel C. Gerould. Crowell: New York, pp. 501–532.

Brustein, Robert. (2005). 'Theater of the Mushy Tushy.' *The New Republic,* 9 May 2005. <http://www.tnr.com/doc.mhtml?i=20050905&s=brustein090505> (accessed 25 May 2005).

Butler, Samuel. (1965). *Erewhon or Over the Range.* Jonathan Cape: London.

Buzacott, Martin. (2004). 'Voices of the Dead Overwhelm the Drama.' *The Australian,* 20 September: 9.

Cane, Scott. (2002). *Pila Nguru: The Spinifex People.* Fremantle Arts Centre Press: Fremantle.

Caruth, Cathy. (1996). *Unclaimed Experience: Trauma, Narrative and History.* The Johns Hopkins University Press: Baltimore.

Castellucci, Claudia, Joe Kelleher, Nicholas Ridout and Romeo Castellucci. (2007). 'The Theatre is not our Home: A Conversation about Space, Stage and Audience.' In *The Theatre of Societas Raffaello Sanzio.* Eds. Claudia Castellucci, Romeo Castellucci, Chiara Guidi, Joe Kelleher and Nicholas Ridout. Routledge: New York, pp. 203–212.

Castellucci, Romeo. (1999). *Genesi.* Program Notes.

—— (2002). *Tragedia Endo-gonidia c.#01.* Program Notes.

Causey, Matthew. (2001). 'Stealing from God: The Crisis of Creation in Societas Raffaello Sanzio's *Genesi* and Eduardo Kac's *Genesis.*' *Theatre Research International,* 26.2: 199–208.

—— (2006). *Theatre and Performance in Digital Culture.* Routledge: London.

Chansky, Dorothy (2004). 'Theatre at the Singapore Arts Festival.' *New York Theatre Wire.* <http://www.nytheatre-wire.com/dc04071t.htm> (accessed 23 August 2005).

Clarke, Arthur C. (1957) *The City and the Stars.* Transworld Publishing: London.

Cohen, Stanley. (2001). *States of Denial: Knowing about Atrocities and Suffering.* Polity: Cambridge.

Cohn, Fred. (2003). 'Three Tales from the Triptych: Steve Reich's Three Tales Comes Out on DVD this Spring.' *Opera News,* 67.9: 50–51.

Conquergood, Dwight. (2002). 'Performance Studies: Interventions in Radical Research.' *TDR,* 46.2: 145–156.

Cosic, Miriam. (2005). 'Drama Drenched in Humanity.' *The Australian,* 14 October: 16.

Critchley, Simon. (1992). *The Ethics of Deconstruction: Derrida and Levinas.* Blackwell: London.

—— (2002). 'Introduction.' In *The Cambridge Companion to Levinas.* Eds. Simon Critchley and Robert Bernasconi. Cambridge University Press: Cambridge, pp. 1–32.

Croggon, Alison. (2005). <http://theatrenotes.blogspot.com/2005/10/miaf-le-dernier-caravanserail-odysses.html> (accessed 9 November 2005).

De Bola, Peter. (2001). *Art Matters.* Cambridge University Press: Cambridge.

De Reuck, Jenny. (2000). 'The Mirror Shattered into Tiny Pieces: Reading Gender and Culture in the Japan Foundation Asia Center's LEAR.' *Intersections.* <http://intersections.anu.edu.au/issue3/jenny3.html> (accessed 24 May 2008).

Derrida, Jacques. (1999). 'Hospitality, Justice and Responsibility: A Dialogue with Jacques Derrida.' In *Questioning Ethics: Contemporary Debates in Philosophy.* Eds. Richard Kearney and Mark Dooley. Routledge: London, pp. 65–83.

Diehm, Christian. (2000). 'Facing Nature: Levinas Beyond the Human.' *Philosophy Today,* 44.1: 51–59.

Dick, Philip K. (1968). *Do Androids Dream of Electric Sheep?* Ballantyne Books: New York.

Diprose, Rosalyn. (2002). *Corporeal Generosity: On Giving with Nietzsche, Merleau-Ponty, and Levinas.* State University of New York Press: Albany.

Dixon, Steve. (2007). *Digital Performance: A History of New Media in Theater, Dance, Performance Art, and Installation.* The MIT Press: Cambridge, Massachusetts.

Dolan, Jill. (2001). 'Performance, Utopia and the "Utopian Performative."' *Theatre Journal,* 53.3: 455–479.

—— (2005). *Utopia in Performance: Finding Hope at the The Theater.* University of Michigan Press: Ann Arbor.

Duffy, Rosemary. (2004). 'Rosemary Duffy – Sandakan Threnody.' *State of The Arts Reviews.* <http://www.stateart.com.au/sota/reviews/default.asp?fid=2944> (accessed 28 October 2004).

Eaglestone, Robert. (1997). *Ethical Criticism: Reading After Levinas.* Edinburgh University Press: Edinburgh.

—— (2004). *The Holocaust and The Postmodern.* Oxford University Press: Oxford.

Eccles, Jeremy. (2002). 'Maralinga Revisited.' *RealTime,* 48: 5.

—— (2002a). 'Poised to Explode.' *RealTime,* 48: 6.

Erikson, Jon. (1999). 'The Face and the Possibility of an Ethics of Performance.' *Journal of Dramatic Theory and Criticism,* 13.2: 5–21.

Felman, Shoshana and Dori Laub. (2002). *Testimony: Crises of Witnessing in Literature, Psychoanalysis, and History*. Routledge: New York.

—— (1992). 'Education and Crisis, or the Vicissitudes of Teaching.' In *Testimony: Crises of Witnessing in Literature, Psychoanalysis, and History*. Eds. Shoshana Felman and Dori Laub. Routledge: New York, pp. 1–56.

Ferreira, Jamie M. (2001). '"Total Altruism" in Levinas's "Ethics of the Welcome."' *Journal of Religious Ethics*, 29.3: 443–470.

Fisher, Mark. (2003). 'Subtitled "From The Museum of Sleep."' In *Genesi: from the museum of sleep*. <http://www.red-noise.com/genesi.html> (accessed 8 May 2008).

Franke, Catherine Anne and Roger Chazal. (1999). 'Between Poetics and Ethics: An Epic Approach to Reality: From an Interview with Hélène Cixous.' In *Collaborative Theatre: The Théâtre du Soleil Sourcebook*. Ed. David Williams. Routledge: London, pp. 147–158.

Gaita, Raimond. (1999). *A Common Humanity: Thinking About Love and Truth and Justice*. Text Publishing: Melbourne.

Gallasch, Keith. (2004). 'Singapore Plays its Own Tune.' <http://www.realtimearts.net/62/gallasch_singapore.html> (accessed 30 August 2005).

Giannachi, Gabriella and Nick Kaye. (2002). *Staging the Post-Avant-Garde: Italian Experimental Performance after 1970*. P. Lang: Oxford and New York.

Gibbs, Robert. (2003). 'Philosophy and Law: Questioning Justice.' In *The Ethical*. Eds. Edith Wyschogrod and Gerald P. McKenny. Blackwell: Oxford, pp. 101–116.

Gibson-Graham, J.K. (2006). *A Postcapitalist Politics*. University of Minnesota Press: Minneapolis.

Gilbert, Helen and Jacqueline Lo. (2007). *Performance and Cosmopolitics: Cross-Cultural Transactions in Australasia*. Basingstoke: Palgrave Macmillan.

Gill, Raymond. (2005). 'Palpable Hit gets State Backing.' *The Age* (Melbourne). <http://www.theate.com.au/news/ars/palpable-hit-gets-state-backing/2005/10/16/1129401145007.html> (accessed 30 October 2007).

Gomez-Pena, Guillermo. (2001). 'The New Global Culture: Somewhere between Corporate Multiculturalism and the Mainstream Bizarre (a Border Perspective).' *TDR*, 45.1: 7–30.

Grehan, Helena. (2000). *Mapping Cultural Identity in Contemporary Australian Performance*. Peter Lang: Brussels.

—— (2000a). 'Performed "Promiscuities": Interpreting Interculturalism in the Japan Foundation Asia Center's LEAR.' *Intersections: Gender, History and Culture in the Asian Context*. 3.6. <http://www.anu.edu.au/intersections/issue3/grehan.html> (accessed 29 May 2008).

—— (2001). 'TheatreWorks *Desdemona*: Fusing Technology and Tradition.' *TDR*, 45.3: 113–125.

—— (2003). Unpublished interview with Andrew Ross, 4 July.

—— (2004). 'Questioning the Relationship between Consumption and Exchange: TheatreWorks' Flying Circus Project, December 2000.' *Positions East Asia Cultures Critique*, 12.2: 565–596.

—— (2005). Personal email correspondence with Susan Moxham, 30 August.

—— (2006). 'Testimony and Ambivalence in *Sandakan Threnody.' ADS,* Special Focus issue on Interculturalism and Emotions, 49: 89–100.

—— (2007). Personal email correspondence with Peter Eckersall, 21 October.

Halliburton, Rachel. (2001). 'From Genesis to Revelation.' *The Independent.* <http://www.independent.co.uk/arts-entertainment/theatre/features/ from-genesis-to-revelation-662198.html?service=print> (accessed 13 March 2008).

Hamilton, Margaret. (2007). *Art and Politics and The Zürcher Theater Spektakel: Maria Magdalena Schwaegermann talks with Margaret Hamilton. Performance Paradigm,* 3. <www.performanceparadgim.net> (accessed 26 May 2007).

Hardt, Michael and Antonio Negri. (2001). *Empire.* Harvard University Press: Harvard.

—— (2004). *Multitude.* The Penguin Press: New York.

Harris, Samela. (2002). 'The Career Highlights of the Mamu.' *Advertiser* (Adelaide), 4 March: np.

Hartman, Geoffrey. (1996). *The Longest Shadow: In the Aftermath of the Holocaust.* Indiana University Press: Bloomington.

—— (2001). 'Tele-Suffering and Testimony in the Dot Com Era.' In *Visual Culture and the Holocaust.* Ed. Barbie Zelizer. Rutgers University Press: New Brunswick, New Jersey, pp. 111–124.

Hatley, James. (2000). *Suffering Witness: The Quandry of Responsibility after the Irreparable.* State University of New York Press: Albany.

Hayles, Katherine N. (1999). *How we Became Posthuman: Virtual Bodies In Cybernetics, Literature and Informatics.* University of Chicago Press: Chicago.

Héliot, Armelle. (2005). 'In Search of Lives: Ariane Mnouchkine Interviewed.' Théâtre du Soleil. 'Program Notes *Le Dernier Caravansérail.'* Melbourne International Arts Festival.

Hilberg, Raul. (1992). *Perpetrators, Victims, Bystanders: The Jewish Catastrophe 1933–1945.* HarperCollins: New York.

Hughes-d'Aeth, Tony. (2002). 'Which Rabbit-Proof Fence? Empathy, Assimilation, Hollywood.' *Australian Humanities Review.* <http://www.lib. latrobe.edu.au/AHR/archive/Issue-September-2002/hughesdaeth.html> (accessed 12 March 2008).

Huyssen, Andreas. (1995). *Twilight Memories: Marking Time in a Culture of Amnesia.* Routledge: London.

—— (2000). 'Present Pasts: Media, Politics, Amnesia.' *Public Culture,* 12.1: 21–38.

Igarashi, Yoshikuni. (2000). *Bodies of Memory: Narratives of War in Postwar Japanese Culture, 1945–1970.* Princeton University Press: Princeton.

Ignatieff, Michael. (2004). *The Lesser Evil.* Princeton University Press: Princeton.

Irigaray, Luce. (1991). 'Questions to Emmanuel Levinas: On the Divinity of Love.' In *Re-Reading Levinas.* Eds. Robert Bernasconi and Simon Critchley. Athlone Press: London, pp. 109–118.

Isherwood, Charles. (2005). 'Lincoln Center Festival Review; Never Touching the Ground in a Constant Search for Refuge.' *The New York Times.* <http:// query.nytimes.com/gst/fullpage.html?res=9807E5D91E30F93AA25754C0 A9639C...> (accessed 20 July 2005).

Jonson, Annemarie, Darren Tofts, and Alessio Cavallaro, Eds. (2003). *Prefiguring Cyberculture: An Intellectual History.* MIT Press: Cambridge, Massachusetts.

Keane, John. (2003). *Global Civil Society?* Cambridge University Press: Cambridge.

Kelleher, Joe. (2002). 'An Organism on the Run.' In *Tragedia Endogonidia: Idioma, Clima, Crono.* Socìetas Raffaello Sanzio, pp. 10–11.

Kelleher, Joe. (2006). 'Human Stuff: Presence, Proximity and Pretend.' In *Contemporary Theatres in Europe.* Eds. Joe Kelleher and Nicholas Ridout. Routledge: London, pp. 21–33.

Kellner, Douglas. (n.d.). 'Globalization and the Postmodern Turn.' <http://www.gseis.ucla.edu/courses/ed253a/dk/GLOBPM.htm> (accessed 20 March 2006).

Kelly, Jem. (2005). 'Auditory Space: Emergent Modes of Apprehension and Historical Representations in *Three Tales.*' *International Journal of Performance Arts and Digital Media,* 1.3: 207–236.

Kent, Rachel. (n.d.). 'Fast Forward: Accelerated Evolution.' <http://www.patriciapiccinini.net/essay.php?id=21> (accessed 8 April 2005).

Kwok, Kenneth. (2004). 'Music Makes the Bourgeoisie and the Rebel.' *theflyinginkpottheatrereviews.* <http://inkpot.com/theatre/04revsandthre.html> (accessed 18 March 2005).

LaCapra, Dominick. (1994). *Representing the Holocaust: History, Theory, Trauma.* Cornell University Press: Ithaca, New York.

—— (2001). *Writing History, Writing Trauma.* Johns Hopkins University Press: Baltimore.

Laub, Dori. (1992). 'Bearing Witness or the Vicissitudes of Listening.' In *Testimony: Crises of Witnessing in Literature, Psychoanalysis, and History.* Eds. Shoshana Felman and Dori Laub. Routledge: New York, pp. 57–74.

Lee, Weng Choy. (2004). 'Authenticity, Reflexivity, and Spectacle; or, The Rise of New Asia Is Not the End of the World.' *Positions East Asia Cultures Critique,* 12.3: 643–666.

Lehmann, Hans-Thies. (2006). *Postdramatic Theatre.* Trans. Karen Jürs-Munby. Routledge: London.

Leverett, James. (2007). 'The New Chinoiserie: Ong Keng Sen Interviewed by James Leverett.' *Theater,* 37.1: 55–68.

Levi, Primo. (1988). *The Drowned and the Saved.* Trans. Raymond Rosenthal. London: Abacus.

Levinas, Emmanuel. (1969). *Totality and Infinity.* Trans. Alphonso Lingis. Duquesne University Press: Pittsburgh.

—— (1985). *Ethics and Infinity: Conversations with Philippe Nemo.* Trans. Richard Cohen. Duquesne University Press: Pittsburgh.

—— (1986). 'The Trace of the Other.' In *Deconstruction in Context.* Ed. Mark C. Taylor. University of Chicago Press: Chicago, pp. 345–359.

—— (1987). *Collected Philosophical Papers.* Trans. Alphonso Lingis. Martinus Nijhoff: The Hague.

—— (1987a). 'Meaning and Sense.' *Collected Philosophical Papers.* Trans. Alphonso Lingis. Martinus Nijhoff: The Hague, pp. 75–108.

—— (1987b). 'Phenomenon and Enigma.' *Collected Philosophical Papers*. Trans. Alphonso Lingis. Martinus Nijhoff: The Hague, pp. 61–74.

—— (1988). 'Useless Suffering.' In *The Provocation of Levinas Rethinking the Other*. Eds. Robert Bernasconi and David Wood. Routledge: London, pp. 156–167.

—— (1989). 'Ethics as First Philosophy.' In *The Levinas Reader*. Ed. Séan Hand. Blackwell: Oxford, pp. 75–87.

—— (1990). 'Judaism and Revolution.' *Nine Talmudic Readings*. Trans. Annette Aronowicz. Indiana University Press: Bloomington, pp. 94–119.

—— (1990a). 'The Name of a Dog, or Natural Rights.' In *Difficult Freedom: Essays on Judaism*. Trans. Seán Hand. The Johns Hopkins University Press: Baltimore, pp. 151–153.

—— (1996). *Emmanuel Levinas: Basic Philosophical Writings*. Eds. Adriaan Peperzak, Simon Critchley and Robert Bernasconi. Indiana University Press: Bloomington.

—— (1998). *Otherwise than Being or Beyond Essence*. Trans. Alphonso Lingis. Duquesne University Press: Pittsburgh.

—— (1999). *Alterity and Transcendence*. Trans. Michael B. Smith. Athlone Press: London.

—— (2001). 'Philosophy, Justice, and Love (1983).' In *Is it Righteous to Be?: Interviews with Emmanuel Levinas*. Ed. Jill Robbins. Stanford University Press: Stanford, pp. 165–181.

—— (2003). *On Escape: De l'évasion*. Trans. Bettina Bergo. Stanford University Press: Stanford.

Llewelyn, John. (1991). 'Am I Obsessed by Bobby? (Humanism of the Other Animal).' In *Re-Reading Levinas*. Eds. Robert Bernasconi and Simon Critchley. Athlone Press: London, pp. 234–245.

Lo, Jacqueline. (2004). *Staging Nation: English Language Theatre in Malaysia and Singapore*. Hong Kong University Press: Aberdeen and Hong Kong.

Lord, Richard. (2004). 'Mourning Becomes Electric: Beauty and Horror Fused in an Arts Festival Offering.' *Quarterly Literary Review Singapore*. <http://qlrs.com/emedia.asp?id=362> (accessed 18 March 2005).

Lyotard, Jean-François. (1984). *The Postmodern Condition: A Report on Knowledge*. Trans. Geoff Bennington and Brian Massumi. Manchester University Press: Manchester.

—— (1988). *The Differend: Phrases in Dispute*. Trans. Georges Van Den Abbeele. University of Minnesota Press: Minneapolis.

Manne, Robert. Ed. (2003). *Whitewash: On Keith Windschuttle's Fabrication of Aboriginal History*. Black Inc.: Melbourne.

Marchitello, Howard. Ed. (2001). *What Happens to History: The Renewal of Ethics in Contemporary Thought*. Routledge: New York.

Marks, Laura. (2000). *The Skin of the Film: Intercultural Cinema, Embodiment and the Senses*. Duke University Press: Durham.

Marshall, Jonathan. (2003). 'The Castellucci Interview: The Angel of Art is Lucifer.' <http://www.realtimearts.net/rt52/castell.html> (accessed 20 July 2007).

Martin, Carol. (2006). 'Bodies of Evidence.' *TDR*, 50.3: 8–15.

May, Todd. (1997). *Reconsidering Difference: Nancy, Derrida, Levinas, and Deleuze.* The Pennsylvania University Press: Pennsylvania.

McEvoy, William. (2006). 'Finding the Balance: Writing and Performing Ethics in Théâtre du Soleil's *Le Dernier Caravansérail*.' *NTQ*, 22.3: 211–226.

Meffan, James and Kim L. Worthington. (2001). 'Ethics Before Politics: J.M. Coetzee's *Disgrace*.' In *Mapping the Ethical Turn: A Reader in Ethics, Culture, and Literary Theory.* Eds. Todd F. Davis and Kenneth Womack. University Press of Virginia: Charlottesville, pp. 131–150.

Melbourne International Arts Festival. (2005). 'Le Dernier Caravansérail.' Festival Brochure.

Mezur, Katherine. (2005). *Beautiful Boys/Outlaw Bodies: Devising Kabuki Female-Likeness.* Palgrave Macmillan: Basingstoke.

Middleton, Carol. (2002). 'Genesi From the Museum of Sleep.' *State of the Arts.* <http://www.stateart.com.au/sota/performing/default.asp?fid=1552> (accessed 20 March 2008).

Midgley, Mary. (1985). *Wickedness: A Philosophical Essay.* Routledge and Kegan Paul: London.

Miller, Judith G. (2006). 'New Forms for New Conflicts: Thinking about Tony Kushner's *Homebody/Kabul* and the Théâtre du Soleil's *Le Dernier Caravansérail*.' *Contemporary Theatre Review,* 16.2: 212–219.

Millner, Jacqueline. (2001). 'Patricia Piccinini: Ethical Aesthetics.' <http://www.patriciapiccinini.net/essay.php?id=4> (accessed 20 October 2005).

Mills, Catherine. (2003). 'An Ethics of Bare life: Agamben on Witnessing.' *borderlands e-journal,* 2.1. <http://www.borderlandsejournal.adelaide.edu.au/vol2no1_2003/mills_agamben.html> (accessed 14 February 2006).

Mills, Jonathan. (2004). 'Composer's Message.' *Sandakan Threnody* Program Notes, Singapore Arts Festival.

Moreton-Robinson, Aileen. (2003). 'I still Call Australia Home: Indigenous Belonging and Place in a White Postcolonizing Society.' In *Uprootings/ Regroundings: Questions of Home and Migration.* Eds. Sara Ahmed, Claudia Castañeda, Anne-Marie Fortier, and Mimi Sheller. Berg: Oxford, pp. 23–40.

Morris-Suzuki, Tessa. (2005). *The Past within Us: Media, Memory, History.* Verso: London.

Moxham, Susan. (2004). <http://inkpot.com/theatre/04reviewsandthre.html> (accessed 18 April 2005).

Murphy, Ann. (2004). 'The Political Significance of Shame.' *borderlands e-journal,* 3.1. <http://www.borderlandsejournal.adelaide.edu.au/vol3no1/murphy_shame.htm> (accessed 28 August 2007).

NACCHO and Oxfam. (2007). 'Close the Gap': Solutions to the Indigenous Health Crisis Facing Australia: A policy briefing paper from the National Aboriginal Community Controlled Health Organisation and Oxfam Australia. <http://www.oxfam.org.au/media/files/CTG.pdf> (accessed 27 September 2007).

National Native Title Tribunal. (2006). 'What is native title?' <www.nntt.gov.au/publications/1035773354_1456.html> (accessed 24 March 2008).

Neale, Imogen. (2006). 'Nature' Little Helper: The Strange World of Patricia Piccinini.' <http://www.lumiere.net.nz/reader/item/476> (accessed 22 April 2008).

Nealon, Jeffrey. (1998). *Alterity Politics: Ethics and Performative Subjectivity.* Duke University Press: London.

Ngapartji Ngapartji. <http://www.ngapartji.org/>

Niedenthal, Jack. (2006). 'A Short History of the People of Bikini Atoll.' <www.bikiniatoll.com> (accessed 15 August 2007).

Nussbaum, Martha. (2003). 'Compassion & Terror.' *Daedalus,* 132.1: 10–26.

Oliver, Kelly. (2001). *Witnessing: Beyond Recognition.* University of Minnesota Press: Minneapolis.

—— (2001a). 'Witnessing Otherness in History.' In *What Happens to History: The Renewal of Ethics in Contemporary Thought.* Ed. Howard Marchitello. Routledge: London, pp. 41–66.

—— (2004). 'Witnessing and Testimony.' *Parallax,* 10.1: 79–88.

Ong, Keng Sen. (1999). *'Lear:* Linking Night and Day.' Director's Notes. Festival of Perth.

—— (2000). 'Director's Notes.' *Desdemona.* Telstra Adelaide Festival.

—— (2004). 'Director's Thoughts.' Program Notes for *Sandakan Threnody.* Singapore Arts Festival.

Oxfam. <http://www.oxfam.org.au/media/files/CTG.pdf> (accessed 24 August 2007).

Pang Khee Teik. (2004). 'Abusing Prisoners of War: How Sandakan Threnody turns 2500 Dead Soldiers into Beautiful Art. How Ah Hock & Peng Yu turn Beautiful Men into Ducks, Monkeys and Squares.' *Kakiseni.com* <http://www.kakiseni.com/articles/reviews/MDUzMA.html> (accessed 11 July 2005).

Papastergiadis, Nikos and Mary Zournazi. (2002). 'Faith Without Certitudes: A Conversation with Nikos Papastergiadis.' In *Hope: New Philosophies for Change.* Ed. Mary Zournazi. New York: Routledge; Pluto Press: Annandale, NSW, pp. 78–95.

Parker-Starbuck. Jennifer. (2006). 'Becoming-Animate: On the Performed Limits of "Human."' *Theatre Journal,* 58: 649–668.

Pavis, Patrice. (2003). 'Afterword: Contemporary Dramatic Writings and the New Technologies.' In *Trans-global Readings: Crossing Theatrical Boundaries.* Ed. Caridad Svich. Manchester: Manchester University Press, pp. 187–202.

Pence, Gregory E. Ed. (1998). *Flesh of My Flesh: The Ethics of Cloning Humans: A Reader.* Rowman & Littlefield: Lanham, Maryland.

Peperzak, Adriaan. (1997). *Beyond: The Philosophy of Emmanuel Levinas.* Northwestern University Press: Evanston, Illinois.

Perera, Suvendrini. (2002). 'What is a Camp...?' *borderlands e-journal,* 1.1. <http://www.borderlandsejournal.adelaide.edu.au/vol1no1_2002/perera_camp.html> (accessed 22 May 2006).

Performance Paradigm. (2007). 'Envisioning Ethics Anew: Rustom Bharucha talks with Performance Paradigm.' *Performance Paradigm.* <http://www.performanceparadigm.net/category/journal/issue-3/> (accessed 12 January 2008).

Peterson, William. (2001). *Theater and the Politics of Culture in Contemporary Singapore.* Wesleyan University Press: Middletown, Connecticut.

Phelan, Peggy. (2001). 'Converging Glances: A Response to Cathy Caruth's "Parting Words."' *Cultural Values,* 5.1: 27–40.

Phelan, Peggy. (2004). 'Marina Abramović: Witnessing Shadows.' *Theatre Journal*, 56.4: 569–577.

Piccinini, Patricia. (2006). 'Artist's Statement.' *In Another Life* catalogue, Wellington City Gallery, Wellington, New Zealand. <http://patriciapiccinini. net/essay.php?id=28&style=printing> (accessed 11 September 2006).

—— (n.d.). 'Artist's Statement: *Nature's Little Helpers*.' <http://patriciapiccinini. net/natureslittlehelpers/print.php?text2show ... titletext=00Natures+Little +Helpers0000&show=00Natures+Little+Helpers> (accessed 11 September 2006).

Picon-Vallin, Béatrice. (2006). 'Reflections on Forty Years of Théâtre Du Soleil.' *Theater*, 36.2: 83–87.

Poirié, François. (2001). 'Interview with François Poirié (1986).' In *Is it Righteous to Be? Interviews with Emmanuel Levinas*. Ed. Jill Robbins. Stanford University Press: Stanford, pp. 23–83.

Pontynen, Arthur. (2006). *For the Love of Beauty: Art, History, and the Moral Foundations of Aesthetic Judgment*. New Brunswick and Transaction Publishers: London.

Powell, Brian. (2002). *Japan's Modern Theatre: A Century of Continuity and Change*. Japan Library: London.

Putnam, Hillary. (2002). 'Levinas and Judaism.' In *The Cambridge Companion to Levinas*. Eds. Simon Critchley and Robert Bernasconi. Cambridge University Press: Cambridge, pp. 33–62.

Quint, Raymond. Dir. (1995). *Return to Sandakan*, Film Australia.

Rae, Paul. (2004). 'Don't Take it Personally: Arguments for a Weak Interculturalism.' *Performance Research*, 9.4: 18–24.

Ramsay Silver, Lynette. (1998). *Sandakan: A Conspiracy of Silence*. Sally Milner Publishing: Bowral, NSW.

Randles, Jackie. (2004). 'Hybrid Life: The Art of Patricia Piccinini.' <http:// www.ethics.org.au/things_to_read/articles_to_read/science/article_0392. shtm> (accessed 1 May 2008).

Rankin, Scott, and Trevor Jamieson. (2002). *The Career Highlights of the MAMU*. Unpublished Playscript.

Read, Alan. (2007). *Theatre, Intimacy & Engagement: The Last Human Venue*. Palgrave Macmillan: Basingstoke.

Reich, Steve. (2003). *Three Tales*. Program Notes, Perth International Arts Festival.

Reich, Steve and Beryl Korot. (2002). *Three Tales DVD and Booklet*. Nonesuch Records: New York.

—— (2003). *Three Tales Libretto*. Distributed at the performance in Western Australia.

Reinelt, Janelle. (2003). 'The Theatre Journal Auto Archive.' *Theatre Journal*, 55.2: 385–392.

Reynolds, Henry. (2001). *An Indelible Stain?: The Question of Genocide in Australia's History*. Viking: Ringwood, Victoria.

Richardson, Owen. (2005). 'Le Dernier Caravansérail (Odysses): Part One – The Cruel River.' *Sunday Age*, 16 October: 30.

Ricoeur, Paul. (1992). *Oneself as Another*. Trans. Kathleen Blamey. University of Chicago Press: Chicago.

Ridout, Nicholas. (2003). 'Out in the Open.' In *Tragedia Endogonidia: Idioma, Clima, Crono*. Socìetas Raffaello Sanzio, pp. 1–2.

——— (2006). 'Make-believe: Socìetas Raffaello Sanzio Do Theatre.' In *Contemporary Theatres in Europe: A Critical Companion*. Eds. Joe Kelleher and Nicholas Ridout. Routledge: London, pp. 175–187.

——— (2006a). *Stage Fright, Animals, and Other Theatrical Problems*. Cambridge University Press: Cambridge.

Robbins, Jill. (1999). *Altered Reading: Levinas and Literature*. University of Chicago Press: Chicago.

Rokem, Freddie. (2000). *Performing History: Theatrical Representations of the Past in Contemporary Theatre*. University of Iowa Press: Iowa.

Rothberg, Mark. (2000). *Traumatic Realism: The Demands of Holocaust Representation*. University of Minnesota Press: Minneapolis.

Salverson, Julie. (1999). 'Transgressive Storytelling or an Aesthetic of Injury: Performance, Pedagogy and Ethics.' *Theatre Research in Canada*, 20.1. <http://www.lib.unb.ca/Texts/TRIC/bin/get6.cgi?directory=vol20_1/&file name=Salverson.htm> (Accessed 12 March 2008).

——— (2001). 'Change on Whose Terms? Testimony and an Erotics of Inquiry.' *Theater*, 31.3: 119–125.

Sartre, Jean-Paul. (2000). 'Beyond Bourgeois Theatre.' In *Brecht Sourcebook*. Eds. Carol Martin and Henry Bial. Routledge: London, pp. 50–57.

Saunders, Alan. (2006). 'Interview with Deborah Bird Rose.' *The Philosopher's Zone*. ABC Radio National. <http://www.abc.net.au/rn/philosopherszone/stories/2006/1672842.htm> (accessed 27 March 2007).

Scavenius, Alette. (2002). 'Searching for Hamlet: An Interview with the Director.' <http://www.theatreworks.org.sg/images/Interview%20OKS.pdf> (accessed 20 March 2008).

Schneider, Rebecca. (2001). 'Hello Dolly well Hello Dolly.' In *Psychoanalysis and Performance*. Eds. Patrick Campbell and Adrian Kear. Routledge: New York, pp. 94–114.

Schumacher, Claude. (1998). 'Staging the Holocaust: The Shoah in Drama and Performance.' Cambridge University Press: Cambridge.

Scott, Ridley. Dir. (1982). *Blade Runner*.

Shepherd, Simon. (2006). *Theatre, Body and Pleasure*. Routledge: London.

Singapore Arts Festival. (2004). Program Notes for *Sandakan Threnody*.

Singleton, Brian. (2003). 'Editorial.' *Theatre Research International*, 28.3: 227–228.

——— (2007). 'Performing Conflict Migration and Testimony.' In *Performing Global Networks*. Eds. Karen Fricker and Ronit Lentin. Cambridge Scholars Publishing: Newcastle, UK, pp. 25–37.

Sobchack, Vivian. (2004). *Carnal Thoughts: Embodiment and Moving Image Culture*. University of California Press: Berkeley.

Sontag, Susan. (2003). *Regarding the Pain of Others*. Picador: New York.

——— (2004). 'Regarding the Torture of Others.' *The New York Times Magazine*. <http://www.nytimes.com/2004/05/23/magazine/23PRISONS.html?ex=1400644800&en=a2cb6ea6bd297c8f&ei=5007&partner=USERLAND> (accessed 24 October 2007).

Sorgenfrei Fisher, Carol. (2005). *Unspeakable Acts: The Avant-Garde Theatre of Terayama Shūji and Postwar Japan*. University of Hawai'i Press: Honolulu.

Stasio, Marilyn. (2005). 'Le Dernier Caravansérail (Odyssees) Parts I & II.' *Variety.com* <http://www.variety.com/review/VE111792711?categoryid=33&cs...> (accessed 27 January 2006).

Stefanova, Kalina. (2004). 'Along the Roads with Ariane Mnouchkine.' *European Cultural Review, 16.* <http://www.c3hu/~eufuzetek/en/eng/16/index.php?mit=mnouchkine> (accessed 28 January 2006).

Stratton, Jon (2000). 'Thinking Through the Holocaust. A Discussion Inspired by Hilene Flanzbaum Ed., *The Americanization of the Holocaust.*' *Continuum: Journal of Media & Cultural Studies*, 14.2: 231–245.

Sullivan, Narelle. (2006). 'Le Dernier Caravansérail (Odyssées): A Case Study of Cosmopolitan Space Between Borders.' *Crossings* 11.2. <http://www.asc/uq.edu.au/crossings/11_2/index.php?apply=sullivan> (accessed 22 April 2008).

Tackels, Bruno. (2001). *Interview with Romeo Castellucci*. <www.theatre-contemporain.net/spectacles/genesi/entreienus.htm> (accessed 17 September 2007).

Taylor, Diana. (1998). 'Border Watching.' In *The Ends of Performance*. Eds. Peggy Phelan and Jill Lane. New York University Press: New York, pp. 178–185.

—— (2001). 'Staging Social Memory.' In *Performance and Psychoanalysis*. Eds. Patrick Campbell and Adrian Kear. Routledge: London, pp. 218–236.

Théâtre du Soleil. (2005). Program Notes, *Le Dernier Caravansérail*. Melbourne International Arts Festival.

TheatreWorks. (2004). *Sandakan Threnody* Flyer. Singapore Arts Festival.

—— www.theatreworks.org.sg

Thomson, Helen. (2002). 'Vivid, Startling Theatre.' *The Age*, March 6. <http://www.theage.com.au/articles/2002/03/06/1015365707592.html> (accessed 3 July 2007).

—— (2004). 'Windschuttling the Right: Some Australian Literary and Historical Adaptations for the Stage.' *JASAL*, 3: 133–142.

Tompkins, Joanne. (2004). 'Locating Maralinga in the Global and Local Landscapes in Two Australian Plays: Scott Rankin and Trevor Jamieson's *The Career Highlights of the Mamu* and Andrea Lemon and Sarah Cathcart's *Tiger Country.*' Symposium on Australian and Canadian Theatre and Globalisation at Meiji Gakuin University, Tokyo, Japan. 20–21 November. Keynote address.

—— (2006). *Unsettling Space: Contestations in Contemporary Australian Theatre*. Palgrave Macmillan: Basingstoke.

Trezise, Thomas. (2001). 'Unspeakable.' *Yale Journal of Criticism*, 14.1: 39–66.

Valentini, Valentina and Bonnie Marranca. (2004). 'The Universal: The Simplest Place Possible.' Trans. Jane House. *PAJ*, 26.2: 16–25.

Veness, Bianca. (2004). 'Verging on the Brilliant: *Sandakan Threnody.*' *M/C Reviews*. <http://reviews.media-culture.org.au/article.php?sid=1037> (accessed 28 October 2004).

Vetlesen, Arne Johan. (1994). *Perception, Empathy, and Judgment: An Inquiry into the Preconditions of Moral Performance*. Penn State Press: Pennsylvania.

Vinebaum, Lisa. (2001). 'Holocaust Representation from History to Postmemory.' <www//Anaxagoras.concordia.ca/vinebaum.pdf> (accessed 7 July 2005).

Virilio, Paul. (2003). *Art & Fear*. Continuum: London.

Wade, Leslie A. (2008). 'Sublime Trauma: The Violence of the Ethical Encounter.' In *Violence Performed: Local Roots and Global Routes of Conflict*. Eds. Patrick Anderson and Jisha Menon. Palgrave Macmillan: Basingstoke, pp. 1–22.

Waldenfels, Bernhard. (2002). 'Levinas and the Face of the Other.' In *The Cambridge Companion to Levinas*. Eds. Simon Critchley and Robert Bernasconi. Cambridge University Press: Cambridge, pp. 63–81.

Wee Wan Ling, C.J. (2004). 'Staging the Asian Modern: Cultural Fragments, the Singaporean Eunuch, and the Asian Lear.' *Critical Inquiry*, 30.4: 771–799.

Wehle, Philippa. (2005). 'Théâtre Du Soleil: Dramatic Response to the Global Refugee Crisis.' *PAJ*, 27.2: 80–86.

Williams, David, Ed. (1999). *Collaborative Theatre: The Théâtre du Soleil Sourcebook*. Routledge: London.

Windschuttle, Keith. (2002). *The Fabrication of Aboriginal History: Volume One, Van Diemen's Land 1803–1847*. Macleay Press: Paddington, NSW.

Wright, Tamara, Peter Hughes and Alison Ainley. (1988). 'The Paradox of Morality: An Interview with Emmanuel Levinas.' In *The Provocation of Levinas: Rethinking the Other*. Eds. Robert Bernasconi and David Wood. Routledge: London, pp. 168–180.

Wyschogrod, Edith. (1995). 'The Art in Ethics: Aesthetics, Objectivity, and Alterity in the Philosophy of Emmanuel Levinas.' In *Ethics as First Philosophy: The Significance of Emmanuel Levinas for Philosophy, Literature and Religion*. Ed. Adriaan Peperzak. Routledge: New York and London, pp. 137–148.

—— (2002). 'Language and Alterity in the Thought of Levinas.' In *The Cambridge Companion to Levinas*. Eds. Simon Critchley and Robert Bernasconi. Cambridge University Press: Cambridge, pp. 188–205.

—— (2004). 'Levinas's Other and the Culture of the Copy.' *Yale French Studies*, 104: 126–143.

Yong Li Lan. (2004). 'Ong Keng Sen's Desdemona, Ugliness, and the Intercultural Performative.' *Theatre Journal*, 56.2. <http://0-proquest.umi.com.prospero.murdoch.edu.au/pqdlink?index=23&did=0000006 ...> (accessed 16 July 2007).

Zylinska, Joanna. (2002). 'The Future...Is Monstrous': Prosthetics as Ethics.' In *The Cyborg Experiments: The Extensions of The Body in the Media Age*. Ed. Joanna Zylinska. Continuum: London, pp. 214–236.

Index